RENAISSANCE MONKS

RENAISSANCE MONKS

A Group Portrait of Monastic Humanism

Franz Posset

Collected Works

Volume 6

WIPF & STOCK · Eugene, Oregon

RENAISSANCE MONKS
A Group Portrait of Monastic Humanism: Collected Works Volume 6

Copyright © 2022 Franz Posset. All rights reserved. Except for brief quotations in critical publications or reviews, no part of this book may be reproduced in any manner without prior written permission from the publisher. Write: Permissions, Wipf and Stock Publishers, 199 W. 8th Ave., Suite 3, Eugene, OR 97401.

Wipf & Stock
An Imprint of Wipf and Stock Publishers
199 W. 8th Ave., Suite 3
Eugene, OR 97401

www.wipfandstock.com

PAPERBACK ISBN: 978-1-6667-3494-2

JANUARY 18, 2022

Cover: *Schotten Closter in Wienn (Vienna, Austria).*
Cloister [of Our Dear Lady] of the Scots in Vienna.

From: *Topographia archiducatus Austriae Inferioris modernae* [1672].
Courtesy Schottenstift, Vienna, Dr. Maximilian Alexander Trofaier.

"Scots Monastery" is a name applied to a monastic foundation of Irish and Scot monastic missionaries on the European continent, particularly to the Scot Benedictines in German-speaking regions. These cloisters are at times also called in German *Schottenstift* (foundation of the Scots). The illustration on the cover showing the monastery in Vienna is employed here in commemoration of the 500th anniversary of its abbot's death on 8 September 1521, Benedictus Chelidonius, who is featured in Chapter Two.

In Memory

of Fr. Terrence Kardong O.S.B. (+ 2019),

Monk of the Assumption Abbey, Richardton, North Dakota.

Editor of *The American Benedictine Review* 1982–2018

Contents

Author's Preface to the Reprint Edition | ix

List of Illustrations | xvii

Foreword by Gerhard B. Winkler, O. Cist. | xix

Author's Preface to the First Edition | xxi

Acknowledgements | xxv

Abbreviations | xxvii

Introduction   1

1. An Editor of Latin Bibles and Works of the Church Fathers: Conradus Leontorius, Monk of Maulbronn | 29

2. A Graecian, Christian Poet, and Playwright: Benedictus Chelidonius, Monk of Nuremberg, Abbot of the *Schottenstift*, Vienna | 63

3. A Historiographer and Distinguished Verse Make: Bolfgangus Marius, Monk of Aldersbach, Bavaria | 93

4. A Latinist, Supporter of Reuchlin, and Editor of Christ–centered Poetry: Henricus Urbanus, Monk of Georgenthal, Thuringia | 109

5. Jack-of-all-Trades: Vitus Bild Acropolitanus, Monk of Saints Ulrich and Afra in Augsburg | 133

6. When Monks Were Eager to Study the Sacred Languages: Nikolaus Ellenbog, Monk of Ottobeuren, Swabia | 155

Conclusion | 173

Select Bibliography | 177

Index of Personal Names | 183

Index of Places | 189

Index of Subjects | 193

List of International Book Reviews of the First Edition of *Renaissance Monks* (2005) | 197

Afterword to the Reprint Edition by Seymour House, Dwyer Chair of Humanities, Mount Angel Seminary, Oregon, USA | 199

Author's Preface to the Reprint Edition

VOLUME 6 OF MY *Collected Works* is a reprint of the book first published in 2005, but for the previous subtitle I chose now "A Group Portrait of Monastic Humanism." Perhaps, its "popularity" has something to do with certain anticipations of scandals in Late Medieval monasteries on the eve of the Reformation involving worldly monks. Be that as it may, the first edition of the book was well-received. Proof for this is the relatively large number of book reviews from all over the world—from Belgium, Germany, Great Britain, Israel, Sweden, and the United States.

Major revisions of the original version are not necessary. Yet, a few minor ameliorations are to be noted:

1. P. ix: In the LIST OF ILLUSTRATIONS: Fig. 5 is not seen on p. 88, but on p. 87.
2. P. 64: The title page of the book could be from a print from Cracow, Poland, 1514 (Courtesy Schottenstift, Vienna, Maximilian Alexander Trofaier).
3. P. 94, Fig. 6, Marius' *Prologus In Annales*. https://html.scribdassets.com/6falildtc05vdagu/images/49-f378405ba6.jpg
4. P. 110, Fig. 8: now available in color online. http://www.literaturland-thueringen.de/wp-content/uploads/2015/01/Rektoratsblatt-Rubeanus-418x548.jpg (accessed 9 November, 2021).
5. P. 166: Pope Clement reigned not up to 1313, but to 1314.
6. P. 175: The very last line of the book has a spelling mistake in the Latin *Hebrai* which must read *Hebraei*, which is given in the context

and translation from Latin as "The Hebrew drink from the source, the Greeks from the rivulets, and the Latins from the swamp."

The concept "Monastic Humanism" still feels somewhat awkward to some readers including historians, but less so perhaps for its German equivalent, *Klosterhumanismus*, the expression being favored by Franz Machilek (1934–2021).[1] This German concept simply draws attention to the fact that around 1500 certain scholars who were Renaissance humanists were living, indeed, in monasteries. Or, from another perspective, monks and civic humanists were actually engaged in extensive correspondence and dialogue.[2]

The very book title, *Renaissance Monks*, may still be an oxymoron to some students of the Renaissance and Reformation since to them the concepts of "Renaissance Humanism" and "Monastic Humanism" seem unrelated. In theological-historical research, the relationship of Renaissance Humanism to the monastic world of the Late Middle Ages remains often neglected because it is perceived, perhaps mistakenly, as a difficult relationship which would be too burdensome to tackle adequately. This may be a consequence of having fallen into the somewhat prejudiced trap laid out by famous men such as "the Preceptor of Germany," Philip Melanchthon (1497–1560), and their aversion to "the monks," or to anything "monkish" which then is used in a pejorative way. To their contemporaries who had joined the Protestant movement, anything related to monasticism had become the epitome of all that was wrong in "medieval" Christendom. Monks supposedly had produced the degeneration of Christianity which needed to undergo reform, as Asaph Ben-Tov succinctly put it in his review of *Renaissance Monks*. Melanchthon despised the period in church history from the fall of the western Roman Empire to the expurgation of doctrine through Martin Luther as the age of the monks. It was a time characterized supposedly by a steep cultural decline, with the fall from pure apostolic doctrine inevitably following at its heels.[3] Such a German-Protestant, lopsided view of monasticism (including the mendicant Orders) is challenged here as it is

---

1. Franz Machilek, "Klosterhumanismus in Nürnberg um 1500," *Mitteilungen des Vereins für Geschichte der Stadt Nürnberg* 64 (1977) 10–45.

2. On this, see Harald Müller's *Habilitationsschrift*, with the title *Habit und Habitus. Mönche und Humanisten im Dialog* (Tübingen: Mohr Siebeck, 2006).

3. See Asaph Ben-Tov. Review of Posset, Franz, *Renaissance Monks: Monastic Humanism in Six Biographical Sketches.* H-German, H-Net Reviews. March, 2007. http://www.h-net.org/reviews/showrev.php?id=12991.

high time to move away from a far too simplistic historiographical working hypothesis of the deformation-reformation model. The "Reformation" can be interpreted to a large degree from the international Renaissance Humanism and the reform efforts within the religious Orders in the Late Middle Ages, and a revisiting of the authentic tradition of the "monastic theology,"[4] such as the one of Saint Bernard of Clairvaux and his theology of grace. In other words, not everything on the eve of the "Reformation" can be naively reduced to some sort of frustration-aggression concept in terms of a ferociously aggressive reaction to a frustratingly abusive or deformed church.

When native speakers of English use the term "monk," one observes not too seldomly a tendency that carelessly includes the mendicant "friars" such as Franciscans, Dominicans, Carmelites, or Augustinians. However, monk and friar are not synonymous terms. "Monks" strictly speaking are contemplative persons and remain stationed in their usually remote monasteries or abbeys of their original choice (*stabilitas loci*). "Friars" are mobile and are sent to cities where their services primarily as preachers are needed most, while residing in friaries of their own Orders. "Friars" usually are members of the so-called mendicant Orders. "Monks" in the West are primarily members of the Orders of the Benedictines or Cistercians, but also of the Carthusians. One of the best-known Carthusian humanists, not included in my *Renaissance Monks*, is Gregor Reisch (c. 1467–1525) who played a role in the conflict over Jewish books between Johann Pefferkorn and Johann Reuchlin.[5] With respect to monks, because of their vow of permanent residency in and allegiance to their local monastery, it is easy to understand that they depended on written communications in their scholarly exchange of thought and of research interests. When the blurring of the distinction between friars and monks in many scholarly and popular writings became apparent over the years, the late Kenneth Hagen felt it necessary to cry out: "Stop it!"[6]

Friars, too, may have been humanists; specifically Augustinian friars, as research done more than a hundred years ago on the spiritual life in the

---

4. Reinhard Schwarz, "Luther's Inalienable Inheritance of Monastic Theology," Franz Posset, trans., in *The American Benedictine Review* 39 (1988) 430–50.

5. Franz Posset, *Johann Reuchlin (1455–1522): A Theological Biography* (Berlin: De Gruyter, 2015), 233–34, 277, 372–73, 834–35.

6. Kenneth Hagen, "So You Think Luther Was a Monk? Stop it!," *Logia* 19 (Eastertide 2010) 35–37. Reprinted in Hagen, *The Word Does Everything. Key Concepts of Luther on Testament, Scripture, Vocation, Cross, and Worm. Also on Method and on Catholicism. Collection of Essays* (Milwaukee: Marquette University Press, 2016), 31–36.

Order of Saint Augustine at the end of the Middle Ages and at the beginning of the modern era showed.[7] We also know, for example, of the German Dominican friar and Grecian, Johannes Cuno (or Cono[n], 1463–1513) who was Johann Reuchlin's (1455–1522) student of Greek in Heidelberg.[8] Furthermore, one of the most famous Italian humanists was the Carmelite friar, Baptist Mantuanus (c. 1448–1516).[9] He was so well-known beyond his homeland that Martin Luther in Germany, too, had read him.[10] From among the Franciscan friars in German-speaking lands, Sebastian Münster (1488–1552) stands out.[11] He later became a Lutheran as he was editing Luther's works for a publisher in Basel, Switzerland, Adam Petri. How important a figure Münster was as a Hebraist, Bible scholar, and cartographer in the cultural history of German-speaking lands can easily be deduced from the fact that his portrait appeared on the 100-Deutsch-Mark bank note (before the introduction of the euro).[12]

Writing biographies has become my favorite way of historiography.[13] With my emphasis on the expression "sketches" in the original subtitle for *Renaissance Monks*, I wanted to draw attention to the fact that these chapters do not claim to be comprehensive biographies which some readers may have expected. There is, indeed, room for further research in order to morph the sketches into full biographies. My sketches raise a number of important questions as one of the book reviewers noted: That some of the questions arising are not awarded a full answer in the biographical sketches

---

7. Hedwig Vonschott, *Geistiges Leben im Augustinerorden am Ende des Mittelalters und zu Beginn der Neuzeit* (Berlin: Ebering, 1915).

8. Martin Sicherl, *Johannes Cuno: ein Wegbereiter des Griechischen in Deutschland; eine biographisch-kodikologische Studie* (Heidelberg: Winter, 1978), 36–40; Posset, *Johann Reuchlin (1455–1522)*, 89.

9. Brocard Sewell, *Blessed Baptist of Mantua, Carmelite and Humanist (1447–1516)* (Aylesford: N.p., 1957).

10. Franz Posset, "'Heaven Is on Sale': The Influence of the Italian Humanist and Carmelite Baptist Mantuanus on Martin Luther," *Carmelus* 36 (1989) 134–44. Posset, *Renaissance Monks*, 8.

11. Stephen G. Burnett, *Christian Hebraism in the Reformation Era (1500–1660): Authors, Books, and the Transmission of Jewish Learning* (Library of the Written Word 19; The Handpress World 13; Leiden/Boston: Brill, 2012).

12. The bank note is depicted as part of my chapter on "Marulus and Luther" in Franz Posset, *Catholic Advocate of the Evangelical Truth: Marcus Marulus (Marko Marulić of Split (1450–1524)* (Collected Works 5; Eugene, OR: Wipf & Stock, 2021), 20.

13. See for example my contribution, "Martin Luther Biographies," in *Biography: An Interdisciplinary Quarterly* 8 (1985) 356–65.

may be due to the fact that the humanist monks studied here are not as well documented as, for example, Abbot Johannes Trithemius (1462–1516),[14] who at times is seen as the example *par excellence* of Monastic Humanism. "Needless to say, scanty sources are an occupational hazard in studying the rank and file of a given intellectual milieu" (Ben-Tov). Since sufficient research on Trithemius is available, I dared to benignly neglect him and draw attention to others, i.e., the six figures presented in this book.

These monastic humanists called themselves in typical humanist fashion by their Grecized or Latinized names: Konrad Töritz from Leonberg (near Stuttgart, Germany) is Conradus Leontorius. Benedikt Schwalbe is Benedictus Chelidonius (Greek for the bird "swallow," German *Schwalbe*). Wolfgang Mayer is Bolfgangus Marius, whereby the Latin "B" is phonetically the closest to the German "W." Heinrich Fastnacht from Orb (or, Urb) is Henricus Urbanus. Veit Bild from Höchstädt is Vitus Acropolitanus (Greek *acropolis* for "high city," i.e., Hochstadt/Höchstädt). Nikolaus Ellenbog is Nicolaus Cubitus (Latin *cubitum* for "elbow," German "*Ellenbogen*").

I agree with one of the reviewers (Seymour House), who wished that I "consolidated these individual studies within the context of the changes even then unfolding in the scholarly world and the wider context of Western Christendom." But such an endeavor would have doubled or tripled the size of the present book. The "context" for the six historical figures is the period called early "Reformation," specifically here, the eve of the Lutheran Reformation: The missed mention of the wider context is the complex matrix, or, the stormy headwaters, from which religious reformers grew or emerged in the early sixteenth century. Some of them joined Friar Martin Luther's movement whereas others remained Catholic while being sympathetic to him.[15] Taking a closer look at the context would have required including, for example, some demythologizing of the German reformer and a search for the historical Luther with a focus on his formative monastic years, i.e., on the young Luther and the humanists.[16] Furthermore, a closer look at Luther's superior, Johann von Staupitz, would have to be included since he was

14. Trithemius was a Benedictine who was visited by Leontorius; see *Renaissance Monks*, chapter 1, 29; N. L. Brann, *The Abbot Trithemius (1462-1516): The Renaissance of Monastic Humanism* (Leiden: Brill, 1981).

15. Franz Posset, *Unser Martin. Martin Luther aus der Sicht katholischer Sympathisanten* (Münster: Aschendorff, 2015); with chapters on Bernhard Adelmann, Caspar Amman, Kaspar Haslach, and Vitus Bild.

16. Helmar Junghans, *Der junge Luther und die Humanisten* (Weimar: Hermann Böhlaus Nachfolger / Göttingen: Vandenhoeck and Ruprecht, 1985).

Luther's beloved, fatherly friend and theological mentor within the Order of Saint Augustine.[17] And, what is often overlooked, the "Bernard Factor" in Luther's theology would have to be taken into serious consideration.[18]

Even though my *Renaissance Monks* does not offer a systematic discussion of exactly what is meant by humanism in the Renaissance period, I am glad to see that one of the younger scholars, in reading the book, pointed out certain "hallmarks of humanism," namely, an interest in the three ancient languages (regardless of the degree of mastery), an interest in Neo-Latin poetry conveying classical imagery and jargon and most importantly, integration into the network of humanist contacts and epistolary friendships. One important feature of the group of German Renaissance monks was the support of their colleague, the lay theologian, Johann Reuchlin, in his adamant advocacy for the preservation of Hebrew books. The group of monks, therefore, deserves "membership in a well–defined humanist milieu." I am also very sympathetic to the observation that our six monks constitute a virtual "group portrait of monastic humanism" (Ben-Tov).

The historical model of the trilingual man (*vir trilinguis*), being well-acquainted with Latin, Greek, and Hebrew, is still a valid ideal today for scholars of the Renaissance and Reformation. This "ideal type" of the trilingual scholar needs to be promoted especially among historians and theologians who specialize in the time period under consideration here, even though the prince of the humanists, the great Erasmus of Rotterdam, himself readily admitted that learning Hebrew was too much for him. He stopped learning it because he was repelled by the strangeness of the language. Later in life he thought it would be risky for young students to learn Hebrew because they might absorb some Judaism in doing so.[19] All the more important is that he readily acknowledged others' polyglot achievements, such as Reuchlin's. Erasmus wrote in his letter to Pope Leo X of May 1515: Reuchlin is almost equally at home in the three languages, Greek, Latin, and Hebrew. "It is quite

17. Franz Posset, *The Front-Runner of the Catholic Reformation: The Life and Works of Johann von Staupitz* (Aldershot: Ashgate: 2003); Lothar Graf zu Dohna and Richard Wetzel, *Staupitz, theologischer Lehrer Luthers. Neue Quellen – bleibende Erkenntnisse* (Tübingen: Mohr Siebeck, 2018).

18. Franz Posset, *Pater Bernhardus. Martin Luther and Bernard of Clairvaux* (reprinted in Collected Works 2; Eugene, OR: Wipf & Stock, 2018). Franz Posset, *The Real Luther: A Friar at Erfurt and Wittenberg* (Saint Louis: Concordia, 2011); Franz Posset, *Luther ist kein Lutheraner. Gesammelte Aufsätze zum historischen Luther* (Paderborn: Bonifatius Verlag, 2019).

19. Nathan Ron, *Erasmus. Intellectual of the 16th Century* (Cham, Switzerland: Palgrave Macmillan, 2021), 90–91.

right that the whole of Germany should admire and venerate this man as its true phoenix and especial glory."[20] Not a monk, Reuchlin was the model of the trilingual scholar whose demise in 1522 was lamented by a learned priest of Würzburg by the name of Vitus Berlerus (1480–1522). He wrote to Willibald Pirckheimer (1470–1530) about "Johann Reuchlin, a man worthy of immortality because of his knowledge of the three languages."[21]

A not very well-known Catholic Hebraist of the first half of the sixteenth century, Georg Witzel (1501–73) warned his audience, in his "Speech in Praise of the Hebrew Language" (*Oratio in laudem Linguae Hebraicae*), not to naively rely on others' translations: One may safely navigate through all the translations—he is speaking primarily of the translations of the Hebrew Bible—only when one is familiar with the original wording. Yet, "new interpreters emerge daily who each translates according to his own taste. If you are not skilled enough to examine them, you may easily fall into error."[22] Witzel proclaimed:

> One cannot sufficiently study theology without the knowledge of this language [Hebrew]. Just as a soldier in battle cannot last long without proper gear. Be persuaded that nothing is more useful, nothing more beautiful, nothing worth striving for more than the study of this language.[23]

In the context of deliberating on the foolishness of relying exclusively on translations and, together with Renaissance humanists, on returning to the sources (*ad fontes*), I am reminded of the Grimm Brothers' fairy tale titled *Hans in Luck* (or, *Clever Hans*; *Hans im Glück*, in the German original): From his honest labors Hans has earned a heavy lump of gold which for our purposes here may be taken as the metaphor for the original Word of God being revealed in the Hebrew language. On his way home Hans finds the lump of gold too heavy to bear. He trades it for a horse to take him home faster,

---

20. Collected Works of Erasmus 3, 109; *Opus epistolarum Desiderii Erasmi Roterodami*, ed. P. S. Allen and H. M. Allen, letter number 335, lines 303–7: *Inter quos est eximius ille vir, Ioannes Reuchlinus Phorcensis, trium linguarum Graecae, Latinae et Hebraicae pene ex aequo peritus; ad haec in nullo doctrinae genere non ita versatus vt cum primis certare possit. Vnde merito virum hunc ceu phoenicem et vnicum suum decus tota suspicit ac veneratur Germania*.

21. Posset, *Johann Reuchlin*, 859.

22. See my rendering of the speech from the Latin original, with the English translation on facing pages, in: Franz Posset, *Respect for the Jews* (Collected Works 4; Eugene, OR: Wipf & Stock, 2019), 154/55.

23. Posset, *Respect for the Jews*, 150/51.

then successively for a cow, a pig, a goose, and eventually a whetstone, which accidentally drops into a river. Step by step, the value of Hans' big gold nugget diminished from transaction to transaction (i.e., for us, any translations) until the last object, the whetstone, got lost in the water.

LIST OF ILLUSTRATIONS

Fig. 1. Church of the monastery complex of Maulbronn, Germany; inscribed on UNESCO's World Heritage List in 1993. Photo of c. 1960 in the private possession of the author 30
Fig. 2. Leontorius' letter of introduction in Johann Reuchlin's book *De verbo mirifico*, 1494. Facsimile reprint of page 6. Courtesy of Verlag Frommann-Holzboog, Stuttgart-Bad Cannstatt, Germany 31
Fig. 3. Title page of *Passio Salvatoris*, Strasbourg, c. 1508. Courtesy of *Schottenstift*, Vienna; Custos Magister Gerhard Schlass 64
Fig. 4. Title page of Chelidonius' morality drama 'The struggle between lust and virtue' (*Voluptatis cum virtute disceptatio*). Courtesy of Österreichische Nationalbibliothek, Vienna 85
Fig. 5. *Triumphal Arch of Emperor Maximilian* by Albrecht Dürer and others (1515–1517) with Latin texts by Benedictus Chelidonius. Courtesy of Österreichische Nationalbibliothek, Vienna 88
Fig. 6. Autograph of Bolfgangus Marius: *Annales sive Cronicon Domus Alderspacensis*. From: *850 Jahre Zisterzienserkloster Aldersbach 1996* (Vilshofen 1996), 53 94
Fig. 7. Tombstone of Bolfgangus Marius, Abbot of Aldersbach, Bavaria. Parish Archive Aldersbach. From: *850 Jahre Zisterzienserkloster Aldersbach 1996* (Vilshofen 1996), 47 107
Fig. 8. Crotus' rectorate page with Urbanus' emblem in the center of the bottom row, c. 1521. Courtesy of Stadtarchiv Erfurt, Germany 110
Fig. 9. Granary of the monastery of Georgenthal. Photo from c. 1902 in the private possession of the author 114

Fig. 10. Title page of Marulus' *Carmen*, edited by
Urbanus (Erfurt: Canappus, 1514), probably patterned
after the woodcut of Urs Graf (see Fig. 11). From:
Charles Béné, *Subina Jedne Pjesme. Destin d'un Poème.
Destiny of a Poem. Carmen de Doctrina Domini Nostri Iesu
Christi Pendentis in Cruce Marci Maruli* (Split 1994),
1:1.3.2 128

Fig. 11. Urs Graf, woodcut in *Passio Christi* by Johann
Geiler von Kaysersberg (Strasbourg: Knobloch, 1506).
From: Anna Scherbaum, *Albrecht Dürers* Marienleben
(Wiesbaden 2004), 311 129

Fig. 12. Title page of pamphlet on the Creed, *Grund vnnd
Schriftliche anzaygungen*, attributed to Vitus (Veit) Bild
Acropolitanus (Augsburg: Philipp Ulhart the Elder,
1525). University of Wisconsin Memorial Library,
Madison, Wisconsin, 3352 Nr. 1605. From Sixteenth
Century Pamphlets on microfiche, pt. 1 (1501–1530).
Fiche 621, nr. 1605. Courtesy of IDC Publishers,
Leiden, Netherlands 134

Fig. 13. Erasmus' letter to Ellenbog of April 1516.
From: *Nikolaus Ellenbog: Briefwechsel*, eds. Andreas
Bigelmair and Friedrich Zoepfl (Münster 1938),
II: 100. Courtesy of *Reuchlin Forschungsstelle*, Pforzheim,
Germany 156

*Every effort has been made to contact all copyright holders. In the event of any
omissions or errors the author asks the copyright holders to inform him so that
the correct credits may be included in future editions.*

FOREWORD

Gerhard B. Winkler, O. Cist.

The title of this book could be deceiving. Some readers might anticipate learning something about decadent clerics and worldly monks of the Renaissance. However, such expectations will be thwarted. In fact, the book deals with the intellectual activities of the so-called 'Northern Humanists' who intended to reform theology, Church, and society through their new education. They focused on the study of ancient authors and the three sacred languages, Hebrew, Greek, and Latin. As humanists in traditional monasteries they formed a stronger group than one might expect. They considered their new endeavours, even their occasional sympathies with Martin Luther, as by no means incompatible with the ideals of a cloistered, contemplative life.

Students of the age of the Renaissance may wonder why, for instance, the most 'silent' of all monks (*numquam deformati* [never deformed], as the saying goes about the Carthusians) attracted great minds and humanists like Willibald Pirckheimer, Thomas More, and Petrus Canisius. Admittedly, the age was keen on discovering hidden manuscripts of ancient authors, pagan and Christian, which were copied and collected in places of cloistered solitude. However, it was certainly not just the libraries that fascinated the scholars of this age, but rather the spirit of contemplation within the milieu of a tremendous 'book culture' that centered on reading. Besides, it might have been the idea of an 'alternative' life that intrigued them. One needs to remember, for instance, that Thomas More depicted his Utopians as industrious 'Puritans,' ascetics, and even as secularized 'monks.' Not by accident, the great Erasmus of Rotterdam, author of the juvenile *Antibarbari* (1498) and quite critical of the 'monks', was rather fond of the sermons on the *Song of Songs* by the monastic theologian Bernard of Clairvaux. Erasmus counted them among the ten best in literature (1522/1523).

Humanists tried to establish an academic alternative to the existing Schools. They attempted a reformation with the help of their new learning (*litterae*) as they were, on the whole, rather disappointed with the scholasticism of many of the friars of the mendicant orders

(Dominicans, Franciscans, etc.). They preferred monastic libraries such as those at Sponheim, Maulbronn, Saints Ulrich and Afra in Augsburg, Saint Emmeram in Regensburg, Aldersbach, Altzelle, or Ottobeuren (all Benedictines and Cistercians) to the those of the 'Schools.'

Saint Benedict demanded of his disciples daily recital of the Bible and the Church Fathers and regular reading of the Christian sources. In this respect the objectives of humanism and the Renaissance meshed with an original monastic claim: back to the sources. Franz Posset, with his six 'portraits' of three Benedictine and three Cistercian monks, presents with skill and learning the rich monastic scenario as it was on the eve of the Reformation and during its early years in German-speaking lands. These German humanists and their colleagues in England, France, Spain, The Netherlands, Bohemia, Slovenia, Croatia, the Ermland, and Poland toiled in the developing humanistic studies. They already formed a united Europe, based on books and letters, on reading and—last, but not least—on a novel approach to the Holy Scriptures, by working from the original biblical languages, Hebrew and Greek.

The six German 'Renaissance Monks' that are presented in this book are from the Benedictine abbeys of Ottobeuren in Swabia, of Saints Ulrich and Afra in Augsburg, of the *Schottenkloster* in Vienna, and of the Cistercian abbeys of Aldersbach near Passau in Bavaria, of Maulbronn near Karlsruhe in Baden-Württemberg, and of Georgenthal in Thuringia. Remarkably, they did not join the Protestant movement. Yet, their lives and works formed an intellectual and spiritual background that, to a large degree, they shared with the reformers at Wittenberg.

The author has already gained a reputation among the leading experts in the intellectual history of the Middle Ages, of monasticism, and of the respective background problems concerning humanism and the Reformation. He represents the group of scholars who vindicate a greater closeness of the spirit of humanism to Martin Luther than is usually acknowledged. From beginning to end, his book is inspiring.

Gerhard B. Winkler, O. Cist.

PREFACE

The principal purpose in writing this book is to draw attention to monastic humanism (*Klosterhumanismus*, in German) at the time of the European Renaissance of the fifteenth and sixteenth centuries. The English term 'monastic humanism' is easily misunderstood in the light of the polemics of present-day 'secular humanism.' Here, however, the term is employed to describe the works of humanists who lived in monasteries around 1500, in contrast to other social groups within the humanist movement. It would be far too simplistic to view all humanists in one camp and the religious orders in the opposing camp.[1] We should also move away from the common historiographical concept of the Deformation-Reformation model, as the Reformation can be explained to a large degree from the matrix of Renaissance humanism and the reform efforts of the religious orders in the Late Middle Ages, and, to a much lesser degree, in terms of a violent reaction to abuses in the Church.

At present there are hardly any publications or biographies of monastic humanists of the Renaissance available in English. Most of the literature is old and in German. For the present project, I have elaborated further on my most recent German lexicon articles in the *Biographisch-Bibliographisches Kirchenlexikon* and the *Verfasserlexikon* of German humanism between 1480–1520, and on some of my previous publications in *The American Benedictine Review* and *Cistercian Studies Quarterly*.

After having investigated over the past two decades the theology and history of the early Reformation and in particular the impact of Saint Bernard of Clairvaux on the Protestant Reformers of the sixteenth century, and after having finished a biography of Johann von Staupitz as the *Front-Runner of the Catholic Reformation*, I felt the need to explore further the humanist matrix of the early Reformation and the spiritual and theological situation on the eve of the Reformation. In this connection, the phenomenon of monastic humanism

---

[1] Such a view is insinuated in Cornelis Augustijn's study of biblical humanism, which otherwise is a most valuable book; see his *Humanismus*, trans. into German by Hinrich Stoevesandt (Göttingen 2003) 108.

presented itself as the major headwater of the Reformation, both Catholic and Protestant. However, instead of theorizing on this issue, I chose to investigate the lives and works of several humanists (for the most part polyglot) and admirers of Christian Latin poetry.

From the numerous candidates for monastic humanism in the religious orders of the Augustinians, Benedictines, Carmelites, Carthusians, Cistercians, Dominicans, and Franciscans, I found the contemplative monks of the Benedictine-Cistercian tradition (and less so the mendicant friars) to be the most under-exposed Renaissance humanists in current historical-theological research. The most recent Catholic lexicon of the Reformation period, *Lexikon der Reformationszeit* (2002), based on the latest edition of the renowned German *Lexikon für Theologie und Kirche*, includes only two of the monks that are dealt with here: the Benedictine Ellenbog and the Cistercian Marius. Yet, other Renaissance monks also deserve similar attention, which will be given them here. However, my presentation is limited to half a dozen monks (three Benedictines and three Cistercians) and to a specific area, that is, the southern regions of the German-speaking lands (Upper Rhine, Swabia, Bavaria, Austria), with the exception of Henricus Urbanus, who lived in the Gotha/Erfurt region.

Most of the information on these monks can be derived from their extensive correspondence in Latin. Whenever available, the critical editions of their works have been used. In typical humanist fashion, these monks called themselves (or were called by colleagues) by their Graecized or Latinized names. For these name changes they sometimes used the name of their birthplace, especially in cases where their original family names were difficult to translate into Greek or Latin: *Konrad Töritz* from *Leonberg* is Latinized as *Conradus Leontorius;* *Benedikt Schwalbe* becomes, in a Latinized/Graecized combination, *Benedictus Chelidonius; Wolfgang Mayer* is Latinized as *Bolfgangus Marius; Heinrich Fastnacht* from *Orb* becomes *Henricus Urbanus; Veit Bild* from *Höchstädt* becomes, in a Latinized/Graecized combination, *Vitus Acropolitanus; Nikolaus Ellenbog* is Latinized as *Nicolaus Cubitus* or *Cubitensis*. The biographical sketches of these six monastic humanists are presented in chronological sequence, according to their dates of birth.

My text contains some words in Greek and Hebrew that help to demonstrate the trilingual ideal that these monks pursued, more or less successfully. Let us remember in this context that the prince of humanists, the great Erasmus of Rotterdam, soon gave up on mastering Hebrew![2] Yet, the enthusiastic attempts of many of these monks to discover the original meaning of the Word of God in the Hebrew and Greek texts of Holy Scripture are truly remarkable. Their search for the 'Greek Truth' and the 'Hebrew Truth' may be the essence of biblical humanism. Their determination to present biblical and historical contents in sophisticated Latin poetic forms that were pleasing to their linguistically sensitive contemporaries is most admirable in terms of pastoral care (*Seelsorge*).

In order to help enlighten and lighten the sometimes complex, perhaps obscure and heavy subject matter, illustrations of interesting title pages of some of the monks' *incunabula* and other visual aids are included.

Franz Posset
Beaver Dam, Wisconsin
Advent Season 2004

---

[2] See Erasmus' letter of December 1504 to John Colet in P. S. Allen, *Des. Erasmi Roterdami Opus Epistolarum* (Oxford 1906) vol. 1:405 (no. 181); Erasmus' letter of 1 April 1516 to William Warham, *ibid.*, vol. 2:218 (no. 396).

ACKNOWLEDGEMENTS

I am most grateful to Professor em. Gerhard Winkler, O. Cist. (University of Salzburg; Stift Wilhering, Austria), for his critical reading of the entire manuscript, for his helpful hints, valuable advice, and for his foreword. I am also very grateful to John R. Sommerfeldt (Dallas) and John Porter (San Francisco) for helping with copy-editing the manuscript, and to the institutions that provided visual source material.

ABBREVIATIONS

ABR	*The American Benedictine Review*
AK	*Die Amerbachkorrespondenz*, ed. Alfred Hartmann, 10 vols. Basel 1942–.
BBKL	*Biographisch-Bibliographisches Kirchenlexikon*
CSQ	*Cistercian Studies Quarterly*
Junghans, *Der junge Luther*	Helmar Junghans, *Der junge Luther und die Humanisten*. Weimar 1984; Göttingen 1985.
RBW 1	*Johannes Reuchlin: Briefwechsel Band I 1477–1505*, ed. by Heidelberger Akademie der Wissenschaften in Zusammenarbeit mit der Stadt Pforzheim, unter Mitwirkung von Stefan Rhein bearbeitet von Matthias Dall'Asta und Gerald Dörner. Stuttgart-Bad Cannstatt 1999; vol. 1 (with letters from 1477–1505).
RBW 2	*Johannes Reuchlin: Briefwechsel Band II 1506–1513*, ed. by Heidelberger Akademie der Wissenschaften in Zusammenarbeit mit der Stadt Pforzheim, unter Mitwirkung von Stefan Rhein bearbeitet von Matthias Dall'Asta und Gerald Dörner. Stuttgart-Bad Cannstatt 2003; vol. 2 (with letters from 1506–1513).
Reformatoren-lexikon	Robert Stupperich, ed. Gütersloh 1984.
StM	*Studien und Mitteilungen zur Geschichte des Benediktinerordens und seiner Zweige*.
VL 2005	*Deutscher Humanismus 1480–1520. Verfasserlexikon*, ed. Franz J. Worstbrock. Berlin and New York 2005.
WA	Weimarer Ausgabe of *D. Martin Luthers Werke. Kritische Gesamtausgabe*. Weimar 1883–. WA Br refers to *Briefe*, the letters of that edition, and WA TR stands for *Tisch-Reden*, the volumes of the Table Talks.

INTRODUCTION

Renaissance humanism around 1500 was an international phenomenon[1] as it was inculturated in the nations of Europe, i.e., 'nationalized'. However, it was not a homogeneous movement.[2] One may differentiate between humanists in general and biblical humanists,[3] but also between 'civic humanists',[4] 'courtly humanists',[5] 'curial humanists' (the latter referring to the 'Roman humanists' at the court of the Renaissance popes),[6] and finally 'monastic humanists' (*Klosterhumanisten*). The main transmitters of Renaissance humanism were not at first the universities but "the monasteries, the ecclesiastical and the secular courts, the urban centres" and then "in due course the universities".[7]

---

[1] "Humanism was becoming an international Phenomenon", Donald R. Kelley, *Renaissance Humanism* (Boston 1991) 56; N. G. Wilson, *From Byzantium to Italy: Greek Studies in the Italian Renaissance* (Baltimore 1992) 24–31; Charles Nauert Jr, *Humanism and the Culture of Renaissance Europe* (Cambridge 1995); Robert Black, "Humanism", in *The New Cambridge Medieval History*, vol. 7, c. 1415–c. 1500, ed. Christopher Allmand (Cambridge 1997) 243–277; reprinted in Robert Black, ed., *Renaissance Thought* (London and New York 2001) 68–94; Peter Burke, *The European Renaissance. Centres and Peripheries* (Oxford 1998).

[2] See Peter Burke, "The Uses of Italy", in Roy Porter and Mikulás Teich, eds., *The Renaissance in National Context* (New York etc. 1992) 6–20, here 6.

[3] See Cornelis Augustijn, "Humanisten auf dem Scheideweg zwischen Luther und Erasmus", in *idem*, *Erasmus. Der Humanist als Theologe und Kirchenreformer* (Leiden and New York 1996) 154–67; *idem*, *Humanismus* (Series: *Die Kirche in ihrer Geschichte. Ein Handbuch*, vol. 2), trans. into German by Hinrich Stoevesandt (Göttingen 2003) (the entire book is dedicated to 'Biblical Humanism'). By the 1540s, however, the ideals of biblical humanism were *passé*; Augustijn, *Humanismus*, 110.

[4] Hans Baron, *The Crisis of the Early Italian Renaissance. Civic Humanism and Republican Liberty in an Age of Classicism and Tyranny*, 2 vols. (Princeton NJ 1955; 1966); James Hankins, *Renaissance Civic Humanism: Reappraisals and Reflections* (New York 2000); Albert Rabil, Jr., "The Significance of 'Civic Humanism' in the Interpretation of the Italian Renaissance", in Keith Whitlock, ed., *The Renaissance in Europe: A Reader* (New Haven 2000) 31–55.

[5] See Friedrich Zoepfl, "Der Humanismus am Hof der Fürstbischöfe von Augsburg", *Historisches Jahrbuch* 62/69 (1949) 671–708 (on the bishops of Augsburg in the 15th and 16th centuries); August Buck, ed., *Höfischer Humanismus* (Weinheim 1989); David Mateer, ed., *Courts, Patrons and Poets* (New Haven 2000).

[6] John F. D'Amico, *Renaissance Humanism in Papal Rome: Humanists and Churchmen on the Eve of the Reformation* (Baltimore 1983); *idem*, *Roman and German Humanism, 1450– 1550. Collected Studies edited by Paul F. Grendler* (Aldershot, Great Britain 1993) I.264.

[7] Lewis W. Spitz, "Humanism in Germany", in *The Impact of Humanism on Western*

Initially, many humanists were marginalized and operated outside the universities. The courts may have been the first to employ the classically-trained men for various administrative services. Functions usually reserved for noblemen were increasingly assumed by civic humanists.[8] These people shared some form of humanist education and were active as Latin secretaries and lawyers at the courts of princes and bishops and in the cities and universities.[9]

We should also not overlook the fact that there were diocesan priests who were humanists, such as the Alsatian Jacob Wimpfeling (1450–1528) or Canon Conradus Mutianus Rufus (1470–1526) at Gotha.[10] There were episcopal humanists[11] such as Bishop Johann von Dalberg (1483–1503) of Worms, who was also the chancellor of the University of Heidelberg.[12] Furthermore, there were humanist laymen such as the Italian Giannozzo Manetti (1396–1459). He found emulators in the two Swabian laymen, Johann Reuchlin (1455–1522) and his grand-nephew Philip Melanchthon (1497–1560), who pursued the well-known ideal of the polyglot scholar. Yet, Reuchlin never joined the Lutheran camp, while his grand-nephew Philip Melanchthon did. Finally, worthy of at least a brief mention is the Croatian layman and patriot Marko Marulić (or Marcus Marulus, 1450–1524), who was an admirer of Erasmus of Rotterdam (1466/69–1536) and a gifted Christian poet and prolific historiographer.[13]

Europe, eds. Anthony Goodman and Angus MacKay (London and New York 1990) 202–219, here 205.

[8] See Eckhard Bernstein, "From Outsiders to Insiders. Some Reflections on the Development of a Group Identity of the German Humanists between 1450 and 1530", in James V. Mehl, ed., *In Laudem Caroli for Charles G. Nauert* (Kirksville 1998) 45–64, here 49; Bernstein, "Vom lateinischen Frühhumanismus bis Conrad Cletis", in *Die Literatur im Übergang vom Mittelalter zur Neuzeit*, eds. Werner Röcke and Marina Münkler (Hansers Sozialgeschichte der deutschen Literatur vom 16. Jahrhundert bis zur Gegenwart, vol. 1) (Munich and Vienna 2004) 54–76, here 62–63.

[9] See Bernstein, "From Outsiders to Insiders", 53.

[10] The medieval ecclesiastical position of 'canons' (German: *weltliches Kanonikerinstitut*, the institution of secular canons) is difficult to define as it depends on the local circumstances; see Guy P. Marchal, "Was war das weltliche Kanonikerinstitut im Mittelalter? Dom- und Kollegiatstifte: eine Einführung und eine neue Perspektive", *Revue d'Histoire Ecclésiastique* 94 (1999) 766–807; 95 (2000) 7–53.

[11] *Humanistenbischof*, as used in Alois Schmid, "Humanistenbischöfe. Untersuchungen zum vortridentinischen Episkopat in Deutschland", *Römische Quartalschrift für christliche Altertumskunde und Kirchengeschichte* 87 (1992) 159–92 (on the bishops of Augsburg).

[12] See Friedrich Wilhelm Bautz, "Dalberg", BBKL 1 (1990) 1195.

[13] A dossier with a biography and English translations of some of his works was published by Bratislav Lučin, ed., *Most/The Bridge. A Journal of Croatian Literature* 1–4 (1999) 3–172. Marulus was famous around the then-known world. One of his poems

Generally, reform-minded, humanist monks are neglected in the research on Renaissance humanism,[14] as the question of the relationship between the scholastics at the universities on one hand and the new type of scholar with humanist education outside or at the margin of academia on the other has dominated recent debate.[15] We must not forget that numerous members of the various religious orders, monks and friars,[16] were humanists along with other priest-humanists.

An informative depiction (see Fig. 8) of the coat of arms of Crotus Rubeanus (c. 1480–1545), a priest-humanist and rector of the University of Erfurt around 1520, demonstrates the various backgrounds and lifestyles of humanists centered at Erfurt,[17] including laymen, secular

---

was published by Henricus Urbanus, the monastic humanist of the Gotha-Erfurt circle of humanists; see Franz Posset, "A Cistercian Monk as Editor of the *Carmen* of the Croatian Humanist Marcus Marulus (died 1524): The German Humanist Henricus Urbanus O.Cist. (died c. 1538)", CSQ 39 (2004) 399–419.

[14] Nicole Lemaitre in her Preface to Jean-Marie Le Gall, *Les moines au temps des réformes: France (1480–1560)* (Seyssel 2001), describes Le Gall's enterprise of investigating the monks at the time of reform as a "no man's land de la recherche historique" (p. 9).

[15] See James H. Overfield, *Humanism and Scholasticism in Late Medieval Germany* (Princeton 1984); Charles G. Nauert, "Humanism, Scholastics, and the Struggle to Reform the University of Cologne, 1523–1525", in James V. Mehl, ed., *Humanismus in Köln/Humanism in Cologne* (Cologne 1991) 39–76; Erika Rummel, *The Humanist-Scholastic Debate in the Renaissance and Reformation* (Cambridge, MA 1995).

[16] German scholars do not usually differentiate between monks and friars; the German word *Mönch* is used for the English 'friar' and 'monk'. On mendicant orders and humanism, specifically on several Franciscans in Vienna, Nuremberg, and Ulm, see Hermann Maschek, "Zur Geschichte des Humanismus im Franziskanerorden", *Archivum Franciscanum Historicum* 28 (1935) 574–579 (on Guilhelmus de Savona, Johannes Lukas Camers, Nicolaus Glassberger, and Johannes von Laudenburg). Another Franciscan was Paul Scriptoris (c. 1460–1505); on him, see Helmut Feld, "Scriptoris", BBKL 9 (1995) 1258–1261. For the order of Saint Augustine, see Rudolf Arbesmann, *Der Augustinereremitenorden und der Beginn der humanistischen Bewegung* (Würzburg 1965). On mendicants in Florence, see Kaspar Elm, "Mendikanten und Humanisten in Florenz des Tre- und Quattrocento. Zum Problem der Legitimisierung humanistischer Studien in den Bettelorden", in Otto Herding and Robert Stupperich, eds., *Die Humanisten in ihrer politischen und sozialen Umwelt* (Boppard 1976) 51–85.

[17] On this so-called 'rectorate page', see Friedrich Kaiser, *Reformations-Almanach 1817* p. LXXXIff., as referred to by August Emil Frey, *Luther und seine Freunde. Erster Theil. Die Freunde Luthers bis zum Beginne der Reformation* (Saint Louis 1884) 66. A depiction of Crotus' emblem is shown in E. G. Schwiebert, *Luther and his times. The Reformation from a New Perspective* (Saint Louis 1950) Plate XL. A more detailed interpretation and depiction is provided by Eckhard Bernstein, "Der Erfurter Humanistenkreis am Schnittpunkt von Humanismus und Reformation. Das Rektoratsblatt des Crotus Rubianus", *Der polnische Humanismus und die europäischen Sodalitäten. Pirckheimer Jahrbuch für Renaissance- und Humanismusforschung* 12 (Wiesbaden 1997) 137–165; depiction of the rectorate page (in color) in Franz Posset, "Polyglot Humanism in Germany

priests, friars, and a monk. Rector Crotus Rubeanus was a friend of Martin Luther (1483–1546); they had been roommates in the *Georgenburse* at Erfurt.[18] In 1515, Crotus contributed to the famous *Letters of Obscure Men*.[19] Crotus' large emblem is framed by sixteen other coats of arms of his humanist colleagues and friends. At the bottom of the page we see the shield/seal of the Cistercian monk Enric[h]us[20] Urbanus (†1538) with two wheels (for a long time, Henricus Urbanus was mistaken for Urbanus Rhegius [1489–1541]). In addition to the monk Henricus there are two Augustinian friars from Erfurt and Wittenberg represented on this page: Johannes Lang (1487–1548) and Martin Luther. Membership of a religious order, however, played no apparent role in the positioning of the coats of arms on this rectorate sheet. The criterion for inclusion was being a 'humanist'. Evidently monks and friars had no problem being accepted in humanist circles of laymen and regulated (canons) or diocesan priests at that time.

Clockwise, starting from the shield of the Cistercian monk Urbanus in the middle of the bottom line, we find the following laymen, clerics, and religious represented: Canon Johannes Draco (or Drach, Draconites, 1494–1566), the layman Johann Reuchlin, the layman Adam Crato (or Krafft, 1493–1558, later a Lutheran preacher), the layman Joachim Camerarius (1500–1574), the priest Jodocus Menius (or Justus Mening, 1499–1558), Friar Martin Luther, the layman Ulrich von Hutten (1488–1532), the layman Eobanus Hessus (1488–1540), Canon Justus Jonas (1493–1555), Erasmus of Rotterdam as the former Augustinian canon regular who was dispensed from his religious vows by Pope Leo X, the layman Philip Melanchthon, Friar Johannes Lang, the layman Peter Eberbach (or Petreius, c. 1480–1531), Canon Conradus Mutianus Rufus, and the layman Georg Petz from Forchheim (or Forchemius, †1522).

Circa 1520 as Luther's Milieu and Matrix: The Evidence of the "Rectorate Page" of Crotus Rubeanus", *Renaissance and Reformation/Renaissance et Réforme* 27 (2003; issue date November 2004) 5–33.

[18] See Schwiebert 133.

[19] The letters in English translation are found in: *On the Eve of the Reformation. Letters of Obscure Men, Ulrich von Hutten, et al. Translated by Francis Griffin Stokes, New Introduction by Hajo Holborn* (New York etc. 1964).

[20] His Latinized first name is rarely used, except for example in Mutianus' letter (1505), Krause 8 (no. 8) (see below with note 23). Usually he is addressed as *H. Urbanus*.

In a way, the iconographical lay-out of this page points to a typical humanist 'sodality' which, however, existed only in Crotus' imagination. Yet it remains remarkable for the figures included on it, namely two friars and a monk, representing monastic humanism around 1520 in the region of Erfurt, Gotha, and Wittenberg. This humanist document shows hand-written polyglot biblical inscriptions and mottos in the three sacred languages of Latin, Greek, and Hebrew. It becomes clear that the association of Greek with Hebrew was primarily a theological rather than a literary one.[21]

Much of the humanists' thought is accessible only through their correspondence. They collected their own letters and those they received. In their view, letter writing was an art form. That the letter form was coming to the fore as a literary genre around 1500 is suggested by two collections of letters that are connected to the great controversy around Johann Reuchlin, who edited the letters of sympathy that he collected. Titled *Clarorum virorum epistolae... missae ad Ioannem Reuchlin*, the volume was first printed in 1514 (*Letters of Famous Men to Reuchlin*). An anonymous editor followed with the collection of fictitious *Letters of Obsure Men*, with its printer falsely given as Aldo Manuzio (Manutius, c. 1450–1515) of Venice.[22] The correspondence is frequently edited in elaborate critical editions.[23] Study of their

---

[21] On Greek and Hebrew and the theological motivation for studying them, see Anthony Levi, *Renaissance and Reformation. The Intellectual Genesis* (New Haven 2002) 291. On the *Collegium trilingue* in Louvain at that time and its challenges for the theologians, see H. de Vocht, *History of the Foundation and the Rise of the Collegium Trilingue Lovaniense 1517–1550* (Louvain 1951); Augustijn, *Humanismus*, 92–93.

[22] See Cecil H. Clough, "The cult of Antiquity: letters and letter collections", in idem, ed., *Cultural Aspects of the Italian Renaissance: Essays in Honour of Paul Oskar Kristeller* (Manchester and New York 1976) 33–67. It is not always evident what a humanist's self-edited letter collection was intended to be. Copyists were at times selective.

[23] For example: *Der Briefwechsel des Mutianus Rufus*, ed. Carl Krause (Kassel 1885); *Konrad Peutingers Briefwechsel*, ed. Erich König (Munich 1923); *Der Briefwechsel des Konrad Celtis*, ed. Hans Rupprich (Munich 1934); *Die Amerbachkorrespondenz*, ed. Alfred Hartmann, 10 vols. (Basel 1942–); hereafter quoted as AK); *Dürer, Schriftlicher Nachlaß*, ed. Hans Rupprich (Berlin 1956); *Jakob Wimpfeling: Briefwechsel*, eds. Otto Herding and Dieter Mertens (Munich 1990); *Johannes Reuchlin: Briefwechsel*, eds. Matthias Dall'Asta and Gerald Dörner (Stuttgart 1999–); *Willibald Pirckheimers Briefwechsel*, vols. 1 & 2, ed. Emil Reicke (Munich 1940–1956), vols. 3–5, eds. Helga Scheible and Dieter Wuttke (Munich 1989–2001); Alfred Schröder, "Der Humanist Veit Bild, Mönch bei St. Ulrich: Sein Leben und sein Briefwechsel", *Zeitschrift des Historischen Vereins für Schwaben und Neuburg* 20 (1893) 173–227; Georg Wolff, "Conradus Leontorius. Biobibliographie", *Beiträge zur Geschichte der Renaissance und Reformation: Joseph Schlecht am 16. Januar 1917 als Festgabe zum Sechzigsten Geburtstag*, L. Fischer et al., eds. (Munich and Freising 1917) 363–410; I am grateful to Matthias Dall'Asta for helpful

correspondence may reveal important insights. For example, in the attempt to reconstruct the biography of the Cistercian Henricus Urbanus, one must depend almost entirely upon the correspondence of his priest-friend Conradus Mutianus Rufus.

The following investigations into the lives of monks on the eve of the Reformation or during its early years are pursued on the working hypothesis that the Reformation of the sixteenth century was not something completely new and revolutionary, but part of a long-lasting process of reform during the Late Middle Ages. There is probably more resemblance and continuity rather than sudden shifts and changes.[24] Religious orders and their reforms played an important role in this development from c. 1450–c. 1550, the 'century of reform'[25] with its 'culture of reform'.[26]

Furthermore, the reformers of religious orders and the monastic humanists of the early sixteenth century stand on the shoulders of reformers of the fourteenth and fifteenth centuries, known for their 'modern devotion' (*devotio moderna*), a designation for a reform movement that started in the Low Countries around 1375 with Geert Grote (1340–1384) in Deventer. Humanists like Rudolph Agricola (1443/44–1485), Conradus Celtis (1459–1508), Conradus Mutianus, Erasmus of Rotterdam, and also Martin Luther, when they were still pupils, are counted among the students who enjoyed the pastoral care of the 'New Devotionalists', the Brethren of the Common Life.[27] They promoted a 'book culture' (*Buchkultur*)[28] and with it the Western

---

bibliographical hints and for providing me with G. Wolff's article. *Kilian Leibs Briefwechsel und Diarien*, ed. Joseph Schlecht (Münster 1909); *Christoph Scheurls Briefbuch, ein Beitrag zur Geschichte der Reformation und ihrer Zeit*, 2 vols., eds. Franz Freiherr von Soden and Joachim Karl Friedrich Knaake (Potsdam 1867–1872; reprint Aalen 1962); Nikolaus Ellenbog, *Briefwechsel*. Einleitung und Buch I–II von Andreas Bigelmair, Buch III–IX und Register von Friedrich Zoepfl (Münster 1938).

[24] See Robert J. Bast and Andrew C. Gow, eds., *Continuity and Change. The Harvest of Late Medieval and Reformation History. Essays Presented to Heiko A. Oberman on his 70th Birthday* (Leiden, Boston, Cologne 2000); Levi, *Renaissance and Reformation*; Alister McGrath, *The Intellectual Origins of the European Reformation* (2nd edition: Malden 2004).

[25] *Reformjahrhundert*, Stefan Ehrenpreis and Ute Lotz-Heumann, *Reformation und konfessionelles Zeitalter* (Darmstadt 2002) 11.

[26] *Une culture de la réforme*, Le Gall 18–21.

[27] See Junghans, *Der junge Luther*, 27–28; Robert Stupperich, "Devotio moderna und reformatorische Frömmigkeit", *Jahrbuch des Vereins für Westfälische Kirchengeschichte* 59/60 (1966/1967) 16–16; Spitz, "Humanism in Germany", in *The Impact of Humanism*, 203; Ross Fuller, *The Brotherhood of the Common Life and Its Influence* (Albany 1995), who apparently coined the English name 'New Devotionalist' (p. xi).

[28] See Thomas Kock, *Die Buchkultur der Devotio Moderna* (Frankfurt 1999).

Christian heritage of the Bible, the Church Fathers and monks, as well as the renewal of the orders and religious life in general.[29]

Indeed, one can say that there would have been no Reformation without monasticism.[30] 'Humanism', 'reformation', and 'monasticism' were not contradictions around 1500, a fact that makes the problematic field of the intellectual and spiritual sources of the Reformation vast and complex. Yet, working with 'Renaissance', 'reformation', and 'humanism' as cultural constructs is unavoidable.[31] For decades, the issue of the relationship between Renaissance humanism and the Reformation has emerged as a region yet to be explored further, where new findings may still be brought to light.[32] A major insight of such investigations has led to the well-founded theory that next to all the abuse and deformation of Church and religion prior to the Reformation, there was genuine Christian life in central Europe on the eve of the Reformation.[33]

The 'decline theory' (malaise of the Church) is actually outdated, if used as an exclusive explanation of the origins and development

---

[29] Rudolf Th. M. van Dijk, "Die Frage einer nördlichen Variante der Devotio Moderna", in *Wessel Gansfort (1419–1489) and Northern Humanism*, eds. Fokke Akkerman, Gerda C. Huisman, and Arie Johan Vanderjagt (Leiden etc. 1993) 157–169.

[30] See Bernd Moeller "Die frühe Reformation in Deutschland als neues Mönchtum", in *Die frühe Reformation in Deutschland als Umbruch. Wissenschaftliches Symposion des Vereins für Reformationsgeschichte 1996*, eds. Bernd Moeller and Stephen E. Buckwalter (Gütersloh 1998) 76–91.

[31] See Levi 370, note 1; on the history of the idea of 'Reformation', see Gerhart B. Ladner, *Idea of Reform. Its Impact on Christian Thought and Action in the Age of the Fathers* (Cambridge, Mass. 1959); Robert Stupperich, Introduction in *Reformatorenlexikon*, 7; Philippe Contamine, "Le vocabulaire politique à la fin du Moyen Âge: L'idée de *reformatio*" in Jean Philippe Genet and Bernard Vincent, eds., *État et Église dans la genèse de l'État moderne* (Madrid 1986) 145–156; Jos E. Vercruysse, "'Reformatio' in Katholischer Perspektive: Drei Beispiele aus dem 16. Jahrhundert", *Ephemerides theologicae Lovanienses* 75 (1999) 142–156 (including the Fifth Lateran Council from 1512–1517).

[32] See Werner Schwarz, "Studies in Luther's Attitudes Towards Humanism", *The Journal of Theological Studies* 6 (1953) 66–76; Lewis W. Spitz, *The Religious Renaissance of the German Humanists* (Cambridge, Mass. 1963); James M. Kittelson, "Humanism and the Reformation in Germany", *Central European History* 9 (1976) 303–322; James D. Tracy, "Humanism and the Reformation", in Steven Ozment, ed., *Reformation Europe: A Guide to Research* (Saint Louis 1982) 33–57. On the history of this issue and related themes, see Helmar Junghans, "Der Einfluss des Humanismus auf Luthers Entwicklung bis 1518" (first published 1970); revised and integrated in his book *Der junge Luther*, 11–62.

[33] See Bernd Moeller, "Religious Life in Germany on the Eve of the Reformation", in Gerald Strauss, ed., *Pre-Reformation Germany* (London 1972) 13–42 (originally published 1965). The idea of a Catholic Reformation before 'the' Reformation stems originally from the Protestant historian Wilhelm Maurenbrecher.

of the Reformation. The religious climate of these years was not simply shaped by disgust with the 'deformed' Church, but more decisively by the will to 'reform' popular and elitist piety. In place of the stereotype of deformation/reformation, we may have to consider a combination of concepts, like 'headwaters' or 'matrix' or the 'heterogeneity' of the Reformation.[34] This issue is also debated in terms of the aptness of the metaphor 'wild growth' (*Wildwuchs*) for the great variety of reform ideas and actions in the 1520s.[35] For instance, the spirituality of Augustinian friars like Luther (and his superior Johann von Staupitz [†1524]) is just one variety within the broad late-medieval spiritual garden. Such spirituality grew primarily on monastic humanism, the fertile ground from which men like Luther developed, but also others,[36] including his opponents. In other words, the Reformation was "not a 'miscarriage' of late scholasticism, but it was a rebirth"[37] ('renaissance'). There was a substantial affinity between the humanism of scholastics and that of monks.[38]

Connected to monastic humanism, Luther's religious ideas and difficulties were often perceived from hindsight and through the later Table Talks. Yet, they were typical of monastic piety "based on spiritual athleticism"[39] in the cloister more than anything else. It is generally overlooked that Luther was much impressed by the monastic humanist and Carmelite, Baptista Mantuan (1448–1516).[40] In other words, Luther was both a man of his age, i.e., of humanism, and a deeply religious genius, "a trained theologian and humanist, immersed in biblical, theological and classical sources".[41] However, he was not as unique as later historiographers made him out to be.[42] He may

---

[34] See Hans-Jürgen Goertz, "Eine 'bewegte' Epoche—zur Heterogenität reformatorischer Bewegungen", in Heiko A. Oberman *et al.*, eds., *Reformiertes Erbe: Festschrift für Gottfried W. Locher zu seinem 80. Geburtstag* (Zürich 1993) 103–25.

[35] See Helmar Junghans: "Plädoyer für "Wildwuchs der Reformation" als Metapher", *Lutherjahrbuch* 65 (1998) 101–108.

[36] See Franz Posset, "Benedictus Chelidonius O.S.B. (c. 1460–1521), A Forgotten Monastic Humanist of the Renaissance", ABR 53 (2002) 426–452, here 426–427.

[37] Spitz, "Humanism in Germany", in *The Impact of Humanism*, 202.

[38] See Richard William Southern, *Scholastic Humanism and the Unification of Europe* (Cambridge, Mass. 1995), vol. 1.

[39] R. W. Scribner and C. Scott Dixon, *The German Reformation* (New York 2003; 2nd ed.) 8.

[40] See Franz Posset, "'Heaven is on Sale': The Influence of the Italian Humanist and Carmelite Baptist Mantuanus on Martin Luther", *Carmelus* 36 (1989) 134–144.

[41] Scribner and Dixon, 13.

[42] Scribner and Dixon, 16.

fit quite well (up to his marriage) into the broadly-conceived group of monastic humanists, avoiding the narrow definition of humanism as Erasmianism.

One of the recent trends in Reformation research has been the further investigation of 'social groups'[43] and their role in the history of the Reformation. One such group has attracted particular attention: the lawyers and administrators of princely courts and imperial cities, such as the layman and city clerk of Nuremberg, Lazarus Spengler (1479–1533).[44] However, the social group of 'monastic humanists'—who were normally far removed from the cities,[45] living in distant monasteries—has not so far found equal attention. The great deficit with regard to this group within early Reformation research is now being recognized; it concerns the Catholic realm.[46] The role of land-owning monasteries in remote, rural areas is underexposed at this stage of Reformation research. By bringing monastic humanists into the scene and thus onto the early Reformation stage a beginning can be made.

A misconception also needs to be corrected: namely, that monks with their ties to one monastic location (*stabilitas loci*) were not in touch with their surroundings and the trends of their times. For example, they did not "turn up their noses at the new technology" of printing as was recently observed.[47] In fact, they used it quite effectively. Monastic humanism and civic and educational humanism

---

[43] See Miriam Usher Chrisman and Otto Gründler, eds., *Social Groups and Religious Ideas in The Sixteenth Century* (Kalamazoo 1978); includes only the nobility, the patriciate, the poor, the universities, refugees, and exiles.

[44] See Harold J. Grimm, *Lazarus Spengler. A Lay Leader of the Reformation* (Columbus 1978); Ehrenpreis and Lotz-Heumann 114f.

[45] The connection between the Reformation and the imperial cities in the German lands has been thoroughly researched in recent years under the leadership of Bernd Moeller; see his *Reichsstadt und Reformation* (2nd German edition: Berlin 1987); English trans.: *Imperial Cities and the Reformation: Three Essays*, ed. and trans. by H. C. Erik Midelfort and Mark U. Edwards, Jr. (Philadelphia 1972; 2nd ed.: Durham NC 1982); Steven E. Ozment, *The Reformation in the Cities: The Appeal of Protestantism to Sixteenth-Century Germany and Switzerland* (New Haven 1975); Berndt Hamm, "The Urban Reformation in the Holy Roman Empire", in Thomas A. Brady, Heiko A. Oberman, and James D. Tracy, eds., *Handbook of European History, 1400–1600: Late Middle Ages, Renaissance and Reformation* (Leiden 1995) vol. 2:193–220; Ehrenpreis and Lotz-Heumann 29–39.

[46] *Katholisch-altgläubige Thematiken*, Ehrenpreis and Lotz-Heumann 113.

[47] Guy-Marie Oury, "The Monks of the Renaissance at the Heart of the Revolution of the Printed Book", CSQ 36 (2001) 163–74; translated from the French by Brian Kerns OCSO.

often went hand-in-hand. Monastic and civic humanists agreed totally on the importance of grammar, rhetoric, logic, and eloquence, and they usually shared a love of poetry. Monks as humanists were open to the reform ideas that were floating around. Although "more reformers were friars than monks",[48] the focus here will be on Benedictine and Cistercian monks rather than on friars.

Monks (and friars) represent what since the nineteenth century has been known as *Klosterhumanismus* (monastic humanism). It means primarily the scholarship that was pursued by monks and friars with humanist tendencies during the Renaissance period from the fifteenth century. The German concept of *Klosterhumanismus* is originally found in the context of the history of literature towards the end of the nineteenth century.[49] Now, it is employed by Church historians and theologians as well.[50]

---

[48] Owen Chadwick, *The Early Reformation on the Continent* (Oxford 2001) 151. An example of an Augustinian friar (later a Benedictine monk) who was open to humanism is Luther's superior in the order, Johann von Staupitz (†1524); see Franz Posset, *The Front-Runner of the Catholic Reformation: The Life and Works of Johann von Staupitz* (Aldershot, Great Britain 2003).

[49] The German concept of *Klosterhumanismus* is found in I. W. Nagl and Jacob Zeidler, *Deutsch-Österreichische Literaturgeschichte* (Vienna and Leipzig 1899) vol. 1:455 (on Chelidonius); Richard Newald, "Beiträge zur Geschichte des Humanismus in Oberösterreich", *Jahrbuch des oberösterreichischen Musealvereins* 81 (1926) 155–223; reprinted in Newald, *Probleme und Gestalten des deutschen Humanismus: Studien* (Berlin 1963) 82–102. The concept is also used by Paul Richter, "Die Schriftsteller der Benediktinerabtei Maria-Laach, mit Textbeilagen. III: Die humanistische Epoche in Maria-Laach mit Rücksicht auf den rheinischen Klosterhumanismus überhaupt", in *Westdeutsche Zeitschrift für Geschichte und Kunst* 17 (1912) 277–340 (Richter deals with, among others, Johannes Trithemius (abbot of Sponheim), Johannes Butzbach (prior of Maria Laach), Jacobus Siberti, and Johannes Curvello); on the Rhenish humanist Curvello, of the monastery of Johannesberg near Bingen, Germany, see F. W. E. Roth, "Johannes Curvello O. S. B. Ein vergessener Humanist des XVI. Jahrhunderts", *Annalen des Historischen Vereins für den Niederrhein* 62 (1896) 209–210; Josef Oswald, "Die Gedichte des Abtes Wolfgang Marius von Aldersbach", *Ostbairische Grenzmarken: Passauer Jahrbuch für Geschichte, Kunst und Volkskunde* 7 (Passau 1964/1965) 310–19, here 312; Franz Machilek, "Klosterhumanismus in Nürnberg um 1500", *Mitteilungen des Vereins für Geschichte der Stadt Nürnberg* 64 (1977) 10–45; Franz Josef Worstbrock, "Aus Gedichtsammlungen des Wolfgang Marius", *Zeitschrift für bayerische Landesgeschichte* 44 (1981) 492; Rolf Schmidt, *Reichenau und St. Gallen: ihre literarische Überlieferung zur Zeit des Klosterhumanismus in St. Ulrich und Afra zu Augsburg um 1500* (Sigmaringen 1985) 11–25; hereafter quoted as Schmidt; Noel L. Brann, *Abbot Trithemius (1462–1516): The Renaissance of Monastic Humanism* (Leiden 1981). Klaus Graf would like to replace the concept of *Klosterhumanismus* with what he calls 'monastic historism'; see his "Ordensreform und Literatur in Augsburg während des 15. Jahrhunderts", in Johannes Janota and Werner Williams-Krapp, eds., *Literarisches Leben in Augsburg während des 15. Jahrhunderts* (Tübingen 1995) 100–59, here 139 and 157; Alois Schmid, "Klosterhumanismus im Augustiner-Chorherrenstift Polling", in Rainer A. Müller, ed., *Kloster*

The concept of monastic humanism may surprise those who think of humanism and monasticism as mutually exclusive opposites, and that humanism was a pagan and an anti-monastic movement. True, some Italian humanists were critical of the monks' and friars' presumptuous claim to the concept of 'religious life' (*religio*), if monks and friars presumed that they themselves were exclusively the true religious people (*religiosi*). Lorenzo Valla (1406–1457) in his work on the profession of the religious (*De professione religiosum*) refuted their claim and suggested that monks and friars in their various orders should call themselves 'sects'. Similar attacks surfaced with Erasmus of Rotterdam and Jacob Wimpfeling.[51] In his book on moral integrity (*De integritate*) of 1505, Wimpfeling attacked the lifestyle (concubinage) and ignorance of the secular clergy and the laziness of the monastic clergy. He included the thesis that the highly-respected Church Father Saint Augustine of Hippo was neither a monk nor a friar, but a canon who had written the *Rule of Augustine*, and that the so-called Augustinian order was a product of later historical developments.[52] The young Augustinian friar Luther questioned Wimpfeling's position.[53]

In the contemplative orders in particular (i.e., in the Benedictine tradition) the study of classical antiquity had probably never disappeared completely, and it was revived in the Renaissance.[54] At that

---

und Bibliothek. Zur Geschichte des Bibliothekswesens der Augustiner-Chorherren in der Frühen Neuzeit (Publikationen der Akademie der Augustiner-Chorherren von Windesheim 2) (Paring 2000) 79–107; Harald Müller and Anne-Katrin Ziesak, "Der Augsburger Benediktiner Veit Bild und der Humanismus. Eine Projektskizze", *Zeitschrift des historischen Vereins für Schwaben* 95 (2002) 27–51, on *Klosterhumanismus*, see 28–38; Anna Scherbaum's dissertation, *Albrecht Dürers 'Marienleben'. Ein Buch im geistigen Umfeld des Nürnberger Klosterhumanismus* (Berlin 2003) published in book form as *Albrecht Dürers* Marienleben. *Form—Gehalt—Funktion und sozialhistorischer Ort. Mit einem Beitrag von Claudia Wiener* (Wiesbaden 2004).

[50] See, for example, the eminent historical theologians Helmar Junghans and Ulrich Köpf who used this concept: Junghans in his groundbreaking study on the young Luther and the humanists, *Der junge Luther und die Humanisten* (1984), 24, and Köpf in his introduction to *Theologen des Mittelalters: Eine Einführung* (Darmstadt 2002) 41.

[51] See Martin Burgdorf, *Der Einfluß der Erfurter Humanisten auf Luthers Entwicklung bis 1510* (Leipzig n.d.) 64–66. Rabelais and others are also known for their anti-monasticism.

[52] See Burgdorf, 73–74.

[53] See WA 9:12; see Reinhard Schwarz, *Luther* (Göttingen 1986) 19.

[54] See Adalbert Horawitz, *Zur Geschichte des Humanismus in den Alpenländern*, 3 vols. (Vienna 1886–1887) vol. 1:4, as referred to by Bernhard Gerhard Winkler, *Die Sonette des B. Chelidonius zu A. Dürers Marienleben und ihr Verhältnis zum Marienleben des*

time, humanistic thought was present in most of the religious orders through members who were trained primarily in Italy, and who brought humanist insights back to their cloisters. These monastic humanists made great contributions to Renaissance thought and scholarship. In terms of content, they were often biblical humanists and at the time of the 'Reuchlin Controversy' early in the sixteenth century they sided with Johann Reuchlin, the Christian Hebraist, Swabian patriot, and defender of Jewish books. Yet, not all monastic humanists became later 'Protestant'[55] Reformers.

Generally viewed, monastic humanism provided inspiration for the young Luther and his early Reformation as a still inner-Catholic reform movement. His theology was shaped largely by the monastic and patristic theology of Bernard of Clairvaux and Augustine. Only in the 1520s did the split along the now familiar denominational lines pro and contra Luther develop.[56] The phenomenon is now called the 'confessionalization' of humanism and the formation of the various Christian denominations.[57] Thus, this view supports the thesis that the Reformation in Germany was not simply a reaction to abuses in the Church (i.e., ecclesiastical de-formation lead-

---

Kartäusers Philipp (dissertation, Vienna 1960) 9. I am grateful to Professor em. Gerhard B. Winkler (Stift Wilhering, Austria) for providing me with a copy of his dissertation.

[55] The term 'Protestant' was originally a political one, designating those who objected in 1529 to the abrogation of previously-granted privileges; see Scribner and Dixon, 3.

[56] See David V. N. Bagchi, *Luther's Earliest Opponents, Catholic Controversialists, 1518–1525* (Minneapolis 1991); Götz-Rüdiger Tewes, "Luthergegner der ersten Stunde. Motive und Verflechtungen", *Quellen und Forschungen aus italienischen Archiven und Bibliotheken* 75 (1995) 256–365 (on Eck, Hochstraaten, Aleander *et al.*).

[57] See Ernst Walter Zeeden, "Grundlagen und Wege der Konfessionsbildung im Zeitalter der Glaubenskämpfe", *Historische Zeitschrift* 185 (1958) 249–299; idem, *Die Entstehung der Konfessionen; Grundlagen und Formen der Konfessionsbildung im Zeitalter der Glaubenskämpfe* (Munich 1965); Wolfgang Reinhard, "Reformation, Counter-Reformation, and the Early Modern State: A Reassessment", *Catholic Historical Review* 75 (1989) 383–404; Anton Schindling and Walter Ziegler, eds., *Die Territorien des Reichs im Zeitalter der Reformation und Konfessionalisierung: Land und Konfession 1500–1650*, 7 volumes (Münster 1989–1998); Heinz Schilling, "Confessional Europe", in *Handbook of European History 1400–1600*, vol. 2:641–681; Franz Machilek, "Die Zisterzienser in Böhmen und Mähren in den konfessionellen Auseinandersetzungen des 15. und 16. Jahrhunderts", in *Zisterzienser zwischen Zentralisierung und Regionalisierung. 400 Jahre Fürstenfelder Äbtetreffen*, eds. Hermann Nehlsen and Klaus Wollenberg (Frankfurt 1998) 113–138; Andrew Pettegree, "Confessionalization in North Western Europe", in Joachim Bahlcke and Arno Strohmeyer, eds., *Konfessionalisierung in Ostmitteleuropa. Wirkungen des religiösen Wandels im 16. und 17. Jahrhundert in Staat, Gesellschaft und Kultur* (Stuttgart 1999) 105–120; Erika Rummel, *The Confessionalization of Humanism in Reformation Germany* (Oxford 2000); Ehrenpreis and Lotz-Heumann, 62–71.

ing to re-formation), but almost an organic result of monastic humanism with its emphasis on the return to sources, biblical scholarship, linguistic expertise in Greek and Hebrew, inner-monastic reforms, and also its interest in historiography, especially local history—all of which we can also observe with regard to other non-monastic Renaissance humanists. Local historiography became a mark of distinction for humanists, monastic and non-monastic.[58]

Occasionally, one encounters the idea of 'national humanism'.[59] However, the use of 'nation' (*natio*) in the period of the Renaissance around 1500 is rather complex and in need of further clarification.[60] At times, the German humanists display their patriotism as an aversion to anything that is not German, by contrasting Germany to the loquacious Greece, the presumptuous Italy, and the quarrelsome France.[61] Especially strong is the anti-Italian attitude of Conradus Celtis and Conradus Leontorius (c. 1460–1511). In addition, these German humanists were opposed to the Italians' perceived homosexual tendencies.[62] A similar aversion is found in the older Luther. In a tirade against cardinals and the contemporaneous Pope Paul III (in office from 1534–1549) he called the cardinals "in their front parts men, in their back parts women". Paul III is a "desperate rascal and scoundrel with his hermaphrodites".[63]

---

[58] See Franz Brendle, Dieter Mertens, Anton Schindling, and Walter Ziegler, eds., *Deutsche Landesgeschichtsschreibung im Zeichen des Humanismus* (Stuttgart 2001). For example, monastic historiographers are Johannes Trithemius, *Chronicon Sponheimense*; Bolfgangus Marius, *Annales sive Chronicon domus Alderspacensis* (see Chapter on Marius), and Angelus Rumpler (c. 1460–1513, Benedictine abbot) and his 1504 history of the monastery of Formbach, *Historia Monasterii Formbacensis*; see Erika S. Dorrer, *Angelus Rumpler Abt von Formbach (1501–1513) als Geschichtsschreiber. Ein Beitrag zur klösterlichen Geschichtsschreibung in Bayern am Ausgang des Mittelalters* (Munich 1965); Kurt Rumpler, "Angelus Rumpler", BBKL 24 (2005) 1250–1264.

[59] See Helmar Junghans, "Der nationale Humanismus bei Ulrich von Hutten und Martin Luther", in *Spätmittelalter, Luthers Reformation, Kirche in Sachsen. Ausgewählte Aufsätze*, eds. Michael Beyer and Günther Wartenberg (Leipzig 2001) 67–90.

[60] See Dieter Mertens, "Nation als Teilhabeverheißung: Reformation und Bauernkrieg", in Dieter Langewiesche and Georg Schmidt, eds., *Föderative Nation. Deutschlandkonzepte von der Reformation bis zum Ersten Weltkrieg* (Munich 2000) 115–134.

[61] For example, the Dominican historiographer Felix Fabri (†1502) who wrote on the *Suevia natio* (the 'Swabian tribe'/'nation'); see Klaus Graf, "Reich und Land in der südwestdeutschen Historiographie um 1500", in Brendle *et al.*, *Deutsche Landesgeschichtsschreibung*, 201–11, here 207.

[62] See Ingrid D. Rowland, "Revenge of the Regensburg Humanists, 1493", *The Sixteenth Century Journal* 25 (1994) 307–22.

[63] See WA 54: 222–223. On Luther's comments in the context of his quoting the Carmelite humanist Mantuan, see Posset, "'Heaven is on Sale'", 142.

We can see a connection between the anti-Italian and anti-Roman humanists and the later confessionalization of humanism north of the Alps. However, humanists in these lands were not always automatically anti-Roman or anti-papal. For example, the monastic humanist Johannes Trithemius OSB (1462–1516), although critical of ecclesiastical abuses, could at times frankly side with the pope.[64] Nevertheless, 'German humanism'[65] came into existence. Or should we say 'humanism in Germany', or 'northern humanism' including 'French humanism', and 'humanism in England', and then also 'Spanish humanism'?[66] In any case, the monastic element in these forms of humanism is rarely taken into consideration.

The contemporary voice of the Nuremberg humanist, Willibald Pirckheimer (1470–1530), may be of help in finding a useful description of monastic humanism. In his view, a true humanist theologian has studied first of all the three ancient languages (Latin, Greek, and Hebrew),[67] including grammar, dialectic, rhetoric, physics and metaphysics, based upon the mathematical sciences (geometry, arithmetic, music, and astronomy). A theologian, furthermore, needs to study history and law. In short, Pirckheimer referred here, without using this terminology, to the study of the humanities and letters (*studia humanitatis ac litterarum*) as a program of education for future leaders.[68] The idea appears to have been introduced to the German lands in 1456 by Peter Luder († c. 1474) during his lectures at Heidelberg.[69]

Such universally-educated people, with moral integrity, were considered by Pirckheimer to be the "true theologians" who do not need training in scholastic speculations, but who should primarily study the Bible and the Church Fathers.[70] The list of names that meet

---

[64] See Walter Ziegler, "Landeschronistik und Kirchenreform", in Brendle *et al.*, *Deutsche Landesgeschichtsschreibung*, 189–200, here 195–95.

[65] Spitz, *The Religious Renaissance*; Eckhard Bernstein, *German Humanism* (Boston 1983).

[66] See Nauert, *Humanism and the Culture* (Cambridge 1995) 95–123. On humanism in France and England, see Werner L. Gundersheimer, ed., *French Humanism, 1470–1600* (London 1969) and James McConica, *English Humanists and Reformation Politics* (Oxford 1965).

[67] *Siquidem praeter grammaticam litteras latinas, graecas et hebreas callere necesse est...*, *Willibald Pirckheimers Briefwechsel*, vol. 3:160, lines 482–562, line 548.

[68] See, for example, Nauert, *Humanism and the Culture*, 12–14.

[69] See Eckhard Bernstein, *Die Literatur des deutschen Frühhumanismus* (Stuttgart 1978) 8, 34–38.

[70] He listed Jerome, Augustine, Ambrose, Hilary, Origen, Basil, Nazianz, Athanasius, and Cyrill, vol. 3:163 (no. 464), lines 586–606. On the humanists' return to the Church Fathers, see August Buck, "Der Rückgriff des Renaissance-Humanismus

Pirckheimer's criteria includes humanist theologians and humanist-trained preachers like the Italian Johannes Pico de Mirandola (1463–1494); the Strasbourg preacher Johannes Geiler von Kaisersberg (1445–1510); the Dominican friar and Graecian of Nuremberg Johannes Cuno (c. 1462–1513); the Benedictine monk Benedictus Chelidonius (c. 1460–1521); the Augustinian Canon Kilian Leyb (or Leib, 1471–1553), who was mentioned explicitly as being learned in the three languages; Erasmus of Rotterdam; Johannes Eck (1486–1543); Johannes Oecolampadius (1482–1531); Johannes Cochlaeus (1479–1552); Thomas Murner (c. 1475–1537); Jacob Wimpfeling; Conrad Pellican (1478–1556); Jerome Emser (1477–1527), and Georg Spalatin (named after his birthplace of Spalt near Nuremberg, 1484–1545). Pirckheimer also listed the vicar-general of the Saxon reformed congregation of the Augustinian order, Johann von Staupitz, superior of Martin Luther, and several members of this order, who were called *sacrae theologiae doctores*, namely Wenceslaus Linck (1483–1547), Martinus Lueder (i.e., Martin Luther), Wolfgang Volprecht, Johannes Lang, and Johannes Fug.[71]

Pirckheimer's definition and examples include priests, friars, and monks, and remarkably, Luther, whom some people might not expect to find in such a list. His list was not meant to be comprehensive. I will concentrate here on a few examples of monks and have picked those that are generally not well known. This lack of information has not improved much since the following statement was written more than thirty years ago in *The American Benedictine Review*:

> We may talk with some justification of a monastic culture of the Renaissance that was also humanistic and hence different in style, if not in ultimate purpose, from the monastic culture of the Middle Ages. We may thus hope to modify, if not to reverse, the prevalent view ... and at least to formulate, if not to solve, a problem whose very existence has been concealed by too literal and narrow a historical perspective ... I can only attempt a kind of outline, hoping that future research will add substance and content to it.[72]

---

auf die Patristik", in Kurt Baldinger, ed., *Festschrift Walther von Wartburg zum 80. Geburtstag 18. Mai 1968* (Tübingen 1968) vol. 1:153–75.

[71] See vol. 3:162, lines 549–580. It is noteworthy that the lay theologian Philip Melanchthon is not mentioned.

[72] Paul Oskar Kristeller, "The Contribution of Religious Orders to Renaissance Thought and Learning", ABR 21 (1970) 1–155; reprinted in *Medieval Aspects of Renaissance Learning. Three Essays* (Durham NC 1974) 95–158. See also Schmidt, 18; Spitz, "Humanism in Germany", in *The Impact of Humanism*, 205.

This *desideratum* of 1970 for further research in this area will be partly fulfilled with the present study of several monastic intellectuals on the eve of the Reformation and in its early phase. The group called monastic humanists would need to include, by today's and by Pirckheimer's own standards, his sister, Caritas (1466/67–1532), a nun and later the prioress of the Sisters of Saint Clare at Nuremberg, but Willibald himself did not mention her in his list of names.[73] She was however herself a monastic humanist.[74]

Although the focus here is on the Benedictine and Cistercian traditions, we should remain aware that while they had humanists in their midst, so did the other contemplative orders, such as the Camaldolese and the Carthusians. The best known early humanist and Camaldolese monk is Ambrose Traversari (1386–1439) of the monastery of Santa Maria degli Angeli in Florence. This monastery was a "favorite place of the third generation of Florentine humanists".[75] In 1425 Traversari organized a course in Greek at his monastery.[76]

Two Carthusians must also be mentioned, though their lives and works will not be dealt with here in any detail. Georg Pirckheimer (†1505) lived at the Charter house in Nuremberg; he was a member of the Pirckheimer clan and the prior of the monastery.[77] The other was one of the best known German Carthusians: Johannes Heynlin von Stein (de Lapide, 1430–1496), a doctor of theology, who in 1470 helped in setting up the first printing press in Paris.[78]

---

[73] Caritas Pirckheimer was prioress from 1503–1532; she would deserve a book of her own. On her, see Georg Deichstetter, ed., *Caritas Pirckheimer: Ordensfrau und Humanistin: Ein Vorbild für die Ökumene: Festschrift zum 450. Todestag* (Cologne 1982); Katharina M. Wilson, ed., *Women Writers of the Renaissance and Reformation* (Athens, GA 1987) 287–303; Martin H. Jung, *Nonnen, Prophetinnen, Kirchenmütter. Kirchen- und frömmigkeitsgeschichtliche Studien zu Frauen der Reformationszeit* (Leipzig 2002) 77–120, here 87 on Caritas as a representative of *Klosterhumanismus*.

[74] *Mulier studiosa et egregie erudite . . . ingenio subtilis et in eloquio Romanae lingue prompta*, Machilek, "Klosterhumanismus", 40.

[75] Cesare Vasoli, "The Theology of Italian Humanism in the Early Fifteenth Century", in Giulio D'Onofrio, ed., Matthew J. O'Connell, trans., *History of Theology. III* (Collegeville, MN 1998) 17–74, here 55. Charles L. Stinger, *Humanism and the Church Fathers: Ambrogio Traversari (1368–1439) and Christian Antiquity in the Italian Renaissance* (Albany 1977); Augustijn, *Humanismus*, 59–60.

[76] See Wilson, *From Byzantium to Italy*, 33.

[77] See Arnold Friedrich Siegfried Reimann, *Die älteren Pirckheimer: Geschichte eines Nürnberger Patriziergeschlechts im Zeitalter des Frühhumanismus (bis 1501)*, ed. Hans Rupprich (Leipzig 1944) 182.

[78] See Max Hossfeldt, "Johannes Heynlin aus Stein. Ein Kapitel aus der Frühzeit des deutschen Humanismus", *Basler Zeitschrift für Geschichte und Altertumskunde* 6 (1907)

He entered the Carthusian monastery at Basel in 1487, and from there he helped publish the works of the Church Fathers.[79] He was also the author of a very popular Mass commentary, first printed in 1492, which was reprinted thirty-eight times up to 1519, and five times more up to the seventeenth century.[80]

A brief historical review of the monastic reform efforts in the German territories needs to be included here insofar as "monastic reforms" preceded monastic humanism.[81] As noted, the headwaters of monastic humanism in the Renaissance are found in the international, inner-monastic reform movements of the fifteenth and sixteenth centuries. The reform of monastic life and the return to the observance of the original monastic rules in the fifteenth century was called *reformatio monachorum*.[82] Often such reformation was tied together with interest in the humanist trends towards the sources of the Christian faith (*ad fontes*). This means that a sharp distinction between the pre-Reformation and Reformation periods is often not possible, as "new perspectives increasingly transcend the divide" between these periods.[83] The late medieval Latin word *reformatio* is opalescent. For example, a Benedictine monk in France wrote in 1503 a defense of monastic reforms under the title *Reformationis monasticae vindiciae seu defensio*.[84] The constitutions of Luther's order, which Johann von Staupitz had printed at the beginning of the sixteenth century, explicitly

---

309–356 and 7 (1908) 79–219, 235–431; Anna Morisi, "Traditionalism, Humanism, and Mystical Experience in Northern Europe and in the Germanic Areas in the Fifteenth and Sixteenth Centuries", in D'Onofrio, ed., *History of Theology. III*, 320–370, here 304; Hans-Josef Olszewsky, "Johannes de Lapide", BBKL 3 (1992) 452–57; Martin H. Jung, "Johannes Heynlin von Stein (de Lapide)", *Religion in Geschichte und Gegenwart: Handwörterbuch für Theologie und Religionswissenschaft* 4 (2001).

[79] See the biographical sketch that accompanies the edition of Lapide's letter to Amerbach in AK, vol. 1:22. Lapide's preface to the *Opera Omnia* of Ambrose (Basel 1492) in AK, no. 23; vol. 1:31–32. On the social context of Amerbach's correspondence and the correspondence itself in English translation, see Barbara C. Halporn, *The Correspondence of Johann Amerbach: Early Printing in its Social Context* (Ann Arbor 2000) 311–15.

[80] *Resolutorium dubiorum circa celebrationem missarum occurentium*, AK, 228, note 2; "Heynlin", BBKL 2 (1990) 810–12.

[81] *Dem Klosterhumanismus ging die Klosterreform voraus*; Richter, "Die Schriftsteller", 277 (see note 49 above). For France, see Marie-Dominique Chenu, "L'humanisme et la réforme au collège Saint-Jacques", *Archives d'histoire dominicaine* 1 (1946) 130–154.

[82] *Reformatorenlexikon*, 7.

[83] See Bob Scribner, "Introduction", in Bob Scribner and Trevor Johnson, eds., *Popular Religion in Germany and Central Europe, 1400–1800* (New York 1996) 1; Posset, *The Front-Runner*, 3.

[84] See Morisi, 305.

contain the idea of *reformatio* in the title.⁸⁵ The German Dominican friars of the fifteenth century spoke of the *Reformacio Prediger Ordens* (Reformation of the Order of Preachers).⁸⁶ In addition to the monastic aspect of *reformatio*, there is the academic aspect. For example, the four leading men at the newly-founded University of Wittenberg were called *reformatores* and had the task of advising the territorial lord on matters of university reform.⁸⁷

*Benedictines*⁸⁸

As may be expected, Italian Benedictines were at the forefront of monastic humanism, particularly those in Padua.⁸⁹ Among the younger ones was Gregorio Cortese (1483–1548), later a cardinal.⁹⁰ Long before Cortese's time, Benedictine humanism had gone hand-in-hand with reforms of the Church and of monastic life, particularly in Austria and Germany, in connection with the reform efforts of the Cistercian Pope Benedict XII (1334–42) and the reform Council of Constance at the beginning of the fifteenth century. In the fourteenth century the Benedictines were organized in numerous provinces, and in the fifteenth century they formed several reform congregations or unions with the purpose of restoring the original discipline of the order. In Italy there was the Congregation of Saint Giustina in Padua, founded in 1412, with Abbot Ludovico Barbo as the leader, while in Spain there was the Congregation of Valladolid, founded in 1450. In the German-speaking lands there were several reform

---

⁸⁵ "Constitutiones fratrum Eremitarum sancti Augustini apostolicorum privilegiorum formam pro reformatione Alemanniae", ed. Wolfgang Günter in Johann von Staupitz, *Sämtliche Schriften. Abhandlungen, Predigten, Zeugnisse*, eds. Lothar Graf zu Dohna and Richard Wetzel, vol. 5 (Berlin 2001); see Heiko A. Oberman, "Martin Luther Contra Medieval Monasticism: A Friar in the Lion's Den", in *Ad fontes Lutheri: Toward the Recovery of the Real Luther: Essays in Honor of Kenneth Hagen's Sixty-Fifth Birthday*, eds. Timothy Maschke, Franz Posset, and Joan Skocir (Milwaukee 2001) 192, note 19.

⁸⁶ See Graf, "Ordensreform", 106 with note 25.

⁸⁷ See Posset, *The Front-Runner*, 79.

⁸⁸ See Ulrich Faust and Franz Quarthal, *Die Reformverbände und Kongregationen der Benediktiner im deutschen Sprachraum* (St. Ottilien 1999).

⁸⁹ See Barry Collett, *Italian Benedictine Scholars and the Reformation: The Congregation of Santa Giustina of Padua* (Oxford 1985).

⁹⁰ See Francesco Ciriaco Cesareo, "Gregorio Cortese and the Reform of Italian Benedictinism", ABR 41 (1990) 36–58; idem, *Humanism and Catholic Reform: The Life and Work of Gregorio Cortese (1483–1548)* (New York etc. 1990).

centers: Kastl with its influence in Bavaria and parts of Switzerland; Melk with its influence in Austria, Swabia, and Bavaria; Bursfeld with its influence in northwestern and central Germany, but also in the southwest (Hirsau [1458] and Alpirsbach [1482], both in the Black Forest),[91] and in Alsace, Holland, Belgium, and Luxembourg. In 1517 (the year that marks the beginning of the Lutheran Reformation in Germany) the Bursfeld Union comprised almost one hundred monasteries.[92]

The monastic reformers in these congregations were open to the new spirit of what is now called 'humanism'. In the contemporary report *Supplementum chronicorum* by the Augustinian friar and humanist from Bergamo, Giacomo Filippo Foresti (†1520), printed at Venice in 1483, we read that in the congregation of Padua there were countless monks who not only studied theology and canon law, but were also skilled in Greek and Latin eloquence.[93] This document shows that the combination of humanist erudition and monasticism was a widespread phenomenon, even though there is a lack of written documentation.

Humanist ideas were brought from Italy by the Benedictine Peter von Rosenheim (1380–1433) to the monastery of Melk in Austria. Peter became a monk in 1413 at Subiaco and was later the prior at Rocca di Mondragone near Capua. In 1416 he participated in the Council of Constance and afterwards became the co-visitator of Melk, which had a reform-minded prior, from 1418 to 1424. From

---

[91] See Klaus Schreiner, "Benediktinische Klosterreform als zeitgebundene Auslegung der Regel. Geistige, religiöse und soziale Erneuerung in spätmittelalterichen Klöstern Südwestdeutschlands im Zeichen der Kastler, Melker und Bursfelder Reform", *Blätter für württembergische Kirchengeschichte* 86 (1986) 105–95.

[92] See Karl Bihlmeyer and Hermann Tüchle, *Church History*, trans. from the 13th German edition by Victor E. Mills (Westminster, MD 1958–1966) 3 vols., here vol. 2: Chapter 151.2. The major work on the Bursfeld Union was done by Paulus Volk, *Die Generalkapitels-Rezesse der Bursfelder Kongregation* (Siegburg 1955–1972) 4 vols. A good summary is found in Adam Wienand, "Die Bursfelder Reformbewegung", in *Und sie folgten der Regel St. Benedikts: Die Cistercienser und das benediktinische Mönchtum*, eds. Ambrosius Schneider and Adam Wienand (Cologne 1981) 381–398; hereafter quoted as Wienand. See also Walter Ziegler, *Die Bursfelder Kongregation in der Reformationszeit: Dargestellt an Hand der Generalkapitelrezesse der Bursfelder Kongregation* (Münster 1968). Roland Behrendt wrote of more than two hundred houses that were influenced by the Bursfeld Union: "The Library of Abbot Trithemius", ABR 51 (2000) 3–23 (reprint of 1959 article).

[93] See Paul Joachimsohn, *Geschichtsauffassung und Geschichtsschreibung in Deutschland unter dem Einfluß des Humanismus* (Leipzig and Berlin 1910) 240, note 23; Junghans, *Der junge Luther*, 24–25.

1423 to 1426 he was the Bible instructor (*cursor biblicus*) and director of studies. Rosenheim's best known book was the *Rosetum memoriale divinorum eloquiorum*, written between 1423 and 1426. In it he summarized the biblical books in verse form (except for the psalms). Thirty manuscripts are extant and almost ten printings from between 1470 and 1570. It was used for memorizing the Bible.[94] He reformed the Benedictine monasteries of Tegernsee and Salzburg. The latter became a stimulating intellectual and spiritual center from the middle of the fifteenth century. No other monastery possessed more texts in the vernacular than the Benedictine library at Salzburg. Its scriptorium reflected the determination of an unknown library director who wanted to make Latin religious literature available to wider circles by offering vernacular translations of works by Augustine (354–430), Bernard (1090–1153), Jean Gerson (1363–1429), Johannes Nider (fifteenth century), Thomas à Kempis (1380–1471), and others.[95]

The ancient Benedictine monastery of Sankt Gallen in Switzerland was another center where monastic reforms took effect under Abbot Kaspar von Breitenladenburg (1442–1457), who had been educated in Italy and who learned of the reforms at Saint Giustina in Padua and at Subiaco. This abbot invited monks from the Melk Union to join his monks at Sankt Gallen. At that time another monk, the humanist and historian Sigismund Meisterlin (c. 1434–c. 1489), joined the community at Sankt Gallen and became its master of novices. He was originally a member of the Benedictine monastery at Augsburg and had spent time at Saint Giustina in Padua.[96] Meisterlin was a pioneer in humanist historiography.[97]

A monk and humanist by the name of Hermannus Piscator at the Benedictine monastery of Saint Jacob in Mainz, which belonged to the Bursfeld Union, became known for his historiography of the local church and city of Mainz with his *Chronicon urbis et ecclesiae Maguntinensis* (written c. 1520). Along with Ulrich von Hutten, he belonged to the

---

[94] See Hellmut Rosenfeld, "Petrus von Rosenheim", BBKL 7 (1994) 377–79. A print by Jakob Thanner is known from Leipzig in 1505.
[95] See Newald (note 49 above).
[96] See Schmidt, 152f.
[97] See Paul Joachimsohn, *Die humanistische Geschichtsschreibung in Deutschland. Heft I: Die Anfänge. Sigismund Meisterlin* (Bonn 1895); reprint in *Gesammelte Aufsätze*, vol. 2, ed. Notker Hammerstein (Aalen 1983) 121–461; Graf, "Ordensreform", 108.

circle of humanists around the Archbishop of Mainz, Albrecht of Brandenburg (1490–1545).[98]

In order to comply with monastic discipline, the founders' Rules were to be kept in mind and for that reason to be made available in print. Within the Bursfeld Union, for example, there was a monastery (not known by name) which possessed a copy of *The Rule of Saint Benedict* from the printer Johannes Schöffer in Mainz in 1528/29. *The Rule* was accompanied by a *Ceremoniale* of the Bursfeld Union. The title page of this Benedictine work shows a woodcut with a motif typical of the Cistercians who are reformed Benedictines: 'The Embrace of Bernard by the Crucified' (*Amplexus Bernardi*).[99] It is the only known edition of *The Rule of Saint Benedict* showing this Cistercian and Christocentric motif. This resembles another woodcut, of 1503, that is attributed to the Renaissance artist Albrecht Dürer (1471–1528). The use of the *Amplexus* motif early in the sixteenth century by non-Cistercians may be interpreted as a sign of the times when monks, too, wanted to return to the sources (*ad fontes*), in this case to the proper observance of their *Rule*. In so doing, they were following the lead of Saint Bernard of Clairvaux, who appears to have been very popular at that time.[100] We can recognize a "powerful movement" for reform that transformed the spirit of numerous Benedictine congregations in Germany, Italy, and Spain at that time,[101] but also in France, especially under the Benedictine humanist Guy Jouennaux.[102]

It is true that some humanist monks left their monasteries at a certain point in their careers. One was Paul Volz (or Volzius, c. 1480–1544), the Benedictine abbot of Hugshofen in Alsace, a monastery of the Bursfeld Reform. He admired Erasmus, who dedicated the 1518 edition of his *Enchiridion* to him. During the Peasants'

---

[98] See Uta Goerlitz, *Humanismus und Geschichtsschreibung am Mittelrhein. Das 'Chronicon urbis et ecclesiae Maguntinensis' des Hermannus Piscator OSB* (Tübingen 1999).

[99] See Wienand, 87.

[100] See Franz Posset, "Saint Bernard of Clairvaux in the Devotion, Theology and Art of the Sixteenth Century", *Lutheran Quarterly* 11 (1997) 309–52. On the history of the *Amplexus Bernardi*, see idem, "The Crucified Embraces Saint Bernard: The Beginnings of the *Amplexus Bernardi*", CSQ 33 (1998) 289–314.

[101] See Jean Claude Margolin, *Humanism in Europe at the Time of the Renaissance*, trans. John L. Farthing (Durham NC 1989) 47.

[102] See Guy-Marie Oury, "Les premiers humanistes et la réforme monastique: Guy Jouennaux", *Province du Maine* 76 (1974) 218–236; Le Gall, 49.

War Volz's monastery was destroyed. He had to seek help, but was refused because he was considered a Lutheran sympathizer.[103] Another such monk was Matthaeus Hisolidus (or Hiscold, Hitzschold) of the Benedictine monastery of Bosau (Posa) near Zeitz, who attended the Leipzig Disputation as Luther's friend[104] and who joined the rebels during the Peasants' War. He had studied in 1519 at Wittenberg while he held the title of prior of his monastery.[105] The two best known Benedictines and later Protestant reformers, however, were Ambrose Blarer (1492–1564) and Wolfgang Musculus (1497–1563). Both were active in southwestern Germany/Switzerland. Musculus was the preacher in the monastery of Lizheim, Alsace, and later became a reformer in Switzerland and southern Germany.[106] Ambrose Blarer was an Erasmian humanist who, from 1521, was the prior of the monastery of Alpirsbach in the Black Forest. He liked Luther's Christ-centered spirituality. In disagreement with his abbot over the Luther issue, he left the monastery in 1522 (without any intention of giving up the monastic way of life, however) and went to Constance, where in 1525 he became a reformer for southern Germany.[107] Also living in a cloister in the Black Forest was Michael Sattler (1490–1527) of the monastery of Sankt Peter. He became an Anabaptist and was executed in 1527.[108] Gottschalk Kruse (born at the end of the fifteenth century, †1527) who had entered the Benedictine monastery of Saint Aegidius in Braunschweig, was another of the reform-minded Benedictines. He received his doctorate in theology from Wittenberg and became a Lutheran reformer in northern Germany.[109]

---

[103] See Gerhard Kaller, "Volz, Paul", BBKL 13 (1998) 69–71; Chadwick 51; Levi 255.

[104] See Schwiebert 398f; Hisolidus wrote a pamphlet so similar to those emanating from Wittenberg that Johann Eck felt compelled to respond to it, *ibid.* 422.

[105] Apparently, after his studies he went to the Benedictine monastery at Oldisleben, and thus did not go back to Bosau; see Gerhard Günther, "Bemerkungen zum Thema 'Thomas Müntzer und Heinrich Pfeiffer in Mühlhausen'", in Gerhard Heitz et al., *Der Bauer im Klassenkampf* (Berlin 1975) 157–82, here 165–174. Hisolidus edited two sermons at Erfurt in 1522.

[106] See *Reformatorenlexikon*, 152.

[107] See *Reformatorenlexikon*, 39; Bernd Moeller, "Ambrosius Blarer als Alpirsbacher Mönch", in *Luther-Rezeption: Kirchenhistorische Aufsätze zur Reformationsgeschichte* (Göttingen 2001) 156–66.

[108] See John Horsch, *Mennonites in Europe* (Scottdale, PA 1942) 70–78; C. Arnold Snyder, *The Life and Thought of Michael Sattler* (Scottdale, PA 1984).

[109] See *Reformatorenlexikon*, 124.

In contrast to these former Benedictines, the learned Abbot Angelus Rumpler (c. 1460–1513) of the Benedictine monastery of Formbach (Vornbach) remained a monk and became known as a historiographer.[110] He did not join the Lutheran movement; nor did the other three Benedictine humanists who are featured here: Benedictus Chelidonius (Nuremberg, later Vienna), Vitus Bild Acropolitanus (Augsburg), and Nikolaus Ellenbog or Cubitus (Ottobeuren in Swabia).

Some of their works have survived. We do not know how much has been lost, possibly gone forever, especially when we think of the 800 out of more than 1,500 Benedictine monasteries in Europe that did not survive the Reformation.[111]

Cistercians

The Cistercians, too, were open to humanism. From the middle of the thirteenth century their General Chapter had always been concerned with the promotion of academic studies. Special attention was given to the College of Saint Bernard in Paris. Those who obtained their degrees from there enjoyed extensive privileges in their home monasteries. During the fifteenth and sixteenth centuries, almost every significant German university recorded Cistercian students. The most frequented among them was the University of Heidelberg, founded in 1386. The faculty of theology was organized by a Cistercian doctor, a graduate of Paris, Reginald of Alna (from the Abbey of Aulne, near Luttich). According to the university records, from its foundation until 1522, the number of Cistercian students totaled 600. When, during the course of the fifteenth century, Heidelberg became a stronghold of nominalism, the Cistercians, as adherents of the doctrine of Saint Thomas Aquinas, gradually abandoned the university. The majority of students were transferred to Cologne; those from southwestern Germany went to Freiburg. Cistercians were also sent to the University of Prague, founded in 1348, but after that faculty became infiltrated by Hussites, the University of Leipzig (founded in 1409) received the largest number of Cistercians. Its records show that some 400 identifiable Cistercians attended the university up to

---

[110] See Dorrer, *Angelus Rumpler* (see note 58 above).
[111] See *Dizionario degli istituti di perfezione* (Rome 1974) vol. 1:1321, as quoted by Le Gall, 17.

the middle of the sixteenth century. In Cologne, the university (founded in 1388) recorded some 100 Cistercian students in attendance up to the middle of the sixteenth century.[112]

The Cistercian monastery of Adwert (Aduard) in the Netherlands was a "lively intellectual centre", where Rudolph Agricola, "the 'father of German humanism' and a 'second Petrarch'"[113] came with others to study and to visit the learned Abbot Henry of Rees. In France, a leader of monastic reform among the Cistercians was the Abbot General, Jean de Cirey (1476–1503).[114] His work is little known and may some day be investigated in greater detail. However, we know that his secretary was Conradus Leontorius whose life and work we will feature in Chapter 1. Furthermore, recent research focused on Spain has demonstrated the relationship of Cistercians there to the humanist movement.[115] We also know of the Swiss Nicholas Wydenbosch (or Weidenbusch) who was a humanist and who called himself Nicolaus Salicetus. Originally he was a medical doctor with a degree from Paris which he gained around 1460, and for a while he was the procurator of the German students in Paris. In 1470 he entered the Cistercian monastery of Frienisberg near Bern in Switzerland. In 1482 Salicetus became abbot of the Alsatian monastery of Baumgarten. He was the author of the widely-read *Antidote for the Soul* (*Antidotarius animae*), first printed in Strasbourg in 1489. In the humanist fashion of the day, the name *Antidotarius* mimicked the ancient technical term for a "book of medication".[116]

---

[112] See Louis Lekai, *The Cistercians: ideals and reality* (Kent, KS 1977); his text is posted on the website of the monks of Spring Bank Abbey, Wisconsin, www.MonksOnline.org

[113] Spitz, "Humanism in Germany", in *The Impact of Humanism*, 205.

[114] See Augustin Renaudet, *Préréforme et Humanism à Paris 1494–1517* (Paris 1916; 2nd, revised edition, 1953) 189.

[115] *Humanismo y Cister: actas de I Congreso Nacional de Humanistas Españoles*, Francisco R. de Pascual, J. Paniagua Pérez, J. F. Domíngez, and Gaspar Morocho Gayo (León 1996).

[116] The full title is *Liber meditationum ac orationum qui anthidotarius animae dicitur*; see Luzian Pfleger, "Nicolaus Salicetus, ein gelehrter elsässischer Cistercienserabt des 15. Jahrhunderts", *Studien und Mitteilungen aus dem Benediktiner- und dem Cistercienser-Orden* 22 (1901) 588–89; E. Mikkers, "Nicolas Salicetus", *Dictionnaire de Spitualité*, vol. 11:299–301; Francis Rapp, "Salicetus", *Nouveau dictionnaire de biographie alsacienne* (no. 32) (Strasbourg 1998) 33–49; Sheryl Frances Chen, "Bernard's Prayer Before the Crucifix that Embraced Him: Cistercians and Devotion to the Wounds of Christ", CSQ 29 (1994) 24–54, with an English version of Salicetus' prayer (25–40); Franz Posset, "The Crucified Embraces Saint Bernard: The Beginnings of the *Amplexus Bernardi*", CSQ 33 (1998) 289–314, here 295–296.

The Cistercian humanist Martin von Lochau, who from 1501 to 1522 was the abbot of Altzelle, near Leipzig and Dresden, was known as a protector of the humanists.[117] His monk Michael Haenlein Meurer (or Michael a Muris Galliculus, †1537) published a manual on music (*Compendium musicae*) in 1514, and a book on the soul (*De statu animae*) in 1519. Michael, however, left the monastery and became a Lutheran.[118] Another, younger, humanist was Antonius Corvinus (or Rabe, 1501–1553) of the monastery of Loccum, later of the monastery of Riddagshausen in northern Germany. He studied at the Cistercian college in Leipzig, but because he sympathized too much with Luther, was evicted from his monastery as "a Lutheran rascal" (*lutherischer bube*). He became known as the 'Reformer of Lower Saxony' and as an 'evangelical martyr' because he was persecuted and died at Hannover shortly after his release from a three-year prison term.[119] Then there was Albert Rizaeus Hardenberg (1510–1574) of the Dutch Cistercian monastery of Adwert, who was a friend of the humanist Philip Melanchthon. Because of his sympathy for the reform ideas of what was later called the Protestant Reformation, Hardenberg was condemned to burn all his books.[120]

Least known are several humanists and poets among the Cistercians in Bavaria who were students of the famous humanist Conradus Celtis[121] in Heidelberg, such as the two Cistercian abbots of Kaisheim, Georg Kassner (1490–1509) and Conrad Reuter (or Reitter, c. 1470–1540),[122] or the abbot of Raitenhaslach, Ulrich Moltzner (†1506), to whom the Cistercian abbot Bolfgangus Marius (1469–1544) dedicated several poems.[123] From among these Bavarian Cistercians, only Marius will be included in the biographical sketches.

---

[117] See Otto Clemen, "Martin von Lochau, Abt von Altzelle", in Ernst Koch, ed., *Kleine Schriften zur Reformationsgeschichte (1897–1944)* (Leipzig and Cologne 1982) 460–466.

[118] See *Reformatorenlexikon*, 145.

[119] See *Reformatorenlexikon*, 62. Friedrich Wilhelm Bautz, "Corvinus", BBKL 1 (1990) 1135–37; Chadwick 147 and 151 mentions Corvinus as a former Cistercian and Reformer.

[120] See *Reformatorenlexikon*, 95f.; Friedrich Wilhelm Bautz, "Hardenberg", BBKL 2 (1990) 523–26.

[121] Celtis was the author of a book on writing poetry, *Ars versificandi* (1496).

[122] On Kassner and Reuter, see Marian Gloning, "Konrad Reuter, Abt von Kaisheim 1509–1540", StM 32 (1912) 450–92.

[123] A brief study on Abbot Moltzner was published early in the 20thC by Fritz Hacker, "Abt Ulrich Moltzner von Raitenhaslach 1502–1506", StM 35 (1914) 347–50.

One of the most infamous former Cistercians was Heinrich Pfeif[f]er (†1525) of the monastery of Reifenstein (Eichsfeld), who renounced his monastic vows in 1521 and became the reform-minded preacher of the church of Saint Mary in the imperial city of Mühlhausen, his birthplace.[124] After Erfurt, this was the second largest city in central Germany, with about 8,000 inhabitants.[125] Pfeiffer eventually led a series of uprisings against the patrician government among well-to-do citizens such as the guild-craftsmen and merchants. This rebellion was part of what became known as the Peasants' War of the 1520s, which in some respects was also a war against land-owning monasteries (*Klosterkrieg; Pfaffenkrieg*); Erasmus saw the revolt in this way.[126] Pfeiffer at first had an ally in the Saxon princes, who had long craved possession of the powerful imperial city. He and his partisans won their first victory in 1523; the spoils fell to the well-to-do citizens, who received a share in the municipal government, while the poor in the suburbs and particularly the peasants came off empty-handed. They, however, had certainly lost none of their confidence, particularly since the arrival of another priest, Thomas Müntzer (1490–1525), formerly the father confessor at the Cistercian monastery for women at Beuditz near Weissenfels, south of Leipzig. These leaders of destruction were decapitated on 27 May 1525 on the command of Duke John of Saxony. Their separated bodies and heads were brought to the city gate of Mühlhausen, were they were exhibited on stakes as a warning to the entire population.[127] Another Cistercian monastery also fell victim to the uprising. This was Georgenthal near Gotha, where Henricus Urbanus was a member and at that time a prominent humanist, whose emblem was included in the aforementioned rector's page of Erfurt University. His biographical sketch will be given in Chapter 4.

In order to better understand monastic humanism around 1500, we must also realize that these monks shared an interest in the study of the biblical languages, as they wanted to return to original sources

---

[124] See Klemens Löffler, "Reifenstein", *Catholic Encyclopedia* (www.newadvent.org).
[125] See Günther, 162.
[126] See Heiko A. Oberman, "Tumultus Rusticorum: Vom Klosterkrieg zum Fürstenkrieg. Beobachtungen zum Bauernkrieg unter besonderer Berücksichtigung zeitgenössischer Beurteilungen", *Zeitschrift für Kirchengeschichte* 85 (1974) 301–316; reprinted in Peter Blickle, ed., *Der Bauernkrieg von 1525* (Darmstadt 1985) 214–236.
[127] Otto Merx, *Thomas Müntzer und Heinrich Pfeiffer, 1523–1525* (Göttingen 1989); Eric W. Gritsch, *Thomas Müntzer* (Minneapolis 1989).

and original meanings. The search for the original meaning of a text was called the search for 'truth' (*veritas*) as the *archetypa veritas*,[128] *hebraica veritas*,[129] or *evangelica veritas*.[130] The expression *hebraica veritas* was picked up by Luther when, around 1510 as a young monastic humanist and instructor, he underlined this expression in his copy of the *Sentences* of Peter Lombard.[131]

Common to most of the Renaissance monks and friars was their interest in polyglotism, i.e., in the "sacred philology"[132] of Latin, Hebrew, and Greek. Related to this was their support for the troubled Christian Hebraist Reuchlin and his defense of Jewish books. Monasteries were often at the forefront of learning these languages, as the example of Nikolaus Ellenbog at Ottobeuren demonstrates. In this connection we must realize that it was a long time before many printers possessed, for instance, Greek type. Oxford did not get Greek type till 1586,[133] while Nikolaus Marschalk (c. 1470–1525) at Erfurt had a Greek textbook printed as early as 1501. It was based on the *Erotemata* ('Questions', grammar book) of Constantine Lascaris (1434–1493/1501), the Greek scholar living in Milan, Italy, and was printed by Aldus Manutius in Venice[134] sometime after the first edition had come out in Milan in 1476.[135]

---

[128] For this expression, see *Briefwechsel des Beatus Rhenanus*, eds. Adalbert Horawitz and Karl Hartfelder (Leipzig 1886, reprint Hildesheim 1966) 577, with note 53; D'Amico, *Roman and German Humanism*, X.241.

[129] This expression may go back to the Church Father Jerome. For a bibliography on 'Hebrew Truth', see Franz Posset, "'Rock' and 'Recognition'. Martin Luther's Catholic Interpretation of 'You are Peter and on this rock I will build my Church' (Matthew 16:18) and the Friendly Criticism from the Point of View of the 'Hebrew Truth' by his Confrère, Caspar Amman, 'Doctor of the Sacred Page'", in *Ad fontes Lutheri*, 214–246, here 227f, note 71.

[130] See the 1523 correspondence between two humanists, Veit Bild and Kaspar Amman, in Alois Wagner, "Der Augustiner Kaspar Amman", *Jahresbericht des Historischen Vereins Dillingen* 8 (1895) 42–64, here 60.

[131] On Liber I, dist. 2, c. 6: *hebraica veritas habet heloym*, Luther crossed out the 'h' in *heloym* and entered in the margin the spelling *elohim* and added notes which he took from Jerome and others; see WA 9,32,9.

[132] Paul Oskar Kristeller, *Renaissance Thought: The Classic, Scholastic, and Humanistic Strains* (New York 1961) 79.

[133] See Chadwick, 5.

[134] See Junghans, *Der junge Luther*, 35. The textbook of Constantine Lascaris was first issued in 1476 in Milan, according to Wilson, *From Byzantium to Italy*, 96, and "a later edition" by Aldus followed in Venice (p. 122), probably in 1494 upon recommendation by Pietro Bembo (1470–1547) (pp. 125–126).

[135] The *Erotemata* type of textbook has a history of its own; see Wilson, *From Byzantium to Italy*, 9f., 42, 95f., 146.

As to Hebrew, very few people knew this language in 1500. When monks north of the Alps wanted to study it, they relied on the layman who wrote an introduction to it in 1506, i.e., Reuchlin and his *Rudimenta hebraica*. He had learned this language from Jehiel Loans, the Jew and personal physician of Emperor Frederick III (1440–1493).[136]

In addition to the polyglot interests of numerous monastic humanists, an interest in Christ-centered poetry was shared by most of them. We shall observe this phenomenon particularly with the Cistercian Bolfgangus Marius and the Benedictine Benedictus Chelidonius.

Altogether six monks are featured: Leontorius, Chelidonius, Marius, Urbanus, Acropolitanus, and Ellenbog. They represent monastic humanism in the Benedictine and Cistercian tradition on the eve of the Reformation and during its early years in the German-speaking territories. Their lives and works demonstrate the close relationship of monasticism, humanism, and reform efforts in the Renaissance. Yet, inner-ecclesiastical reforms may not always have been their first priority, and much of their criticism of the Church may actually have been a fashion,[137] in contrast to Luther, who began to draw practical conclusions and took action.

---

[136] See Chadwick, 28f.

[137] *Rhetorische Phrase*, according to Walter Ziegler, "Landeschronistik und Kirchenreform", in Brendle *et al.*, *Deutsche Landesgeschichtsschreibung*, 200.

CHAPTER ONE

AN EDITOR OF LATIN BIBLES AND WORKS OF THE CHURCH FATHERS: CONRADUS LEONTORIUS, MONK OF MAULBRONN

In two books on ecclesiastical writers and famous Germans of his time, the humanist and Benedictine abbot Johannes Trithemius[1] entered certain biographical data for Konrad Töritz who called himself Conradus Leontorius, after his birthplace of Leonberg near Stuttgart in Swabia, in southwestern Germany. Leontorius was thus of the German nation (*natione teutonicus*), and a monk of the Cistercian monastery of Maulbronn, also in Swabia, during the reign of Emperor Maximilian (1469–1519) (*sub Maximiliano imperatore*). He was a scholar of Holy Scripture, who knew the three sacred languages, Latin, Greek, and Hebrew (*trium principalium liguarum peritus; hebraice et graece non ignarus*). He was also a philosopher, learned in secular matters, an orator, and a poet.[2] Leontorius visited Abbot Trithemius at his monastery, and both made excursions together.[3] Trithemius explicitly mentions Leontorius' activities as a writer of verse and prose, including his help with a commentary on the work of the Carmelite friar and humanist Baptista Mantuan. This commentary was begun by another priest-humanist, Sebastian Murrho (1450/52–1494) of Colmar,

---

This Chapter is an expansion in English of my entries on "Leontorius" in BBKL 19 (2001) 896–900 and in VL (forthcoming).

[1] *Liber de scriptoribus ecclesiasticis* (Basel: Amerbach, 1494; with reprints in 1512, 1531, and more frequently later) fol. 134 and the *Catalogus illustrium virorum Germaniam suis ingeniis et lucubrationibus omnifariam exornantium* (Mainz: Peter von Friedberg, 1495). See Roland Behrendt, "The Library of Abbot Trithemius", ABR 10 (1959), reprinted in vol. 51 (2000) 3–23.

[2] In the following I rely on the information provided by Trithemius as quoted in the still-valuable study by Georg Wolff, "Conradus Leontorius. Biobibliographie". That Leontorius is virtually forgotten these days may be seen from the fact that in the *New Catholic Encyclopedia* the entry in the earlier edition of the *Catholic Encyclopedia* (edited at the beginning of the 20thC) was deleted. Only with Barbara C. Halporn's book, *The Correspondence of Johann Amerbach*, does the significance of the Cistercian monk and humanist come to the fore again.

[3] See Wolff's note 21.

Fig. 1. Church of the monastery complex of Maulbronn, Germany. Photo of c. 1960 in the private possession of the author.

In laudem disertissimi atq̃ triũ principaliũ linguarũ peritissimi uiri Ioannis Reuchlin Phorcensis:librorũq̃ quos de Verbo Mirifico nuper edidit:comen/ titia Conradi Leontorij Mulbrunneñ.Epistola.

Conradus Leontorius:Iacobo Vinphelingo.S.P.

Vt primum a te Moguntiaco discessi:statim in meipso sum expertus uulgatum aud Gallos nostros puerbiũ: Nusq̃ cum amico satis nec præsens: nec absens. præsens enim cum essem:nõ satis te pro nostra amicitia sum usus:qd̃ amātibus nnibᵘ accidere solet:qui in digressu sentiunt se plæraq̃ omisisse: quæ se factu/ is aut dicturos animo destinauerāt.Sed quod omisi: resartient litterulæ : qua/ m cõmercio utinam sæpius tecũ essem. Colloquebamur de libello clarorum rorum domini Spanhemeñ. quem impressioni Basilæam datũ esse dicebas. terrogaui de doctore Ioanne Reuchlin:esset ne insertus:qd̃ ipsum cum sub/ ubitares:negaresq̃:sum demiratus. Quem enim i omni genere doctrinæ hac mpestate clariorem existimare posses: si tibi penitus esset familiaris & notus: peures neminē. Eũ ergo non sine magna iniuria & iactura germani nominis ætentibus tuaq̃ abbasq̃ tuᵒ. Est enim triũ linguarũ peritissimᵘ interpres: Græ/ cæ:Hebraicæ & Latinæ. Adde etiam si ius Gallicæ: quã Aurelianis dũ iuris stu/ o nauaret opera perdidit.Transtulit plæraq̃ orationes adolescens: quarum iquæ nisi fallor fut Xenophontis in Socratis defensione cõfictæ. Cõdidit car/ ma multa & iucunda:cõscripsit plærasq̃ epistolares disputationes:quas sente is Græcorũ etiã hebræorũ refersit. Vt autem hebræorũ secreta dogmata pe/ ctraret:multis annis enixissime laborauit : atq̃ ita omnē eorum bibliothecam soluit: ut quem hebræox̃ sibi opponas:nõ facile reperies. Hac ingenij & do/ rinæ fœlicitate & ubertate inductus: ad scribendũ dialogum se cõtulit: quem aprion: seu de uerbo Mirifico inscripsit:quo nihil unq̃ uidi:nec facundiᵘ: nec irabilius. In tris autem libros diuidit́. Primus omnia secreta philosophiæ sub omine Sidonij explicat. Secũdᵒ. Baruchiã iudæũ omnia illa secreta nomia & ortentifica & alia multa hebræorũ enodantem confingit. Tertius Capnionē: dem christianã ex præscriptis duobus approbantē & demonstrantē inducit: 'bi omia uerba mirifica ad nomē Iesus ita applicat: ut illud ineffabile tetragra/ aton: tam effabile factum esse demonstret. Quẽ si legeris dialogum: affirma/ s nullũ:neq̃ philosophũ:neq̃ iudæum : neq̃ christianũ Ioanni Reuchlin iure ræferri posse.Hunc talē non omnibus Italis opponere nobis fuerit perpetuus udor. Quare mi Iacobe cum Augustam sim petiturus: & nesciam quo tem/ ore Basilæã peruenia : uelim summa cura & diligētia scribas Ioanni Amorba/ no impressori:ut in Catalogo:suum Ioanni Reuchlin Phorceñ. locũ assignet. 'ale mi iucũdissime Iacobe lætus & fœlix.Spiræ.xj.Kal̃.Maias.M.cccc.xciij.

Fig. 2. Leontorius' Letter of Introduction in Johann Reuchlin's Book *De verbo mirifico*, 1494. From facsimile reprint (Stuttgart: Frommann-Holzboog, 1964) 6.

who died on 19 October 1494.[4] Leontorius composed the epitaph for Murrho's grave that ends with the line "And Murrho may live for ever in your mouth".[5] There is no doubt that Leontorius was a leading humanist. The famous Alsatian humanist Jacob Wimpfeling writes of him as "one of theirs" in a letter to his friend, the 'archhumanist' Conradus Celtis.[6]

We can assume that Leontorius was born about 1460, and that he studied at the University of Heidelberg. Here the Cistercians maintained Saint Jacob's College (from 1387 to 1523),[7] where students from the monastery of Maulbronn usually pursued their studies. We know for sure that Leontorius had become a monk at Maulbronn, but we do not have a date of entry. In 1492 he was listed for advanced studies in Heidelberg, as *Conradus Leontorius Mulbronnensis*.[8] Bolfgangus Marius, who later became abbot of the Cistercian monastery of Aldersbach, may have been his fellow student. In Marius' collection of poems,[9] there are three poems composed by Adam Werner von Themar (1462–1537) which are dedicated to Leontorius. Adam Werner was connected to the circle of humanists at Heidelberg, and also dedicated poems to the French humanist Robert Gaguin (1433–1501).[10] All these poems can be dated to the years 1489–1495. Adam Werner himself repeatedly asks Leontorius to send him his poems, as he was already a celebrated poet. Of course, as a human-

---

[4] *Commentarios in Baptistam Mantuanum Carmelitam* [Sebastian Murrho] *incepit... eosque Conradus Leontorius monachus Mulbronnensis terminandos suscepit et prope diem imprimendos concedet.* Wolff, 378–379; Lina Baillet, "Murr (Mörer, Murrho) Sebastian", *Nouveau dictionnaire de biographie alsacienne* (no. 27) (Strasbourg 1996) 27–87. Peter Walter opines that it was Wimpfeling who had reworked Murrho's comments on Mantuan; see "Johannes von Dalberg und der Humanismus", in *1495. Kaiser—Reich—Reformen. Der Reichstag zu Worms* (Koblenz 1995) 139–171, here 146 (no mention of Leontorius).

[5] *Et vivat Murrho semper in ore tua*, quoted after Wolff, 408. For an overview of Leontorius' poems, see Wolff, 383–86, 409.

[6] The letter may be dated January 1496 or 1497; edited in Joseph Knepper, "Jakob Wimpfeling (1450–1528). Sein Leben und seine Werke nach den Quellen dargestellt", *Erläuterungen und Ergänzungen zu Janssens Geschichte des deutschen Volkes* (Freiburg 1902; reprint Nieuwkoop 1965) vol. 3:1–375; hereafter quoted as Knepper.

[7] The Cistercians also maintained colleges at other universities, such as that in Paris founded in 1245, in Prague in 1374 and in Vienna after 1385.

[8] See Reinhard Schneider, "Maulbronns kulturelle Ausstrahlung im Mittelalter", in Peter Rückert and Dieter Planck, eds., *Anfänge der Zisterzienser in Südwestdeutschland: Politik, Kunst und Liturgie im Umfeld des Klosters Maulbronn* (Stuttgart 1999) 135.

[9] See Franz Josef Worstbrock, "Aus Gedichtsammlungen des Wolfgang Marius", *Zeitschrift für bayerische Landesgeschichte* 44 (1981) 491–504, here 500f.

[10] See Worstbrock, "Aus Gedichtsammlungen", 501.

ist, he asks in verse form.[11] The three poems by Adam Werner that are dedicated to Leontorius are a carmen of four distiches, dedicated to him as the *commissarius* (that is, secretary to the Abbot General of the Cistercians), a poem consisting of three Sapphic stanzas, and one of fifteen hexameters which starts with a reference to Calliope, the beautiful-voiced muse of poetry.[12]

At that time, Leontorius was secretary to the reform-minded Abbot General of the Cistercian order at Cîteaux, Jean de Cirey (†27 December 1503), who held this office from 1476 to 1501.[13] Leontorius was his secretary for about six years, from 1489 to 1495,[14] and was involved in the reform efforts promoted by Cirey. In November 1493 King Charles VIII (1483–1498) created a commission for the reform of monasteries. Cirey, as abbot of Cîteaux, was a member of this commission along with other abbots such as that of Cluny.[15] The

---

[11] *Te celebris magnum depromit phama poetam*
Fac precor, ignotos ut videam numeros.
Si tibi religio, si Pyerides tibi charae,
Te rogo, discipulo carmina mitte tuo.
Garrulus ipse licet Choridon, taciturnus Alexis
Neu sis, ne saeuum te mea Clyo vocet.
Quis sim, forte roges. Heydelbergensis alumnus
Sum modo. Nuper Adam rector in urbe noua, as edited by Karl Hartfelder, "Werner von Themar, ein Heidelberger Humanist", *Zeitschrift für die Geschichte des Oberrheins* 33 (1880) 1–101, here 23 (no. 10); see Wolff, 407.

[12] Here is the latter:
Ad Calliopen carmen, ut fratrem religiosum divino numine afflatum Conradum Leontorium ad rescribendum incitet.

Maxima Musarum mea Calliope rogitata,
I[n]?cita rumpe moras, accede virum mihi phama
Notum immortali, sacer ipse est relligione [sic]
Pyeridesque colit, humiles praemitte salutes,
Ut tua germana mea Musa domi modo moeret,
Deinde refer tristis verecundaque velat amictu
Ore nigro, cytharam nec Phoebi audire sonoram
Euterpesve Iyram juvat horrescitque sorores,
Ut despecta latet nec vult prodire in apertum,
Dum sibi responsum mittatur amabire carmen,
Ergo virum blandis movens iterumque movebo
Suppliciter precibus; eius miserescat honestas
Reddere jamque vices ne dedignetur, et ipsam
Te rogo, speratum referas carissima carmen.
Tandem vive vale, dic, o divine poeta;
as edited in Wolff, 407, note 91.

[13] On Cirey, see Renaudet, *Préréforme et Humanisme*, 189; Le Gall, *Les moines*, 73, 89, 272, 467, 474f, 482, 485, 601.

[14] See Leontorius' letters from Dijon of 1491, AK, nos. 18 and 19; Halporn, 59–62.

[15] See Le Gall, 72–73.

Cistercians considered King Charles VIII to be the new King David or the new King Solomon.[16] During his reign, in 1493, Cirey restored the studies at the College of Saint Bernard in Paris. In the same year the reform text *Articula parisiensis a patribus cisterciensibus* was written, which included the desire of the order's founders to restore the purity of the Rule and return to the life of the holy fathers.[17] In 1494, Cirey summoned a general chapter of his order at Paris in order to finalize the statutes of reform.[18] Secular servants were no longer to be accepted.[19] Pastoral care at churches in the vicinity of a Cistercian monastery was discontinued, as monks were no longer to celebrate mass outside the monastery in any neighboring churches, except for those of the nobility.[20] If a monk needed to be outside his monastery, he had to wear his habit, and not carry arms.[21] Monks were no longer allowed to appeal to secular authorities against their superiors or the general chapter.[22] Cirey also fought the system of commendatory monasteries,[23] in place since the eighth century, by which kings gave monasteries to loyal laypeople or non-monastic clerics who became abbots (*in commendam*), using the monasteries as *beneficium* for their own gain. However, the decisions of the chapter meeting in Paris in 1494 do not mention anything about the *commenda* system or the reform of the higher clergy. Only the reform of its members appears to have won priority.[24]

As Cirey's secretary, Leontorius apparently traveled with him in France and Germany. He also accompanied him to Italy and Rome, as we know from his first letter to Johann Reuchlin from the Eternal City, dated 7 March 1489.[25] As a humanist, he collected the clas-

---

[16] See Le Gall, 125.
[17] See Manuscript 1652, fol. 242, of the Bibliothèque Sainte-Germaine, Paris, as referred to by Le Gall, 244, note 6.
[18] See Le Gall, 601.
[19] See Manuscript 1652, fol. 250, Paris, as referred to by Le Gall 319, note 8.
[20] ... *nisi esset pro nobilibus personis*; Manuscript 1652, fol. 250, as referred to by Le Gall, 359, note 1.
[21] See Manuscript 1652, fol. 250, as referred to by Le Gall, 392, note 5.
[22] See Latin Manuscript 13116, fol. 66v, of the Bibliothèque Nationale, Paris, as referred to by Le Gall, 272, note 11.
[23] See Latin Manuscript 13116, fol. 65, as referred to by Le Gall, 474, note 5; William J. Telesca, "The problem of the commendatory monasteries and the order of Cîteaux during the abbacy of Jean de Cirey, 1475–1501", *Cîteaux* 22 (1971) 154–177.
[24] See Le Gall, 410.
[25] See **RBW** 1, 97–98 (no. 31); this letter and no. 68 (to be quoted below) have not been available in any modern edition since the 16thC.

sics, such as the works of Virgil (Publius Vergilius Maro, *Opera*) with the commentaries of Servius Maurus Honoratus, Aelius Donatus, and Christophorus Landinus (1424–1498/1504),[26] edited by Demetrius Chalcondylas (1423–1511; a Greek scholar and refugee from the fall of Constantinople living in Florence in 1487) and printed by Bernardinus Nerlius. We know this from his inscription in his copy, extant and listed in the Catalogue to the Travers Books in Sussex, England.[27]

On 27 November 1493, Leontorius wrote a poem which was included in the notebook (dated 1504) of the Nuremberg physician, Hartmann Schedel (1440–1514). Among several anti-Italian and anti-homosexual poems in Latin is one by Leontorius, meant as a confutation of an Italian proverb about the drunkenness of the Germans and simultaneously a criticism of homosexual activities among Italian men, being contrary to natural law. Leontorius calls it an "unpolished" (not "impolite") song.[28] The synecdochic Italian male is called *spurci[di]cus Cynaedus*, derived from the Greek/Latin *cinaedus*, which means somebody indulging in unnatural lust; *spurci[di]cus* is to be translated not simply as 'filthy' but as 'talking obscenely'. Leontorius rather prefers his Germans in worshipping Bacchus: "It won't shame us Germans to worship Bacchus".[29]

---

[26] See the index volume on the Latin literature of the Renaissance by Ute Ecker, Dorothee Gall, Peter Riemer, and Clemens Zintzen, *Cristoforo Landino* (Hildesheim 1998). Landino was the fifteenth-century commentator on the classics, such as Horace and Virgil.

[27] *F[rater] Conradus T Leontorius uulgar Leonberger Mulbron[ens]ÿ R[everendissi]mi D[omini] Cistercie[ns]ÿ Secretarius: Florentie Comparauit 1489*, as given on the internet: www.sussex.ac.uk/library/rare/travcat.html This edition is the first to include the commentaries of Cristoforo Landino. On the study of Greek in the West, see Wilson, *From Byzantium to Italy*; Leighton Durham Reynolds and Nigel Guy Wilson, *Scribes and Scholars: A Guide to the Transmission of Greek and Latin Literature* (Oxford and New York 1991; 3rd ed.).

[28] *Confutatio Proverbii Italici de Germanorum Ebrietate In Pedicones Italos Carmen Impolitum phalenticum Conradi Leontorii Quinto Kalendas Decembris Ex tempore Argentine*. See Ingrid D. Rowland, "Revenge of the Regensburg Humanists, 1493", *The Sixteenth Century Journal* 25 (1994) 307–22. The Latin version is edited in the appendix on p. 321 (based on the original in the Bavarian State Library in Munich, Cod. Lat. 716, cc. 158 (154)v–159 (155)r); an English translation is provided on pp. 310–11. Rowland did not indicate that Leontorius was a Cistercian monk, speaking of him and of "his female partners" (313). Leontorius' poem was written in *Argentine*, the Latin name for Strasbourg, Alsace, and not for Regensburg (which would be *Castra Regina*).

[29] We may wonder whether the monk Leontorius would agree with the vulgar expressions used in the English translation which includes the obscene four-letter word three times for the Latin *futire* (*futuere*) which means 'to have intercourse'.

From Leontorius' extant correspondence we learn that in the spring and summer of 1491 he stayed at Dijon, where it seems the printing press for the Cistercian order was located.[30] His letter from Rome reveals his friendship with Reuchlin, in whom he saw both great *humanitas* (kindness) and familiarity with Latin and Greek eloquence and poetry.[31] No mention is made, however, of Reuchlin as a Hebraist. This changed six years later, in another letter to Reuchlin, of 30 March 1495, probably from Maulbronn, in which Leontorius mentioned that he had received gratis from the printer Johannes Amerbach (c. 1440–1513) in Basel Reuchlin's brand-new book *De verbo mirifico*.[32] This edition includes Leontorius' letter of praise for Reuchlin, dated 21 April 1494, which he had written to his priest-friend Jacob Wimpfeling. The printer made it the frontispiece for Reuchlin's book, and introduced Leontorius' letter with these words:

> In praise of Johann Reuchlin of Pforzheim, the most eloquent man, most skilled in the three main languages, and of his book *De verbo mirifico* which is now edited with a letter of introduction by Conradus Leontorius of Maulbronn.
> Conradus Leontorius to Iacobus Vinphelingus [Wimpfeling] with many greetings.[33]

This letter of praise has now been re-edited as part of the Wimpfeling correspondence.[34] Written from Speyer, it reveals that Leontorius knew Reuchlin's name was not included in the publication project of Abbot Trithemius.[35] Leontorius strongly recommended that Reuchlin should be included in the final version of *De scriptoribus ecclesiasticis*, which then happened.[36] Johannes Amerbach published it sometime

---

[30] Leontorius' letters to Amerbach of 22 April 1491, AK, no. 18, and of 21 June 1491, AK, no. 19; Halporn, 59–62. Leontorius was also at Colmar (Alsace) in November 1494 and November 1502, as his letters from there demonstrate: AK, no. 32; Halporn, 68–69, and AK, no. 175 (6 November 1502).

[31] See RBW 1, 97 (no. 31).

[32] See RBW 1, 213 (no. 68).

[33] *In laudem disertissimi atque trium principalium liguarum peritissimi uiri Ioannis Reuchlin Phorcensis: librorumque quos de Verbo Mirifico nuper edidit: comendaticia Conradi Leontorij Mulbrunnen. Epistola. Conradus Leontorius: Iacobo Vinphelingo. S[alutem] P[lurimam] dicit]*, Facsimile reprint of Johannes Reuchlin, *De verbo mirifico. 1494. De arte cabalistica. 1517. Faksimile-Neudruck in einem Band* (Stuttgart-Bad Cannstatt 1964) [6]. See Fig. 2.

[34] See Otto Herding and Dieter Mertens, eds., *Jakob Wimpfeling: Briefwechsel* (Munich 1990) vol. 1:220–23 (no. 40); hereafter quoted as Herding and Mertens.

[35] i.e., the catalogue of ecclesiastical writers, as he had the opportunity to talk about this forthcoming book with Wimpfeling in Mainz.

[36] See Wimpfeling's letter of 4 May 1494 to Amerbach, with which Leontorius'

between 28 August and 19 November 1494.[37] Leontorius pointed out that Reuchlin had command of not only Greek, Hebrew, and Latin, but also of French, which he learned when he studied law at Orléans in 1479. With Leontorius as the promoter of Reuchlin's work, it comes as no surprise that the monks at Clairvaux seemed to devour it. They also loved the *Praise of Folly* and the *Enchiridion* of Erasmus, and the *Ship of Fools* by Sebastian Brant (1457/58–1521).[38]

Reuchlin's extensive study of Hebrew had prepared him well to write his book, which deals with the name of God (the *tetragrammaton*) and the name of Jesus. Those who read this book will affirm that:

> with right nobody from among the philosophers or the Jews or the Christians will be preferred to Johann Reuchlin. It would be our perpetual shame not to place him [Reuchlin] next to all the Italians [humanists].[39]

Leontorius writes to Reuchlin (in the above-mentioned letter of 30 March 1495) that this new book will help to increase the fame of German scholarship in Italy, where so far it has not been held in high esteem at all. National pride is on the rise. Leontorius writes further that he "read, thoroughly surveyed, and reread" the book with the greatest admiration, particularly for what Reuchlin says about the name of Jesus, something that is not known at all to any of the Latins.[40] Leontorius means, of course, Reuchlin's Chapter (Book) Three on the name of God in Hebrew, יהוה (IHVH, the four-letter word, *tetragrammaton*).[41] Reuchlin explains that when one enters the Hebrew consonant שׁ (š) into God's name to read יהשוה (IH š VH), now a five-letter word, we have the Hebrew name for Jesus, *Ihsuh*,[42] which allows the name of God to be pronounced, and therefore it is the "wonder-working word", *verbum mirificum*, the title of Reuchlin's book. Only thanks to Christ's redemption did the

---

letter of praise was forwarded, Herding and Mertens, 220–223 (no. 40); AK, no. 28; Halporn, 63–64.

[37] For this time span, see Herding and Mertens, 221, note 5.

[38] See Le Gall, 212.

[39] Reuchlin, *De verbo mirifico. 1494. De arte cabalistica. 1517*, [6]; Herding and Mertens, 222 (no. 40).

[40] See RBW 1, 213 (no. 68).

[41] *Sunt autem quattuor solae: IHVH: quib[us] Tetragrammaton ineffabile constat*... Reuchlin, *De verbo mirifico. 1494. Faksimile-Neudruck* [73]–[103], here [92].

[42] Reuchlin, *De verbo mirifico. 1494. Faksimile-Neudruck* [94].

ineffable name of God become utterable through the letters that make up the name of Jesus. "In his attempt to construct a biblical theology Reuchlin uses the interpretational techniques of the Cabala and dissolved Hebrew theosophy into a christosophy".[43]

In the eyes of Leontorius (himself a Swabian), the multi-lingual Swabian Reuchlin is to be preferred to the Roman Cicero. Leontorius recognized Reuchlin's shining significance for the humanist movement in Germany. He makes his point perfectly clear when he writes that he bought five more copies of Reuchlin's book[44] for distribution, probably within the Cistercian order. With proper monastic humility, he further writes that it was against his will that Amerbach printed his private letter to Wimpfeling (of 21 April 1494) as the *frontispicium* (frontispiece) to the Basel edition, that is, the letter containing his high praise for Reuchlin's book.[45] Nevertheless, Leontorius is happy that his and Reuchlin's names are now closely connected. Apparently Amerbach learned of this letter at the very time when Reuchlin's text went to the press, and thought it would be quite useful for marketing the book. Leontorius concludes his letter to Reuchlin with the information that the monks of Maulbronn want him back. Therefore he is returning from France against the wishes of the Abbot General Jean de Cirey, who swears to call him back to his service by the end of the year.[46] In September 1495, Leontorius assisted Abbot Jacob of Morimond with the visitation of the monastery of Heilsbronn near Nuremberg.[47]

Friendships were cherished among the humanists. They sought each others' acquaintance, often by letter. Such a friendship developed between Leontorius and Wimpfeling, and it survived despite their divergent personalities. They are "a study in contrasts".[48] Wimpfeling was a secular priest who was often critical of the monas-

---

[43] Anna Morisi, "Traditionalism, Humanism, and Mystical Experience in Northern Europe and in the Germanic Areas in the Fifteenth and Sixteenth Centuries", in D'Onofrio, ed., *History of Theology III.*, 320–370, here 348.

[44] *Ego te trilinguem, immo quinquilinguem Suevum Romano Tullio non aequo tantum, sed etiam praefero, tanti existimo ex hac barbarie in tantam eruditionem emergere potuisse. Sed de hoc satis. Redeo ad mirificum illud opus tuum, quod statim quinquies emptum...*, RBW 1, 213 (no. 68).

[45] See RBW 1, 213 (no. 68).

[46] *... sed contra voluntatem reverendissimi domini Cisterciensis, qui me honore et veneratione plus debito prosequutus est. Iuravitque me post annum revocaturum ad se;* RBW 1, 214 (no. 68).

[47] See Wolff, 369, note 11.

[48] Halporn, 113.

tic orders; he was bellicose, aggressive, and provocative. Leontorius as a Cistercian monk was pacific and compassionate.[49] In fall and winter of 1503/04, Wimpfeling stayed with Leontorius at Engental, from where they wrote occasional joint letters to Amerbach in Basel.[50]

From other extant humanist correspondence we discover that Leontorius was friends not only with Johann Reuchlin and Jacob Wimpfeling, but also with Peter Schott (1458/60–1490),[51] a young priest, canon lawyer, and poet at Strasbourg, whose early death from the plague at the age of thirty-one, on 12 September 1490, Leontorius lamented.[52] Leontorius contributed a poem on his death that was printed with Schott's *Lucubratiunculae*, as edited by Wimpfeling, on 27 July 1498.[53]

Schott was about Leontorius' age, born into a patrician family in Strasbourg. He attended the famous school at Schlettstatt, probably at the same time as Sebastian Brant. After completing his schooling at Schlettstatt, Schott began his studies at the University of Paris, where he graduated with a bachelor's degree in 1475. Among his teachers was the theologian Johannes Heynlin von Stein (later a Carthusian in Basel). Schott continued his study of law at the University of Bologna, then a great center for humanistic studies. There he learned Greek under Antonius Manlius Britonoriensis.[54] Schott no longer wanted to pursue a civic career and, with the permission of his father and the support of Geiler von Kaisersberg, the cathedral

---

[49] See *ibid*.

[50] Wimpfeling wrote a letter to Amerbach on 30 October 1503 with a note added by Leontorius that he was anxious to learn of new books on display at the Basel book fair; AK, no. 210; Halporn, 115–116; Knepper, 175–176.

[51] See Schott's singular letter to Leontorius as the *cancellarius* of the Cistercians of 23 December 1489, printed in *Petri Schotti Argentinensis Patricii: Juris utriusque Doctoris consultissimi: Oratoris et Poetae elegantissimi: graeceque linguae probe aeruditi: Lucubratiunculae ornatissimae* (Strasbourg: Martin Schott, 1498); *i.e.*, his 300 letters and poems, with a preface and conclusion by Wimpfeling; Schott's texts are edited by Murray and Marian L. Cowie, *The Works of Peter Schott (1460–1490)*, 2 vols. (Chapel Hill 1963–1971); Schott's letter to Leontorius is found in vol. 1:146–147 (no. 126); Cowie has the misspelling *Leontarius*. Leontorius' letter of 19 November 1494, written as *secretarius Cisterciensis* from Colmar to Amerbach also mentioned Schott's work, AK, no. 32; Halporn, 68–69.

[52] See Leontorius' letter of 12 September 1490 to Wimpfeling, Herding and Mertens, 159 (no. 20); also in Cowie vol. 1:311 (no. 291).

[53] See the edition of *Lucubratiunculae* in the library of *Jesuitenkolleg* in Graz, Austria (website: www.kfunigraz.ac.at/ub/sosa/inku/s.html). *Lucubratiunculae* are 'small studies produced by lamp-light'.

[54] *Me in grecorum litteris erudisti*, Schott's letter to him in his *Lucubratiunculae*, Cowie, vol. 1:79–80 (no. 73).

preacher at Strasbourg, he turned to the study of theology while completing his law studies in September 1480. He was ordained to the priesthood in December 1482.[55] Evidently, Leontorius and Schott shared not only their ordination to the priesthood, but also a great interest in humanist studies and in mastering the Greek language. Abbot Trithemius included a short biography of Schott in his book on ecclesiastical writers, reprinted in Schott's *Lucubraciunculae*,[56] edited posthumously by Wimpfeling. Trithemius called Schott a man experienced in Holy Scripture, most learned in civil and ecclesiastical law, and very erudite in the humanities; a philosopher, rhetor, and celebrated poet, who wrote, for example, a *carmen* to the three Johns: the Baptist, the Evangelist, and Chrysostom, and a prose eulogy of Jean Gerson, the famous chancellor of the University of Paris.[57]

Leontorius was also a friend of the Alsatian Conrad Pellican, twenty years younger, who called Leontorius his "unique friend".[58] Pellican was a Franciscan from 1493 to 1525, a known Hebraist, author of the *Commentaria bibliorum*, and later a reformer at Basel and Zurich.[59] Other close friends were the book printers and distributors Anton Koberger (1445–1513)[60] and Johannes Amerbach.[61] Leontorius appears to have been especially close to Amerbach as he signed off his letters to him with "your friend" or "your brother".

According to Trithemius, Leontorius was the author of many poems (*carmina multa*). In a list of Swabian poets (*oratores atque poetae Suevi*) Leontorius is ranked in first place.[62] This list includes among others Heinrich Bebel (1472–1518) and Jerome Emser (1447–1527). In 1493 Leontorius, as secretary to the Cistercian Abbot General, expressed his admiration for Wimpfeling's poem on the triple brilliance of Mary (*De conceptu et triplici candore Mariae virginis*)[63] with an ode to Wimpfeling's

---

[55] See Cowie, xxii–xxxi.
[56] *Ex libro Abbatis Spanheymensis de Ecclesiasticis Scriptoribus*, Cowie, vol. 1:11 (no. 5).
[57] On the three Johns, see Cowie, vol. 1:274–78 (no. 241); on Gerson, see Cowie, vol. 1:258–62 (no. 232).
[58] *Amicus singularis meus Conradus Leontorius*, AK, no. 452, 419 with note 2.
[59] See *Reformatorenlexikon*, 164.
[60] See Wolff, 377.
[61] For his biographical data, see Friedrich Wilhelm Bautz, "Amerbach, Johannes", BBKL 1 (1990) 144; Halphorn, 1–12 (Introduction).
[62] See Wimpfeling's and others' letter of early 1506, Herding and Mertens, 534 (no. 203).
[63] Printed in Strasbourg in 1493, in Basel in 1494; Wolff, 408; Knepper, 55. In

work, *Phoebe divinum*.⁶⁴ Apparently Leontorius shared Wimpfeling's conviction of the Immaculate Conception of Mary,⁶⁵ and thus these humanists demonstrate their religious sensibilities once again. Indeed, the doctrine and devotion of the Immaculate Conception was a 'trademark' of the early humanists.⁶⁶

In 1494, Leontorius paid tribute to the humanist lawyer Dietrich Gresemund (1477–1512) with an introduction in poetic form to his first work, *Lucubratiunculae*, printed by Martin Schott in Mainz, and dedicated to Trithemius. Gresemund's work does not deal with issues of law, but with the value of humanistic studies in the seven liberal arts. The book includes a dialogue on the Mainz carnival. Erasmus of Rotterdam eulogized Gresemund in his 1516 edition of Saint Jerome's works.⁶⁷

The two books by Trithemius of 1494 and 1495 include works known up to that time, but apparently Trithemius was unaware of Leontorius' role in editing and printing the list of privileges of the Cistercian order; this was published by the Augustinian Peter Metlinger⁶⁸ in Dijon on 4 July 1491. This work, *Collecta quorundam*

Knepper's appendix VIII, we find the conclusion of the Latin poem including a call upon Mary as the leader in the war against the "raging Turks":

In saevos, belli ductrix fortissima, Turcos
Fac celerem, genitrix, experiamur opem!
Fac, o catholicae spes et patrona salutis
Hostes nos tandem vincere posse tuos! (Knepper, 337).

⁶⁴ *Sapphicum Conradi Leontorii Suevi Mulbronnensis Reverendissimi domini Cisterciensis Secretarii*. It is a Sapphic ode, that is, verses in imitation of the Greek poetess Sappho who is said to have invented this type of verse. The reprint of two strophes (1 and 30) is found in Wolff, 408:

Phoebe divinum pater alme vatum
Fronde daphnea redimite crines
Primus argutis resonare doctus
  Carmina nervis.

Ipsa nil praeter resonet Mariam
Ipsa reginam celebret Mariam
Teque nos omni veneremur aevo
  Virgo Maria.

⁶⁵ Peter Schott also wrote a poem in praise of Wimpfeling's poem to the Virgin Mary: *Carmen Eligiacum De Conceptu et triplici candore Diue Marie*, Cowie, vol. 1:306 (no. 279). The doctrine of Mary's Immaculate Conception was also accepted by the Benedictine humanist Chelidonius; see Winkler, 4 (and see Chapter on Chelidonius).
⁶⁶ I am grateful to Gerhard Winkler for this insight.
⁶⁷ See Klemens Löffler, "Dietrich Gresemund", *Catholic Encyclopedia* (www.newadvent.org).
⁶⁸ Identified as such by Leontorius in his letter of 4 March 1504 to Amerbach, AK no. 216; Halporn, 119.

priuilegiorum ordinis Cisterciensis, is a valuable source for the historiography of the Cistercian order.[69] Abbot General Jean de Cirey had this collection published to defend his order against attacks on its privileges and possessions, and also as a reminder for its members on the proper conduct of monks. Leontorius concluded the edition with these lines:

> F. Conradus Leontorius Mulbronensis benivolo lectori salutem.
> Quisquis es accipies istum qui forte libellum
> Ordinis eximii, quisquis amator ades...[70]

In the conclusion, Leontorius himself is mentioned by name, that is, only those printed copies carrying his signature were to be recognized as official documents.[71] Leontorius then appended his poem for this 1491 edition under the title *Carmen rithmicum in laude Cistercii.* The opening line reads: *Gaude felix mater Cistercium firmamenti spera stelligera* ("Be glad, mother of Cîteaux, be hopeful, star-bearer of the sky"). In the poem he mentions that Abbot General Jean de Cirey had financed the printing from his own resources.[72]

Late in 1494, Leontorius must have returned to Maulbronn, as on 19 November that year he was still in Colmar, from where he sent a letter to Amerbach which he signed as *secretarius Cistercienis.*[73] During his stay there he kept in touch with his humanist friends, as

---

[69] The University Library in Graz, Austria, has the copy owned once by the monastery of Heiligenkreuz (*Inkunabelkatalog* 9275): *Privilegia ordinis Cisterciensis* (Dijon: Petrus Metlinger, 1491). I am grateful to Dr. Hans Zotter (Graz) for providing me with the text of Leontorius' poem and the image of a woodcut showing the Virgin Mary as Patroness of the Cistercians (Mother of Mercy motif, *Schutzmantel-Madonna*), which is placed at the end of the booklet.

[70] Wolff, 381.

[71] *Et decernimus nullam fidem esse adhibendam nisi codicibus per fratrem Conradum Leonbergensem monasterii nostri Mulbronnensis professum, secretarium nostrum, aut per alium a nobis instituendum signatis.* Wolff, 381.

[72] *Quare age sub tuto latebras hoc ordine querens*
  Nobiscum semp[er] delituisse velis.
 Sed tu, qui legis haec, merita qua laude Johannem
  Cistercii abbatem concelebrare potes.
 Ille etenim nulli sacra virtute secundus,
  Ordinis et divae religionis apex,
 Is tibi, sed proprio confingens aere libellum,
  Pontificum cartas innotuisse dedit.
 Hunc tu perpetuo carum venerare parentem
  Et vivat memori semper in ore tuo.
See also Wolff, 381 and 407.

[73] AK, no. 32.

his letters to Reuchlin of 30 March 1495, to Wimpfeling of 1496[74] and to Amerbach of 17 November 1497[75] show. Around 1500 Leontorius must have read or at least been in possession of the manuscript of Reuchlin's comedy *Sergius vel Capitis caput*, as in January 1500 he promised Sebastian Brant that he would send him a copy.[76] The comedy, written in verse form, was composed at the end of 1496, but was not available until 1504, when it was printed at Leipzig.[77] In it Reuchlin deals in a satirical way with an influential former Augustinian friar at the court of the territorial lord.[78] The work was written for Reuchlin's patron, Johannes von Dalberg, prince-bishop of Worms.[79]

Along with Reuchlin and others, Leontorius had access to Dalberg's episcopal court. In 1496 he was invited as a guest and entertainer to Dalberg's residence in Heidelberg, as the bishop had also been chancellor of the university since 1481. While Reuchlin had to work as a translator of anything the bishop wished translated from Greek into Latin, Leontorius and Wimpfeling were expected to produce spontaneous verses while they were drinking at parties. The prelate persuaded Leontorius' superior to grant him a leave of absence from the monastery for several months in order to be of service to him. All this information is found in a letter of Heinrich Spiess (Cuspidius) to Conradus Celtis of 13 May 1496.[80] Occasionally these friends

---

[74] See Herding and Mertens, 258–60 (no. 67).
[75] See AK, no. 66.
[76] This promise is mentioned in Brant's letter to Reuchlin of 13 January 1500: *comoedia, quam Leontorius noster mihi sese transmissurum pollicebatur, sed nondum videre merui*. RBW 1, 329 (no. 102). See also Reuchlin's letter to Brant of 3 June 1503, with editorial note 6 in RBW 1, 391–92 (no. 125); Hugo Holstein, *Johann Reuchlins Komödien. Ein Beitrag zur Geschichte des Lateinischen Schuldramas* (Halle 1888; reprint Leipzig 1973) 130 with note 2.
[77] See RBW 1, 330 (no. 102) with note 4.
[78] The friar's name was probably Dr. Conrad Holzinger, at the court of the Duke of Württemberg; on Holzinger, see Dieter Stievermann, "Der Augustinermönch Dr. Conrad Holzinger—Kaplan, Rat und Kanzler des Grafen bzw. Herzogs Eberhard d. J. von Württemberg am Ende des 15. Jahrhunderts", in *Mittel und Wege früher Verfassungspolitik*, ed. Josef Engel (Stuttgart 1979) 356–405, here 390.
[79] See Holstein, 135. On Dalberg, see Karl Morneweg, *Johann von Dalberg, ein deutscher Humanist und Bischof* (Heidelberg 1887); Peter Walter, "Johannes von Dalberg und der Humanismus", in *1495. Kaiser—Reich—Reformen. Der Reichstag zu Worms* (see note 4 above).
[80] *Officium Joannis Reuchlin est transferre e Graeco in Latinum nostrum sermonem, quae volet Episcopus... Officium Conradi et Jacobi est cudere carmina; quae cudunt et in mediis ipsis poculis*. Hans Rupprich, *Der Briefwechsel des Konrad Celtis* (Munich 1934) 185 (no. 110); hereafter quoted as Rupprich.

went on excursions, for instance to Sponheim for a visit to Abbot Trithemius.[81] Bishop Dalberg of Worms was the center of a humanist literary sodality called *Sodalitas Litterarum Rhenana*, founded by Celtis around 1495. The transition from scholastic to humanistic culture at Heidelberg was decisively effected by the sodality. Among the members were Johann Reuchlin, Johannes Trithemius, Jacob Wimpfeling, and Conradus Leontorius.[82] Similar sodalities were founded elsewhere.[83]

Leontorius stayed at Maulbronn until 1503, when Abbot Johannes Burrus was deposed. He had been in office since 1491 (and held office again from 1518 to 1521).[84] Apparently the monks of Maulbronn were discontented with his strict reforms, which we know not from Leontorius himself, who is silent on the issue, but from his priest-friend Wimpfeling, who wrote to Amerbach in 1504 that "they, out of hatred born of great trifles, manoeuvered to get rid of their abbot, who was as pious as he was holy".[85] The military occupation of their monastery by Duke Ulrich of Württemberg during a local conflict is seen as punishment for the unruly monks.[86] At that time Leontorius was already in Switzerland, as Wimpfeling says "You and C. Leontorius can reply to me" through a third person.[87]

Leontorius left Maulbronn in order to become the father confessor of the Cistercian nuns at Engental,[88] near Basel. This job left him enough time to pursue humanistic studies, and, living close to Basel as one of the great centers of scholarship, he was able to contribute greatly to the advancement and fame of monastic and biblical humanism. He was considered well-versed in ancient literature,

---

[81] See letter of Heinrich Spiess (Cuspidius) to Celtis of 13 May 1496; Rupprich, 185 (no. 110); Wolff, 372, note 23.

[82] See letter of Heinrich von Bünau to Celtis of 8 December 1495; Rupprich, 164 (no. 100), note 1. See also Knepper, 133, who listed additional members of this sodality.

[83] At Cracow, Celtis had founded a learned society called the *Sodalitas Litterarum Vistulana*, and another, entitled the *Sodalitas Litterarum Hungarorum*, in Hungary. The name of the latter association was afterwards changed to *Sodalitas Litterarum Danubiana*, and its seat was transferred to Vienna in 1494. See Joseph Sauer, "Conrad Celtes" [sic] in *Catholic Encyclopedia* (www.newadvent.org).

[84] See Wolff, 370, note 11.

[85] AK, no. 233; Halporn, 122.

[86] See Halporn, 121.

[87] See AK, no. 233, Halporn, 122.

[88] Nunnery and church were plundered during the Peasants' War of 1525 and completely razed in later years; Wolff, 370 with note 13. On Leontorius in Engental, see Halporn, 113.

so that in April 1504 Wimpfeling asked him (via Amerbach, the printer in Basel) to tell him the place in Pliny where faith in the immortality of the soul is ridiculed:

> P.S.: Tell C. Leontorius that I once read a statement in Pliny, laughing at the idea of a human soul as immortal. I cannot find the citation again anywhere in Pliny. If he knows it, have him write me.[89]

In the fall of 1503 Leontorius was in contact with another prelate, Christoph von Utenheim (c. 1450–1522),[90] who had been the reform-minded bishop of Basel since 1 December 1502. In 1503 Leontorius wrote a panegyric, *In sacram synodi celebritatem F. Conradi Leontorii Mulbronnen[sis] lyricum dedicatum*, for the edition of the new statutes on the reform of the clergy of the Diocese of Basel, *Statuta synodalia Basiliensia/ Christophori episcope Basilien./ ad clerum suum oratio*.[91] Wimpfeling had compiled the statutes and contributed the prologue, in which he made use of Saint Bernard's *Letter 42 On the conduct of bishops*.[92] This edition included a speech which the bishop had delivered to his clergy; it was printed by Amerbach in 1503.[93] As part of his reform plans, the bishop included the directive that every one of his priests should possess the Mass explanation by the Carthusian Johannes Heynlin (de Lapide), who appears to have been Leontorius' teacher at some point.[94] Heynlin's book was so popular that on 10 November 1504 Leontorius asked Amerbach to provide him with a copy.[95]

In 1503 Leontorius, as editor, was privileged to write the prefatory ode[96] to the latest edition of a textbook on humanist rhetoric,

---

[89] Herding and Mertens, 456–57 (no. 157); AK, no. 220; Halporn, 121. Leontorius also stayed in touch with Wimpfeling during a controversy with the Dominicans in Basel; see Herding and Mertens, 483–84 (no. 178, letter from Engental, dated 14 May 1505).
[90] On him, see Ursula Olschewski, "Christoph von Utenheim", BBKL 12 (1997) 988–989.
[91] Printed by Amerbach in 1503; Leontorius' poem is found on fol. XXII; see Knepper, 173, note 2.
[92] See Wimpfeling's mention of his Prologue in his letter to Bishop Albrecht of Strasbourg of 1506: *Prologus statutorum synodalium Basiliensium in fine, ubi sanctum Bernardum citavi*, Herding and Mertens, 566 (no. 216); see Bernard's *Epistola 42, De moribus et officio episcoporum*, in *Opera Sancti Bernardi*, eds. Jean Leclercq and Henri Rochais (Rome 1957–1977) vol. 7:100–131, here 127. Wimpfeling used the edition of Bernard's letters that was printed by Kessler at Basel in 1494.
[93] See AK, 198 (no. 210), note 1.
[94] See Junghans, *Der junge Luther*, 110.
[95] See Leontorius' letter from Engental, AK, no. 241.
[96] Edited in Wolff, 384, notes 56 and 409.

letter writing, and orations, called *Margaritha poetica*, i.e., 'literary pearls'. It was written by the early German humanist Canon Albrecht von Eyb (1420–1475), of Eichstätt in Bavaria, who was educated at the University of Pavia (1444–1447) and the University of Bologna (1448–1451).[97] The trio of printers in Basel (Johannes Amerbach, Johannes Petri, and Johannes Froben [1460–1527]) reprinted it in 1503, basing it on both the first edition—which had come out in Nuremberg in 1472—and the 1495 edition, provided by Amerbach. The 'literary pearls' consisted of examples in prose and verse from Latin authors, enriched by specimens of humanist eloquence.[98]

Leontorius evidently did not mind at all using pagan authors for the purpose of education, while his friend Wimpfeling disagreed.[99] However, Leontorius would have preferred to give the work a new title, such as 'The Maxims of Famous Orators', since the poets are not very well represented in it. In Leontorius' view, Eyb's intention was not to introduce poetry to the young, but to instruct them in good letter writing.[100] The number of printed copies of this book must have been very high, for in 1506 the book distributor Koberger bought 1,600 of them.[101]

Leontorius was not only interested in ancient rhetoric, but also in ancient history. In particular he wanted to read *De Roma triumphans* by Flavio Biondo of Forli (1388–1463), which was first published in 1473 and then republished in 1503. Our Cistercian wanted his friend Amerbach to track it down for him at the Frankfurt Book Fair, at any cost: "I want it so much that I will pay whatever it takes", the monk wrote in the spring of 1504.[102] In November 1508 he still did not have a copy, so he asked Amerbach if he could borrow his copy.[103]

Sometime in the spring of 1505 Wimpfeling was stirring controversy with his book *De integritate*, in which he proposed that Augustine was not a monk. The Augustinians, including the young Martin

---

[97] See Joseph Anthony Hiller, *Albrecht von Eyb, Medieval Moralist* (dissertation Washington, DC 1939) 8–14; Johannes Madey, "Albrecht von Eyb", BBKL 16 (1999) 474.
[98] The table of contents is given in Hiller, 70–74.
[99] See Halporn, 116.
[100] See Leontorius' letter to Amerbach of 23 February 1504; AK, no. 215; Halporn, 116–117.
[101] See letter of 23 February 1504; AK, 203 (no. 215), note 1.
[102] Letter to Amerbach of 4 March 1504; AK, no. 216; Halporn, 119.
[103] See letter of 15 November 1508; AK, no. 401; Halporn, 131.

Luther,[104] and the Dominicans, including the prior of the Dominican friars at Basel, Wernher von Selden, were offended, as the Dominicans also follow the Rule of Saint Augustine. Since Leontorius was a good friend of both the controversial secular priest Wimpfeling and the Dominican prior of Basel, he wanted to mediate. In a letter of 9 May 1505 to Amerbach, written from Engental, he says:

> For there is some controversy (*controversia*) afoot between our Jacob and a doctor, a dear friend of mine, that I want to put to rest, and a certain writing erased (for there will be a great fire from this little flame unless the water of peace is not poured on quickly). I will tell you the cause when I can speak with you alone.[105]

While this controversy was going on, Leontorius had some monastic-spiritual business to attend to, as a nun of Engental had asked him to get a hair shirt which she wanted to wear for doing penance. Simultaneously we get a glimpse of Leontorius himself as a person, as he wrote about this request and about himself in his letter to Amerbach of 17 December 1506. Evidently his previous request to a Carthusian friend at Basel had been left unanswered. Therefore he asked Amerbach to get him the hair shirt, be it new or used, for the Cistercian nun. A bit irritated, he wrote of her that the Cistercian order seemed to suit her so little that she wanted to try the Carthusian way of life. Amerbach would not have believed him, if he had asked for such a shirt without the explanation that it was not for him but for a nun in the monastery where he was the father confessor: "You would not believe that I want a hair shirt since I am used to wear sometimes shirts of linen".[106] He jokingly added that Amerbach's influence in matters of religion was not so strong on him that Amerbach could suspect him of wanting a hair shirt. If Amerbach was able to procure such a shirt for the nun, he should wrap it in paper when sending it in order to keep the other nuns from seeing it and gossiping.[107]

In the spring of 1507 the young Boniface Amerbach (1495–1562), aged about twelve, was sent temporarily to Leontorius at Engental to be tutored in Latin together with another boy, as an epidemic

---

[104] See Junghans, *Der junge Luther*, 195, 212–213.
[105] First edited by Knepper, 360 (no. 15); AK, no. 262; Halporn, 125.
[106] AK, no. 326; Halporn, 129.
[107] See *ibid.*; Halporn, 130.

had broken out in Basel.[108] As a teacher, Leontorius was concerned that the young Amerbach should master the humanist script; we know this from a message from Leontorius that Johann Amerbach passed on to his sons, namely that they should not "disfigure their handwriting with barely civilized gothic script, but apply a modest measure of attention to forming their Latin letters in roman style".[109]

Leontorius was a diligent and kind teacher of the two boys, who were eager to learn. Of Boniface, he wrote to his father in Basel that he was of a gentle nature and did not want to be driven like a slave, something the teacher appreciated as "more laudable and more acceptable in a young person of good breeding than to be forced by sharp rods in the barbaric custom of the Germans".[110] On 22 May 1507, Leontorius added a postscript to a letter from young Amerbach to his father. It gives us insight into the tutor's ordinary life at the nunnery of Engental. The major part of the text is given here verbatim:

> Yesterday evening, doing as good a job as I could, I composed a brief letter in German for your son and for his very diligent little companion. As I was about to go hear the confessions of our sisters, I instructed each to translate it into Latin out of his own head. On returning I found that both of them had translated the letter, both of which I send you and which you are reading, without any corrections from me, as I warned them I would do when I left. I read them with pleasure, but I do not doubt that you read them with unusual satisfaction. Wherefore, my dear Amerbach, if the weather is mild, come to visit us in the precincts sacred to the muses...[111]

The reference to the muses means that Leontorius gave the two boys lessons in writing poems. At the end of the year 1507 he wrote a little guidebook on the lyrics of Horace and some Christian poets for Amerbach's twelve-year-old son, primarily in gratitude for the father's generosity towards him as a tutor and a scholar. Leontorius apparently gave this manuscript to the boy as a New Year's gift. It has a prefatory note that he signed with the initials C(onradus) T(uus) L(eontorius) E(ngental):

---

[108] See letter of 12 May 1507; AK, no. 337; Halporn, 279–280; AK, no. 336; Halporn, 285. On Boniface, see Peter Walter, entry "Amerbach, Bonifatius", in *Lexikon der Reformationszeit* (Freiburg, Basel, Vienna 2002) 26.

[109] See Johann Amerbach's letter of 22 May 1505 to his son Bruno, living at the College of Bourgogne; AK, no. 265; Halporn, 194.

[110] Letter from Engental from the beginning of May; AK, no. 336; Halporn, 285.

[111] AK, no. 340; Halporn, 286.

These kinds of poems, my young scholar Bonifacius, I have collected together in one place for you, for your pleasure and instruction in good literature, so that you can easily recognize the genres of the poems of Horace and others. With it you can scan poetry wherever you encounter it in the course of reading; I have done this in appreciation of your learned father who has honored me with unusual affection and generosity beyond what I deserve. Farewell and take care that you do your duty, as everything is supplied for you by others, especially by your indulgent father. C.T.L.E.[112]

Also in the year 1507, Leontorius wrote the preface to an edition of a work by the medieval monk Gunther of Pairis (c. 1150–c. 1220), the Cistercian monastery in Alsace, where Leontorius appears to have been stationed for some time. Gunther's devotional work on prayer, fasting, and almsgiving was printed by Michael Furter in Basel in 1507.[113] This medieval monk is better known today, however, for his historiography of the crusades.[114]

Having knowledge of manuscripts of the Bible and other texts in the libraries of various Cistercian monasteries (in particular Maulbronn and Heilsbronn),[115] Leontorius began to work on a critical edition of the texts. He could not stand the carelessness of many editors and, therefore, chastised them, as they undermined "the divine art of printing" by their ignorance and corrupt practices.[116] He had been prompted by Amerbach to locate manuscripts of Hugo Cardinalis a Sancto Caro (†1263), the famous Bible commentator of the Order of Preachers, in the Maulbronn library. In response, Leontorius wrote to Amerbach on 17 November 1497 that his abbot would send him

---

[112] AK no. 365; Halporn, 293. An illustration of his handwritten text is given in Holger Jakob-Friesen, Beat R. Jenny, and Christian Müller, eds., *Bonifacius Amerbach, 1495–1562: Zum 500. Geburtstag des Basler Juristen und Erben des Erasmus von Rotterdam* (Basel 1995) 41.

[113] *Opus pulcherrimu[m] de tribus vsitatis christianoru[m] actibus: oratione videlicet: ieiunio [et] elemosyna: continens libros tredecim: venerabilis p[at]ris Guntheri ordinis diui Benedicti p[ro] sermonib[us et] collationibus publice faciendis ... diu absco[n]ditu[m] s[ed] nup[er] inuentu[m et] impressu[m]/Guntherus <Ordinis Divi Benedicti* (Basel: Furter, 1507). See *Patrologia Latina*, vol. 212:97–221.

[114] See Francis R. Swietek, "Gunther of Pairis and the Historia Constantinopolitana", *Speculum* 53 (1978) 47–79; Bruno W. Häuptli, "Gunther von Pairis", BBKL 22 (2003) 481–484.

[115] See Wolff, 383. For instance, Leontorius knew of a codex by the ancient author Martianus Capella (5thC), *De nuptiis Philologiae et Mercurii*, with a commentary, extant in his monastery at Maulbronn, and he recommended consulting it before Amerbach edited this work; see AK, no. 18; Halporn, 59f. Leontorius helped with editing, particularly with explanations of Greek words; see Haporn, 62 and 68.

[116] See AK, no. 145; partly translated in Halporn, 2.

(Amerbach) from his own library what he had of Hugo Cardinalis for him to see, read, and use.[117] After he had finished this letter, he remembered that some of the required manuscripts by Hugo might still be at the monastery of Pairis, where his own brother Henricus was prior from 1480 to 1504. Amerbach should contact him directly on this matter.[118]

Eventually, the project came to a fair conclusion because the distributor Koberger brought together "the three finest and most accomplished printers among the Germans: Johannes Amerbach, Johannes Petri, and Johannes Froben".[119] Amerbach had taken the lead in editing and producing the first printed reference Bible (in Latin) that contained the postils of Hugo Cardinalis (*Biblia latina cum postillis Hugonis a S. Caro*).[120] He edited this Bible, with commentary, between 1498 and 1502, and the Nuremberg book dealer Koberger financed and distributed it. This edition comprised seven volumes and was the first complete edition of its kind.[121] Leontorius noted that almost no library possessed the complete manuscript, but now it was made available in many copies.[122] In Amerbach's words, Hugo's interpretations referred to "the old and new law in both historical and mystical senses", made "with the greatest diligence and the highest wisdom, and left nothing unexplained". Hugo inserted many comments that were "suitable for preaching to the people", simply a "splendid treasure". "The old law will become clear; the new law will go forth in light; the religion of Christ will be firmly grounded and clear".[123]

Contrary to Koberger's expectations, this work sold badly. He thought that it would sell better if an index was included.[124] Therefore, the second edition appeared in 1503–1504 with an index[125] by the

---

[117] See the second letter of 17 November 1497, AK, no. 66; Halporn, 217f. Halporn wrote of Heilbronn (an imperial city on the Neckar River) instead of Heilsbronn (a Cistercian abbey near Nuremberg).

[118] See AK, no. 67; Halporn, 218.

[119] Leontorius' letter from Colmar to Koberger of 4 November 1503; Halporn, 255.

[120] See the description of it in Walter Arthur Copinger, *Incunabula biblica; or, The first half century of the Latin Bible* (London 1892) 193–197.

[121] See Wolff, 382–383.

[122] See Leontorius' letter from Colmar to Koberger of 4 November 1503; Halporn, 255.

[123] Amerbach's letter to Koberger of 28 September 1498 (preface to the edition); Halporn, 220.

[124] See AK, no. 202; Halporn, 253.

[125] *Repertorium postillarum utriusque Testamenti domini Hugonis cardinalis* (Basel 1504); see AK, no. 176: Amerbach to Koberger on 7 November 1502; Wolff, 409–10.

Dominican friar Georg Epp (†1507 or 1510), from Güglingen near Wimpfen[126]: *Biblia Latina continens textum biblie cum postilla domini Hugonis [de Sancto Charo] Cardinalis*. For this second edition, dated 16 November 1504, Leontorius wrote the eulogy for Epp as the author of the index (*repertorium*), in verse, of course,[127] but veiling the fact that sales were lacking.[128] He referred to the work as Hugo's 'commentary' on the entire Old and New Testament (*commentarius totius veteris et novi instrumenti*). Incidentally, Leontorius also provided the preface (dated 3 April 1506) to Epp's book *De illustribus viris ac sanctimonialibus O.P.*, on famous members of the Dominican order, possibly printed by Amerbach.[129] For this second edition of the Bible with the cardinal's comments, which Koberger again financed, and which the three Basel printers Amerbach, Petri, and Froben produced, Leontorius played the key role, as he was now the sole editor. As an introduction to volume one he used his letter to Koberger of 4 November 1503, and as a conclusion at the end of volume six he used a letter of 23 August 1504 to the same.[130] Leontorius' prefatory letter heaps praise on Koberger as the financier of the project:

> For, Anton [Koberger], jewel of the wealthy city of Nuremberg, you have won much genuine glory by the beneficent generosity of your good self. With a liberality different from that of Cimon, the famed leader of Athens, who generously provided his poor citizens with food, clothing, and money, you have lavishly provided all those hungry for knowledge who are scattered through Christendom with the nourishment that grows and multiplies with use, and shines with wear; the more they exercise their minds, the more vigorous they become.[131]

He adds effusively that the new edition "could be thought to have appeared not from a printing shop but in a heavy shower from the heavens".[132]

In 1506, Leontorius took care of a new edition of the Bible Concordance by Conradus de Alemannia (Conrad of Halberstadt)

---

[126] Epp had studied theology in Paris in 1490. From 1503 he was father confessor of the Dominican sisters in Basel, at the convent of St. Mary Magdalene *an den Steinen*, i.e. outside the city wall.
[127] See Wolff, 383 and 410 with partial edition of Leontorius' poem for Epp.
[128] See Halporn, 254.
[129] See AK, no. 121.
[130] See Wolff, 383; Knepper, 179.
[131] Leontorius' letter of 4 November 1503 from Colmar to Koberger; Halporn, 254–255.
[132] *Ibid.*

and Johannes de Ragusa (Johannes of Dubrovnic) with the *Prologus in concordantias/Sacrae paginae doctoris eximij Ioannis de secubia* (Johannes de Segovia) in the second part, again printed by Amerbach, Petri, and Froben. Leontorius' edition is the improved version (i.e., "done with the greatest care") of an edition first printed in 1496 by the same printers, but edited at that time by Sebastian Brant. Leontorius provided the introduction to the 1506 Bible Concordance,[133] in which he made perfectly clear who had provided the emendations, as he signed off with his name "from Engental on the Birs River near Basel".[134]

Initially the Bible with the traditional glosses, the postil of Lyra, the additions of Paul of Burgos (†1435) and the Franciscan friar Matthias Thoring (Döring, 1390/1400–1469) had been published at Basel in 1498 and edited by Brant, under the title *Textus biblie/Cu[m] Glosa ordinaria/Nicolai de lyra postilla/Moralitatibus eiusdem/Pauli Burgensis Additionibus/Matthie Thoring Replicis*. It was published in several parts, printed by Petri and Froben. Amerbach joined them for the second printing, which appeared in 1502, and for the third, which started to appear in 1506 and was completed in November 1508. This third printing was edited by Leontorius.[135] His name, *F. Conradus Leontorius*

---

[133] *Concordantie maiores/biblie tam dictionu[m] declinabiliumq[ue]; indecli/nabilium de de nuouo summa diligentia cu[m] textu/vise ac scd'm veram orthographiam eme[n]d/atissime excuse. F. Conradus Leontorius Mulbrunne. Be/niuolo Lectori Salutem & foelicitatem optat.*

[134] *Ex Artaualle ultra Birsam Basileanam*; Wolff, 393–96.

[135] *Textus biblie: Cum glossa ordinaria, Nicolai de Lyra postilla, moralitatibus eiusdem, Pauli Burgensis additionibus, Matthie Thoring replicis* (Basel 1506–1507).
Textus biblie / P. 1 / Et sunt in ea hec scilicet: Genesis, Exodus, Leviticus, Numerorum, Deuteronomius (Basel 1506).
Textus biblie / P. 2 / In se continens glossam ordinariam cum expositione Lyre litterali et morali necnon additionibus ac replicis super libros Josue, Judicum, Ruth, Regum, Paralipomenon, Esdre, Neemie, Tobie, Judith, Hester (Basel 1506).
Textus biblie / P. 3 / In se continens glossam ordinariam cum expositione Lyre litterali et morali, necnon additionibus ac replicis, super libros Job, Psalterium, Proverbiorum, Ecclesiasten, Cantica canticorum, Sapientie, Ecclesiasticum (Basel 1506).
Textus biblie / P. 4 / In se continens glossam ordinariam cum expositione Lyre litterali et morali, necnon additionibus ac replicis super libros Esaie, Hieremie, Threnorum, Baruch, Ezechielis, Danielis, Osee, Johelis, Amos, Abdie, Jone, Michee, Naum, Abacuk, Sophonie, Aggei, Zacharie, Malachie, Machabeorum (Basel 1507).
Textus biblie / P. 5 / In se continens glossam ordinariam cum expositione Lyre litterali et morali, necnon additionibus ac replicis, super libros Matthei, Marci, Luce, Johannis (Basel 1507).
Textus biblie / P. 6 / Cum glossa ordinaria et expositione Lyre litterali et morali necnon additionibus ac replicis super epistolas ad Romanos, . . . Actus apostolorum, super canonica Jacobi . . ., Apocalypsim (Basel 1508).
Textus biblie / [P. 7] / Repertorium alphabeticum sententiarum praestantium contentivum decerptarum ex glossa ordinaria, interlineari, ex Nicolai de Lyra litterali-morali postilla . . . super vetus et novum testamentum (Basel 1508).

Mulbronnen, appears on the back of the title page of the first volume (containing the books of Genesis, Exodus, Leviticus, Numbers, and Deuteronomy). In his introduction, Leontorius points out the advantages of the new edition compared to the earlier ones. His name reappears in the third volume,[136] the fourth volume (the Minor Prophets), the fifth volume (the Four Gospels), and the sixth volume (the Epistles and Acts). He also provided an introduction to the volumes of the New Testament, dated 1507, which he adorned with seven distiches (couplets) on the four evangelists.[137]

He also contributed a postscript at the end of volume six in which he indicates how important the Church Fathers are for the better understanding of the Scriptures. The concluding volume seven is his biblical index in alphabetical order, called *repertorium alphabeticum*, which also includes his report on the difficulties of producing the index and its usefulness; it, too, carries his name, the location, and date: Engental, 8 November 1508.[138]

Leontorius spent much of his time at Engental proof-reading the Bibles and the texts attached to them. Besides this tedious job he helped with the emendation of the editions of the works of the Church Fathers Augustine and Ambrose. These "monumental publications"[139] are based upon manuscripts that took many years to assemble, edit, and finally print.[140] The Augustine edition of eleven volumes was soon in trouble, as shortly after production began the

---

[136] *Tertia pars huius operis* (1506); copy in Madison, WI, Memorial Library, BS 1415.3.

[137] *Bis duoquinta novae pars evangelia legis*
Quattuor et Christi continet illa rotas;
Undique plena oculis animalia quattuor ista
Circumstant solium nocte dieque Dei.
Hebraeo Levi profert sermone Matthaeus
Humanam faciem publico ab officio.
Interpres Petri Marcus, leo fortis et urbis
Praesul Alexandri, scribit in Italia.
Tertius est medicus Lucas, qui Syrus Achaeis
Sub specie vituli virgineo ore canit.
Ultimus altivolans aquila caelebsque Johannes
Antistes Asiae scripsit ad ecclesias.
Quattuor irriguum faciunt haec flumina mundum,
Hi perflant venti quattuor omne solum. Wolff, 402, note 85.

[138] See Wolff, 396–405.

[139] Halporn, 11.

[140] We know, for instance, that a monk from the Benedictine monastery of St. Blasien in the Black Forest called Alexius Stab provided manuscripts by Augustine and Jerome from this cloister for the printer at Basel; see Halporn, 72.

editor died; his successor lasted less than a year. It took several years to finish the edition.[141]

Amerbach invited Leontorius to supply prefatory letters for some of the volumes.[142] Leontorius agreed to this task for the Augustine edition if nobody else could do a better job.[143] He wrote the introduction and conclusion to the Augustine edition and in 1504 and 1505 worked on volume seven, which included Augustine's *The City of God*. It was published in October 1508 and was based on the earlier Amerbach edition of the individual book of the *De civitate Dei* of 1489 and 1490. A reprint of Leontorius' edition of *De civitate Dei* was arranged by Adam Petri of Basel in 1515, which was again funded by Koberger of Nuremberg; but Leontorius was no longer mentioned by name. The same is true for another reprint funded by Koberger, but printed by Jacques Sacon at Lyon in 1520.[144]

The eleven volumes of Augustine's *Opera* were ready after 22 January 1506. Leontorius had added the chapter headings with brief summaries (*argumenta*), further glosses, and a much larger index. On the reverse of the title page a woodcut print shows Saint Augustine at his desk, and at the bottom of the page Leontorius' poem on Augustine's book is given.[145] In June 1506 Leontorius reminded Amerbach that he expected a complete set in exchange for his scholarly contributions. The volumes were to be sent to Engental.[146] The market value of this edition was the equivalent of one fifth of the living expenses of a student in Paris at that time.[147] Therefore, only the major contributors received a complimentary complete set. Minor contributors had to be happy with a discount. Of the 2,100 copies that were printed, Koberger, the distributor, bought 1,600.[148]

Around that time (September 1506) Leontorius was in need of spectacles (*specilla*), which he hoped to receive from Froben via Amerbach. He was also awaiting the reprint of the *Dictionarium Ambrosii*

---

[141] See *ibid*.
[142] For translations see Barbara Halporn, *Johann Amerbach's Collected Editions of St. Ambrose, St. Augustine, and St. Jerome* (dissertation Indiana University 1988).
[143] See his letter to Amerbach of 12 or 19 April 1505; AK, no. 259; Halporn, 326–327.
[144] See Wolff, 389.
[145] Included in *Augustini librorum pars septima* (Basel 1504/1505); Wolff, 410, and 386–388.
[146] See his letter to Amerbach of 8 June 1506; AK, no. 313; Halporn, 335.
[147] See Halporn, 334.
[148] See Halporn, 335.

Calepini Bergomatis (Venice 1506; earlier prints in 1503 and 1505), by the Augustinian friar Ambrose Calpinus (1435–1511).[149]

Thus far, the works of the Church Father Ambrose had not been available in a complete edition. No library had a complete set of manuscripts of all his works. In 1492 the first complete edition appeared, by Amerbach. In 1506, Leontorius worked on the improvement of this Ambrose edition, printed in three parts: *Diui Ambrosij Ep[iscop]i Mediolanen[sis] O[mn]ia opera denuo accuratissime reuisa et nouiter impressa* [microform]: [Woodcut] [*Paulinus de vita Ambrosii: registru[m] in tripertitu[m] opus librorum Ambrosii . . . / C. Leontorius*].[150] Leontorius provided a new, expanded index of the collected works of Ambrose, and he made sure that a woodcut print showing Ambrose in his study was included after the title page. Once again, he wrote the introduction and conclusion, indicating at the end of the introduction his name, the location, and date: *F. Conradus Leontorius Mulbronne . . . Ex arta valle vltra basileanam birsam . . . Septembres: Anno domini. M.D.VI* (1506). His name appears once more in the preface to the index volume, with the date of the memorial day of Saint Augustine's baptism, as the spiritual son of the most blessed Ambrose. Leontorius concluded the Ambrose index volume with another of his poems.[151]

In his letters, the ageing and ailing Leontorius began to talk about his needs, illnesses, and cures. He had once asked Froben to procure him glasses, as mentioned. Now he asked Amerbach the same favor. After he finally received them, he thanked him in a letter of 30 November 1507, writing that the new spectacles were the kind he wanted, namely the thicker type of glass and more curved:

> For when I put two pairs of these spectacles together on my nose, I see much further and more clearly; if I add a third, they are almost equal to a thicker and more curved lens.[152]

He complains that Amerbach and another friend, a schoolmaster, never visit him in Engental, and jokingly adds that he would chastise the schoolmaster, if he had a long leather belt hanging at his side for a spanking, like Plautus' *Pyrgopolinices*.[153]

---

[149] See AK, no. 317 with notes.
[150] Microfilm, Madison, WI, Memorial Library.
[151] Printed in *Registrum florigerum in tripertitum opus librorum beati Ambrosii* (Basel 1506); Wolff, 410, and 390–393.
[152] AK, no. 362; Halporn, 130.
[153] See AK, no. 362; Halporn, 131.

Evidently the sickly monk started to read medical authors of old such as Aulus Cornelius Celsus (c. 25 BC–40/50 AD), whose work was first printed in 1478 and several times afterwards.[154] Leontorius also knew where the book could be found, as he advised Bruno Amerbach to read it in his father's library, when he wrote of kidney stone problems:

> For if kidney stones could be cured without an incision, Cornelius Celsus, that eloquent doctor, would never have undertaken it. Yet he even mentions the surgical instruments that these moderns think they invented although they were invented in the time of Augustus.[155]

Old and new medical treatments are his topic again in his letter of the summer of 1508: surgeons of old used their hands to grasp a kidney stone with great danger and pain for the patient. Contemporary physicians begin to use small instruments without pain and risk. As Leontorius recommended these new procedures to the Amerbach family, he asked for the exact date of surgery so that he could offer a Mass to God and the nuns could pray on that day for a successful operation.[156] In the same letter he inquired about Dr. Johann Silberberg, a doctor of arts, law, and medicine, who was on the law faculty in Basel and had a medical practice. On his next visit to Basel Leontorius planned to see him 'about numerous ailments' which seemed hopeless.[157] In another letter from the beginning of 1509 to the young Bruno Amerbach, Leontorius wrote that he was sending a servant with a urine sample and upon its analysis he expected to receive medication to be picked up at the apothecary in Basel; the servant was expected to be back by dinner time.[158]

He and his amanuensis must have left Engental/Basel in the spring of 1509. On his journey from Switzerland to southern Germany, Leontorius was to act as Amerbach's messenger to Reuchlin concerning editorial work on the edition of the works of the Church Father Jerome.[159] Amerbach needed scholars who were capable of reading Hebrew and Greek. Reuchlin was the only man who could

---

[154] See Halporn, 300.
[155] Letter to Bruno Amerbach from Engental of 7 January 1509; AK, no. 406; Halporn, 301.
[156] See letter from Engental to Amerbach of 14 August 1508; AK no. 387; Halporn, 297–298.
[157] See AK, no. 387; Halporn, 298.
[158] See letter from Engental; AK, no. 408; Halporn, 302.
[159] See AK, no. 426; Halporn, 135.

help him, and Leontorius was the one who could deliver this request convincingly. This he did in person, handing over Amerbach's letter of 27 June 1509 to Reuchlin who was then visiting at the Benedictine abbey of Hirsau in the Black Forest, which belonged to the reformed Benedictine congregation of Bursfeld.[160] Leontorius reached him after having experienced shipwreck on the Rhine and a short sojourn at his home abbey of Maulbronn, and after an uncomfortable overland journey through the Black Forest to Hirsau.[161] In the letter to Reuchlin we read that Amerbach had copied the dubious passages, which he had enclosed for Leontorius to deliver:

> I have given all of these to Conradus Leontorius, the monk well known to you... Whatever recompense you ask for your labors I will gladly give. But if you let me down, I know of no one in Germany who can help me, and the work will remain incomplete.[162]

This letter is included in the collection of *Letters of Famous Men to Reuchlin* (1514).

Reuchlin reacted favorably to the Jerome project and approved of Leontorius' preface for the Jerome edition that Leontorius asked him to critique.[163] However, Reuchlin was unable to get to work on this edition right away. But he finally agreed to do the task, if Amerbach would buy from him the remaining 700 copies of his Hebrew grammar, *Rudimenta hebraica*. Reuchlin would even travel to Basel and stay there for a time at his own expense in order to finish the job.

Reuchlin traveled to several monastic libraries in search of manuscripts, including that of the Cistercian abbey of Bebenhausen.[164] At the same time he recommended Johannes Cuno (or Cono, 1463-1513), the Dominican friar and Graecian, to help out at Basel. Cuno was then enlisted as a substitute to assist in editing the works of Jerome.[165]

---

[160] See AK, no. 425, p. 390, note 5; Halporn, 345.
[161] See Leontorius' letter to Amerbach of 1 August 1509; AK, no. 425; Halporn, 344-345.
[162] AK, no. 420; Halporn, 343.
[163] See AK no. 425; Halporn, 345. see Reuchlin's letter to Amerbach of 26 March 1510, AK no. 434; Halporn, 346f.
[164] See Reuchlin's letter to Amerbach of 6 April 1511, AK no. 451; Halporn, 354. Other Swabian monasteries that he searched were Maulbronn, Hirsau, Denkendorf, and Lorch; see his letter of 31 August 1512, AK no. 469; Halporn, 358.
[165] See Reuchlin's letter to Amerbach of 1 December 1510; RBW 2, no. 173; AK, no. 443; Halporn, 350-351.

Reuchlin also recommended that Matthaeus Adrianus († c. 1520), a known Jewish-Christian Hebraist and physician, should be invited to work on the Jerome edition.[166] Yet Amerbach himself did not see the finished nine-volume edition of Jerome's works, as he died on Christmas Day, 1513.[167]

In 1509, during his stay at the Benedictine abbey of Hirsau, Leontorius wrote to Amerbach on 19 September that he had had an accident which caused him trouble in his right shin, which the surgeon had not treated well enough. Therefore, he was now in the care of an excellent lay brother at Hirsau who had treated his wounds, and who "toils daily with great concern and diligence to restore me to health". Leontorius slowly recovered, "at the pace of a tortoise". He gives a gory description of his injuries. Even certain medications were imported for him from a very capable physician at Tübingen, but to little avail.[168] Therefore, he decided to try a cure of the sulphurous waters at the famous nearby *Wildbad* (in German), and *thermae ferinae* in Latin translation, literally "wild baths".[169] Leontorius went there with Abbot Johannes Hesmann of Hirsau, who was originally from Calw, a town in the Black Forest. Both Leontorius and Hesmann had been born in Leonberg.

Leontorius further informed his friend in Basel that his superior at Maulbronn, Michael Scholl from Vaihingen (abbot from 1504 to 1512),[170] had ordered him to return to Maulbronn. Therefore, Leontorius sent his servant, who was well-known to Amerbach, back to Switzerland in order to collect his possessions in an appropriate container, as he could not do without the books he had collected: partly gifts from Amerbach, partly purchased at his own expense.

---

[166] See Pellican's letter (from Pforzheim) to Amerbach of 22 January 1513; AK, no. 476; Halporn, 359–360; see also AK, no. 475. Adrianus, however, is not mentioned in the printing as an editorial assistant; Halporn, 561.

[167] See Halporn, 362. Erasmus, who arrived in Basel in August 1514, finished the work on Jerome in 1516; however, he did it for the Froben Press at Basel: *Omnium operum divi Hieronymi Stridonensis*.

[168] See letter of 19 September 1509; AK, no. 426; Halporn, 133–36.

[169] *Verum quoniam ego ad recuperandum corporis mei ferme deperdita membra cum domino meo Hirsaugiensi [sum] circa dies sancti Galli ad thermas illas ferinas (si uulgo bene loquar) sum iturus.* Leontorius' letter from Hirsau, dated 1 August 1509; AK, no. 425; Halporn, 344–345. Halporn assumes that Leontorius and the abbot of Hirsau went to Enz. However, the correct place is *Wildbad*, a popular spa up to this day.

[170] On him, see Johannes Wilhelm, "Die Wandmalereien des Klosters Maulbronn und ihre historischen Restaurierungen", in Rückert and Planck, eds., 211–220, here 213 (see note 8 above).

He noted that they were scattered over several monasteries, "first at Cîteaux, second, at Maulbronn, third, at Pairis [Alsace], fourth at Engental", where he had thought he would die in the company of his books, and where he wanted a place dedicated to him and his muses, as he, the Cistercian monk, immodestly wrote to his friend. He continued that he must see to it that his bags were packed according to the advice of Francis Petrarch (1304–1374), because the necessity of moving elsewhere shortly was rushing upon him. Apparently our monk had sufficient funds to purchase the container for his books, as he noted: "I will repay whatever the container costs".[171]

At Basel, Amerbach's son Bruno was of great help in the publishing business, as he had studied Greek in Paris, although not Hebrew. He now had to learn this language on his own after his return to Basel. In this endeavor he followed the example of Leontorius by using Reuchlin's *Rudimenta hebraica* of 1506, which was the only textbook available. This book may be Reuchlin's most important work as it instigated a new, scholarly impulse to the study of the Old Testament in the original Hebrew. In addition, Leontorius sent Hebrew study materials. However, no details are known, except that the same material was used by Leontorius' deceased humanist friend in Colmar, Sebastian Murrho. Apparently, Leontorius had inherited it from him, and now passed it on to the younger Hebraist in the making at Basel. In the same letter with this information, Leontorius revealed that the beginnings of his own Hebrew studies went back to Colmar, where a certain baptized Jew by the name of Paul had taught him the Hebrew alphabet. The same teacher had copied the Pentateuch in German for Reuchlin. From this very manuscript the sheet was taken that he was sending along. Its last paragraph contains notes from the pen of Murrho, copied from Reuchlin's texts. Leontorius encouraged the young Amerbach to use these materials; if used "thoughtfully" they would be of help to him.[172]

The year and place of Leontorius' death is given variously. Wimpfeling writes in his death notice to Amerbach on 29 April 1511: "To you, especially, I commend the spirit of our Conradus Leontorius",[173]

---

[171] See AK, no. 426; Halporn, 134–135, reads 'Paris' instead of Pairis, the Cistercian monastery in Alsace, in the diocese of Basel.

[172] Letter from Engental of 7 January 1509; AK, no. 406; Halporn, 301.

[173] *Conradi nostri Leontorii animam unice tibi commendo. Vale*; the Latin original is printed in Knepper, 359 (no. 13); AK, no. 452.

without indication of the location. Pellican also notes his death for the year 1511, but at Engental,[174] which is unlikely. According to the necrology of the monastery of Pairis, Leontorius died there, but in the year 1507.[175] The greatest likelihood is 7 January 1511 at Pairis or Maulbronn.

The great Christian Hebraist Reuchlin left us a literary monument in honor of Leontorius. He sent this to Leontorius in the form of a poem in humanist Latin, datable to 25 June 1510.[176] In this poem, Reuchlin imitates Horace, one of Leontorius' favorite Latin authors, employing Horace's metrics.[177] In 1507 Leontorius had written, as mentioned, a little guidebook on the metrics of Horace for Amerbach's son. Perhaps Reuchlin knew of Leontorius' text or his favorite poet when he made use of Horace's metrics and also one of his expressions (*Acroceraunia*, the "thundering mountains").

Reuchlin's opening line 'O, you my closest hope' may refer to the fact that Leontorius had been the carrier of the galley proofs of the edition of Jerome's works that Amerbach had sent to Reuchlin for emendation. They had needed many corrections, particularly with regard to the Greek and Hebrew words, and the improved edition would make Reuchlin's own textbook *Rudimenta hebraica* more marketable[178] (Reuchlin had financed this project with his own funds, at a financial loss thus far). In his poem Reuchlin excused himself for not writing a more extensive letter. In place of a long explanatory letter Reuchlin sent him a container (*canna*, reed-pipe), be it of copper (*aerea* = *aenea*), silver (*argentea*), or brass (*orichalcea*), with writing

---

[174] *Huius anni initio obiit amicus singularis meus Conradus Leontorius Mulbrumiensis* [sic; Maulbronn] *monachus*... in *Das Chronikon des Konrad Pellikan*, ed. Bernhard Riggenbach (Basel 1877) 41; AK, 419 (no. 452), note 2; see Martin Sicherl, *Johannes Cuno: ein Wegbereiter des Griechischen in Deutschland. Eine biographisch-kodikologische Studie* (Heidelberg 1978) 135; Herding and Mertens, 680 (no. 275). The PhD dissertation (Columbia University 1950) by Frederick Christian Ahrens is a translation of the *Chronikon: The Chronicle of Conrad Pellican, 1478–1556*.

[175] *Memoria fr. Conradi Töritz de Leonberg, dicti Leontorii. Secretarii D. Johannis abb. Cistercii et compilatoris privilegiorum ordinis, professus Mulbrun., conventualis in Pa[i]ris et confessor sacrarum virginum nostrarum in arcta valle vulgo Engental* 1507; edition of Clauss in *Bulletin de la Société pour la conservation des monuments historiques d'Alsace* 2. F., 22 (1908) 76.

[176] Edited in RBW 2, 140–141 (no. 166). On 'humanist Latin', see Eckhard Bernstein, "Humanistische Standeskultur", in *Die Literatur im Übergang vom Mittelalter zur Neuzeit*, 97–129, here 104–106.

[177] Metrics such as *glykoneen*; on this, see the editorial notes in RBW 2, 141–143 (no. 166).

[178] See RBW 2, no. 156.

utensils (*calamus*), which he mentioned at the end of his poem. Reuchlin was so swamped with various legal cases at the court in Stuttgart that he had no time for writing, as he indicated in his short poem. He felt like Aikos (*Aëacus*), Rhadamanthys, or Minos, the three sons of Zeus who were judges in the nether world, having to pass judgments quickly. Only a humanist could understand what he was alluding to with his references to Greek mythology and geography (*Pelion* and *Ossa*, two names of the Thessalian mountains).

> *Ioannes Reuchlin Phorcensis S. P. D. Conrado Leontorio dicto Leobergensi.*
> *O mi spes mea proxima,*
> *Non curis potero scribere subrutus*
> *Insanique fori iugo.*
> *Nunc erecta tribunalia principis,*
> *Nunc causae popularium*
> *Producuntur. Ego clamito, clamito*
> *In raucosque cado sonos.*
> *Fas et iura loquor solvoque iurgia.*
> *Frendunt Acroceraunia,*
> *Tanguntur tonituru, Pelion Ossaque*
> *Fumant maxima summaque.*
> *Concurrunt fremitus. Aecus arbiter*
> *Librat sollicitudines,*
> *Hinc lites movet et vox Rhadamanthyos,*
> *Minos assidet arbiter.*
> *Talis vita meis esse sodalibus*
> *Ad subsellia dicitur.*
> *Tractamusque ea nos iura solemnia.*
> *Talis regia curia.*
> *Hiis ita non potero scribere subrutus.*
> *Pro his, canna tamen aerea*
> *Sive argentea sit sive orichalcea,*
> *Hos mitto calamos tibi.*
> *Vale foeliciter. Ex Stutgardia VII. Kal[endas] Iulias, in occupationibus nimiis.*[179]

Leontorius' greatest achievement may be his work as a biblical humanist, as with his linguistic skills he helped to spread knowledge of the Scriptures through his editions of the Bible which included Lyra's glosses and Hugo's postils. Leontorius, along with others like Brant and Wimpfeling, contributed to the vast number of editions of the Scriptures that came into existence in the German lands around 1500. No less than fifty-eight incunabula of the complete Latin Bible

---

[179] RBW 2, 140–141 (no. 166).

were published in the German lands (including Basel in German-speaking Switzerland). Leontorius and his like-minded humanist friends applied new methods for the recovery and publication of sacred texts, "but their enthusiasm did not yet find expression in a new religious thinking".[180] They painstakingly edited the Bible. This generation of Greek and Hebrew scholars tried with the help of their new tools to emend the Vulgate text that had been badly corrupted through the centuries by a great number of copyists and printers, the latter mainly in the fifteenth century. These editions appear to have been much worse than those of the twelfth century.[181] Therefore the text they published was always that of the Paris edition of the Vulgate, going back to the end of the twelfth century. They revised it, annotated it, and cross-referenced it, but they did not retranslate it from the original languages,[182] a need that became increasingly clear and which these scholars wanted to meet, as they tried to master the sacred languages of Greek and Hebrew. Leontorius with his work on the Bible cleared the way for the climaxing (*Blütezeit*) of biblical humanism between 1510 and 1520, its golden years, represented by scholars such as Jacobus Faber Stapulensis (Lefèvre d'Étaples, 1455–1536), Erasmus, Reuchlin, Melanchthon, Jacobus Latomus (c. 1475–1544), and Luther.[183] The latter may have used the Latin bibles which Leontorius helped to revise.[184]

---

[180] Morisi, "Traditionalism", 347 (but without mention of Leontorius; only Brant and Wimpfeling are mentioned).
[181] I am grateful to Gerhard Winkler for this hint.
[182] Erasmus translated the Greek New Testament into a novel, humanist Latin, differing at times considerably from the Vulgate.
[183] "Blütezeit des Bibelhumanismus, die Jahre von 1510 bis 1520", Augustijn, *Humanismus*, 70; "Die goldenen Jahre: 1510–1520", 78–100 (though without mention of Leontorius).
[184] See Sachiko Kusukawa, *A Wittenberg University Library Catalogue of 1536* (Binghamton 1995) 17.

CHAPTER TWO

A GRAECIAN, CHRISTIAN POET, AND PLAYWRIGHT:
BENEDICTUS CHELIDONIUS, MONK OF NUREMBERG,
ABBOT OF THE *SCHOTTENSTIFT*, VIENNA

The monk, Benedikt Schwalbe (c. 1460–1521), was born in Nuremberg during the Renaissance. He is better known by the Graecized family name of Chelidonius; *Chelidón* means 'swallow' (the bird) in Greek (*Schwalbe* in German). In his earlier years, he was also called by his Latinized name, *Hirundo* (swallow). He received or gave himself the surname *Musophilus*, 'lover of the muses'. He was a son of Nuremberg, one of the most important cities in Germany in the Middle Ages. It was home to the Benedictine monastery of Saint Aegidius[1] to which he belonged earlier in his monastic career.[2] Nuremberg was a center of monastic humanism, as evidenced by a study of the monastic libraries at Nuremberg.[3] The Carthusians and the Augustinian friars of Nuremberg also possessed contemporary, up-to-date libraries.[4]

Chelidonius may have joined the Benedictines in about 1485 at Nuremberg's so-called *Schottenkloster*, Saint Aegidius. In 1514 he transferred to the *Schottenstift*[5] in Vienna where he became abbot from

---

For initial information I thank the Custos, Magister Gerhard Schlass, Schottenstift in Vienna, Austria. This chapter is the revised and expanded version of my article "Benedictus Chelidonius O.S.B. (C. 1460–1521), A Forgotten Monastic Humanist of the Renaissance", ABR 53 (2002) 426–52. See also Stephan Füssel, "Chelidonius" in *Literaturlexikon. Autoren und Werke deutscher Sprache*, ed. Walther Killy, vol. 2 (Munich 1989) 404; Johannes Staub, "Chelidonius", in *Lexikon für Theologie und Kirche* 1.2 (1994) 1032–1033; Claudia Wiener, "Chelidonius", in VL 2005.

[1] Dissolved in 1525, a few years after Chelidonius' death.
[2] No biographical details of the young Chelidonius are known; see Wiener, "Chelidonius", in VL 2005.
[3] See Franz Machilek, "Klosterhumanismus in Nürnberg um 1500", 10–45.
[4] See Bernhard Gerhard Winkler, *Die Sonette des B. Chelidonius zu A. Dürers Marienleben und ihr Verhältnis zum Marienleben des Kartäusers Philipp* (dissertation Vienna 1960) 9. I am grateful to Professor Winkler for sending me a copy of his dissertation.
[5] *Schottenkloster* and *Schottenstift* are designations of Benedictine monasteries in the German-speaking lands that trace their origins back to Irish-Scottish monks as their founders; see Helmut Flachenecker, *Schottenklöster: Irische Benediktinerkonvente im hochmittelalterlichen Deutschland* (Paderborn 1995).

Fig. 3 Title Page *Passio Salvatoris*, today at *Schottenstift*, Vienna; likely a book printed in Cracow, Poland, 1514.

1518 to 1521.⁶ Chelidonius probably moved to Vienna in order to be close to the court of Emperor Maximilian I.⁷ Already in the manuscript of his elegy for Celtis on the occasion of the latter's death in 1508, Chelidonius openly recommended himself to the emperor as the court poet.⁸ This text is known to us from the handwritten copy of Hartmann Schedel, *Elegia F. Benedicti Chelidonii Norici de fato Conrado Celtis protrucii [sic] poete Laureati*.⁹

In Chelidonius' day, his Viennese monastery had already belonged to the Melk reform movement within the Benedictine order for one hundred years. It was a time when good relations existed between the monks and the University of Vienna¹⁰ and its humanist milieu.¹¹ Chelidonius was called from Nuremberg as the compromise candidate to succeed Abbot Johann VIII (Krembnitzer), who had resigned.¹² After the Nuremberg monk was elected, and after no objections were raised when he was presented to the general public, Chelidonius was confirmed in his new position as Abbot Benedict I by Bishop George Slatkonia of Vienna.¹³

In his literary works Chelidonius treated of two major devotional topics: the suffering and death of Christ, and the life of the Virgin Mary. At that time people were greatly interested in the suffering and death of Christ and its meaning for them. Preaching on this subject was more or less a matter of routine. Johann von Staupitz and Martin Luther both preached and wrote on these central Christian themes.¹⁴ The Passion of Christ was also the subject of religious

---

⁶ He signed then as *D. Benedictus Chelidonius Abbas ad Scotos Viennae* (Lord Benedictus Chelidonius, abbot of the Scots in Vienna).
⁷ See Anna Scherbaum, *Albrecht Dürers Marienleben. Form—Gehalt—Funktion und sozialhistorischer Ort*. Mit einem Beitrag von Claudia Wiener (Wiesbaden 2004) 118.
⁸ See Wiener, "Chelidonius", in VL 2005.
⁹ See Wiener, "Chelidonius", in VL 2005.
¹⁰ See www.schottenstift.at/archiv.html, the monastery's home page.
¹¹ On the history of the reception of the humanist movement in Vienna, see Alfred A. Strnad, "Die Rezeption von Humanismus und Renaissance in Wien", *Humanismus und Renaissance in Ostmitteleuropa vor der Reformation*, eds. Winfried Eberhard and Alfred A. Strnad (Cologne, Weimar, and Vienna 1996) 71–135.
¹² See Winkler, 10.
¹³ I have no further biographical data on this bishop. His figure appears in the *Triumphal Procession of Maximilian* as the music conductor; his honorific title was 'arch-musician'; see Nagl and Zeidler, *Deutsch-österreichische Literaturgeschichte*, 49.
¹⁴ For background information, see Bernd Moeller, "Piety in Germany around 1500", *The Reformation in Medieval Perspective*, ed. Steven Ozment (Chicago 1971); Franz Posset, "Preaching the Passion of Christ on the Eve of the Reformation", *Concordia Theological Quarterly* 59 (1995) 279–300.

poetry. Two names of humanist monks stand out (although they are generally unknown): Bolfgangus Marius, the abbot of the Cistercian monastery of Aldersbach from 1514 to 1544[15] with his poem *Christi Fasciculus*, and our Benedictine monk and later abbot, Benedictus Chelidonius, who published a booklet at Strasbourg (perhaps in 1508, printed by Johann Knobloch), called *The Passion of Jesus Christ, the Savior of the World*. It is illustrated (see Fig. 3) by Johannes (Hans) Wechtelin († c. 1526).[16] Its title page, a woodcut, shows the crucifixion with Mary and John. Its caption is identical to that of the better known *Little Passion* or *Little Passion on Wood* of 1511 with its images by Albrecht Dürer.[17] The dedication to the famous humanist Willibald Pirckheimer of Nuremberg is included in both editions. Dürer is given prominence on the title page of *The Little Passion*, which declares "The Passion of Christ in effigies by Dürer". Chelidonius' poems in various styles are mentioned in second place: *Passio Christi ab Alberto Durer* [sic] *Nurenbergensi effigiata cu[m] varij generis carminibus Fratris Benedicti Chelidonij Musophili* (the usual spelling of the artist's name is Albrecht, not Albert; the family name is spelled with a German *Umlaut*). It was printed in 1511, by Hieronymus Höltzel at Nuremberg. A later edition (1526) is known as *Passio Jesu Christi amarulenta, certis & primarijs effigiata locis, uario carmine Benedicti Chelidonij, & tandem Christiani*

---

[15] See Marian Gloning, "Aus der Gedichtesammlung des Abtes Marius von Aldersbach", StM 33 (1912) 76–89; Willibald Hauer, "Wolfgang Marius, der Humanistenabt von Aldersbach (1514–1544)", in Robert Klugseder, ed., *850 Jahre Zisterzienserkloster Aldersbach, Festschrift zur Feier der 850. Wiederkehr des Gründungstages* (Vilshofen 1996) 43–48 (see Chapter 3).

[16] *Passio Jesu Christi saluatoris mundi vario Carminum genere F. Benedicti Chelidonij Musophili doctissime descripta. Cum figuris artificiosissimis Ioannis Vuechtelin* [Wechtelin]. See Manfred Knedlik, "Chelidonius", BBKL 20 (2002) 293–96; Scherbaum, *Albrecht Dürers Marienleben*, 181; 204, 312–313 with plates 80 and 81 that show image and text on facing pages; Wiener, "Chelidonius", in VL 2005. The edition of the text is found in M. Kisser, *Die Gedichte des Benedictus Chelidonius zu Dürers Kleiner Holzschnittpassion. Ein Beitrag zur Geschichte der spätmittelalterlichen Passionsliteratur* (dissertation Vienna, 1964); idem, in Horst Appuhn, *Die Kleine Passion von Albrecht Dürer* (Dortmund 1985) 85–137.

[17] The former edition is referred to as the 1508 edition. Its caption starts with *Christus ad Peccatorem* ('Christ [speaking to] the sinner'), while *The Little Passion on Wood* does not have this line; however, it includes the addition after the caption: *Cum priuilegio*. Both editions share the following wording in the caption:

    O mihi tantorum, iusto mihi causa dolorum
      O crucis O mortis causa cruenta mihi.
    O homo sat fuerit, tibi me semel ista tulisse,
      O cessa culpis me cruciare nouis.

Austin Dobson, *The Little Passion of Albrecht Dürer*, with an introduction by Austin Dobson (London and New York 1894).

Ischyrij illustrata, and was published by Peter Quentell in Cologne.[18]

Chelidonius also compiled an anthology of poetic texts collected from various religious poets who wrote on the subject of the Passion of Christ: *Passio domini nostri Jesu ex hieronymo Paduano. Dominico Mancino. Sedulio. et Baptista Mantuano per fratrem Chelidonium collecta cum figuris Alberti Dureri Norici Pictoris.*[19] This book is now known as the *Large Passion* of 1511 (because of the size of the prints, 11 by 15 inches), for which Dürer created woodcuts. The artist's creations were mentioned in secondary place and again he is called Albert, the Bavarian painter (*Noricus Pictor*). The poems collected by Chelidonius from various religious or monastic writers were the main theme, and the artist's pictures appear to be the illustrations for them.

Dürer produced still more woodcuts and copperplates on the Passion of Christ that are world-famous today. They confirm the thesis that on the eve of the Reformation, cross-centered piety was flourishing. From the age of twenty-three until his death at fifty-seven, Dürer worked on at least six different versions of Christ's Passion.[20] However, to most people today little or nothing is known of the Benedictine monk whose poems accompanied Dürer's images or, indeed, who used the woodcuts as illustrations for his own collection of religious texts on this subject.

In the dedications in *The Little Passion* (1511), no mention at all is made of the artist, nor did he receive any poem of acknowledgement. Nevertheless, his name is found on the title page. After Chelidonius' dedications to two friends, Willibald Pirckheimer and Johannes Cochlæus, both of Nuremberg, some return-verses were written by them in praise of Chelidonius. Pirckheimer (spelled *Vuildualdus Pirchamerus*) was one of the very few Graecians who was able to appreciate Chelidonius' poetic efforts in correlating the central Christian themes of salvation history with aspects of pagan, Greek, and Latin antiquity. Chelidonius handed his story of Christ over to Pirckheimer for any necessary revisions (*limae*).[21] In his three-liner (*tetrastichon*)

---

[18] See Wiener, "Chelidonius", in VL 2005.

[19] Its title page is a hand-colored woodcut which is displayed on the internet: www.lcweb.loc.gov/exhibits/dres/dres3.html It is called the Saxon edition as it is kept, in a deluxe edition, in the Saxon state library. Another copy has the title page in black and white, and was displayed in an exhibition at Harvard University; see catalogue and internet display from the Gray Collection of Engravings: www.art-museums.harvard.edu/exhibitions

[20] See Jordan Kantor, ed., *Dürer's Passions* (Cambridge, Mass 2000) 2 vols.

[21] The same wording to Pirckheimer is found in the 1506 edition.

Pirckheimer refers to Chelidonius as an Athenian born of Pandion, king of Athens, a title borrowed literally from Ovid (*Pandione nata*). Pandion was the father of Procne, the wife of Tereus. To prevent her husband from killing her for being garrulous (*garrulitate* is the reference word in Pirckheimer's verse), she was changed into a 'swallow', which is, of course, our poet's family name! However, our poet is not garrulous like Pandion's daughter; the poem is written in praise of God that Chelidonius pours out his songs (*carmina*) from his learned mouth, in order to raise the strong celestial roof of God's house.[22]

There is really no explanation for the absence of Dürer's name in the mutual expressions of appreciation among the humanist writers. We may suppose that poetry to these men may have been more important than the illustrations made by a craftsman (as a woodcutter was classified at that time). This is in stark contrast to our modern view of the greater significance of the craftsmanship and art of Albrecht Dürer. The colophon, however, gives additional credit to him as a picture-maker/painter (*pictor*), namely, that the book was printed by 'Albert [Albrecht] the painter' in the year of the Lord 1511.[23] Chelidonius' name appears on the title page not only of the 1508 edition and of *The Little Passion*, but also of the *Large Passion*. The title page of the 'Saxon copy' of the *Large Passion* indicates that the images by Dürer are secondary and apparently meant as illustrations for Chelidonius' anthology of poetic texts in his *Passio Domini*.

Chelidonius selected poems on the Passion of Christ from the fifth-century *Carmen paschale* of Coelius Sedulius[24] and from several contemporary works: Dominicus Mancinus' *Carmen de Passione*,[25] Hieronymus

---

[22] Quoting from the British Museum edition:
Vuildbaldi Pirchameri in carmina Fratris Benedicti Chelidonij
Tetrastichon
Quae fuert quondam volucris Pandione nata
Tecta subit hominum garrulitate sua.
Carmina sed doctor fundit Chelidonius ore
Tangere quae valeant tecta superna dei
(also found in the 1508 edition).

[23] *Impressum Nurnberge per Albertu[m] Pictore[m] Anno christi Millesimo quingentesimo vndecimo*. The colophon includes a caveat directed primarily at an Italian engraver by the name of Marcantonio Raimondi; see Linda C. Hults, *The Print in the Western World. An Introductory History* (Madison, WI 1996) 89.

[24] The principal work of Sedulius (5th C) is his *Carmen paschale* in five books. The first book contains an overview of the Old Testament; the four others a summary of the New Testament.

[25] *De Passione domini nostri Jesu Christi. Oratio ad Virginem* (Paris: Baligault, no date,

Paduanus' *Iesuida seu De passione Domini*,[26] and Baptista Mantuan's *Parthenice* and *Libri tres de calamitatibus temporum*, of which several editions were available.[27] The latter was Baptist Spagnoli of Mantua (Mantuan[us]), a Carmelite friar, humanist, and poet; he was well-known and published all over Europe around 1500 and was called the 'new Virgil'.[28]

The title page of *The Little Passion*, as found in the British Museum, shows a variation of Dürer's 'Man of Sorrows', i.e., a simpler version with the composition in black and white, depicting Christ alone,[29] while the *Large Passion* in the Saxon Staatsbibliothek shows a hand-colored woodcut with an additional figure next to Christ, apparently a soldier mocking him, all within an elaborate framework. This edition appears to have had the primary purpose of publishing the artist's woodcuts, with Chelidonius' poems placed on the back of the cuts.[30] Does this mean he had written his poems with the prints in front of him? Or, were his poems written first, independently of Dürer's images? Comparing the two *Passions* that include Dürer's pictures (leaving aside the 1505 edition) we notice that they share the major twelve incidents that represent the core of the artist's repertoire of scenes from the story of Christ's Passion.

Let us look in detail at *The Little Passion*. It was edited in a reproduction from stereotypes of the original blocks.[31] The booklet contains thirty-seven woodcuts and poems on the history of salvation,

---

possibly 1478–1491); microform, Center for Research Libraries, Chicago. MF-1553 reel 114 item 3. It is also known as *Tractatus de passione Domini*.

[26] Printed at Leipzig by Jacob Thanner, 1500, also known as Hieronymus de Vallibus, †1443. Another text by this author is on the resurrection: *Scriptum de resurrectione domini* (today at the library of Melk, Austria).

[27] See Thea Hillmann, "Benedictus Chelidonius von St. Ägidien in Nürnberg", StM 58 (1940) 139–45, here 140–141 with note 5.

[28] See Franz Posset, "'Heaven is on Sale'. The Influence of the Italian Humanist and Carmelite Baptist Mantuanus on Martin Luther", *Carmelus* 36 (1989) 134–144; Mantuan's *Aeglogae* were reprinted early in the 16thC in Bonn, Brussels, Deventer, Paris, Leipzig, Koblenz, Frankfurt, Tübingen, Erfurt, Wittenberg and also in Strasbourg, see 136; in the Alsatian capital Strasbourg Mantuan's *Carmen contra poetas impudice loquentes* was first published in 1501. The Alsatian Wimpfeling edited Mantuan's *Bucolica* three times (1510, 1511, and 1517) and his *Fastorum libri* once in 1518. Another Alsatian, Sebastian Brant, edited his *Opera* in three volumes at Paris in 1513. On Mantuan's fame in England, see Lee Piepho, *Holofernes' Mantuan. Italian Humanism in Early Modern England* (New York etc. 2001); Scherbaum, *Albrecht Dürers Marienleben*, 123–124.

[29] See Dobson's edition of the copy in the British Museum.

[30] See Dobson, 7. Could it be that the poems came first and pictures were added?

[31] See Dobson, 6.

including the title page (CHRIST AS THE MAN OF SORROWS). The title page unequivocally proclaims that the publication enjoys a privilege (*cum priuilegio*), which is explained in the colophon as having been granted by the most glorious Roman Emperor (of the German Nation) Maximilian.[32] The images are inspired primarily by biblical themes. Four, however, are non-biblical. The woodcuts 'Christ departing from his mother' (no. 8), 'Veronica and her handkerchief (*sudarium*), flanked by Saints Peter and Paul' (no. 23), and 'The risen Christ appearing to his mother' (no. 31) are based on legends. Chelidonius evidently shared a generally-accepted opinion that Veronica's *sudarium* with the image of Christ impressed on it was kept in Rome.[33] The woodcut 'Descent into hell' (no. 26) is based not so much on a biblical narrative but on the Apostles' Creed with the line 'he descended into hell', based on 1 Peter 3:18–20 ("Put to death in the flesh, he was brought to life in the spirit. In it he also went to preach to the spirits in prison who had once been disobedient while God patiently waited in the days of Noah"). The entire booklet resembles an expanded series of the later popular 'Stations of the Cross' (with the traditional fourteen stations). However, they are framed by the opening story of *Adamus & Aeua* (as Adam's and Eve's names are spelled by the poet) and by the closing scene of the Last Judgment with Mary and John the Baptist as intercessors (the iconographic *deësis* motif).

In the concluding lines of the poem on Christ crucified, a mystical element is introduced when Chelidonius uses the expression *amplexus* (embrace) for the mystical experience of the encounter with God:

> Behold, [Christ] offers his breast for the embrace, for the kisses on the forehead, he opens his heart. With tears he calls you and calls you again.[34]

The *amplexus* is based on the medieval interpretation of the Song of Songs (on the kisses and the embrace), an interpretation that Saint Bernard of Clairvaux made popular. The medieval Bernard legend and iconography refers to the *Amplexus Bernardi*, i.e., Bernard in prayer

---

[32] *Scias eni[m] a gloriosissimo Romanoru[m] imperatore. Maximiliano. nobis co[n]cessum esse.*
[33] *Diua nunc Romae residens imago.*
[34] *Pectus ad amplexus.en* [sic] *praebet ad oscula frontem Cor aperit. lachrymis te vocat atq[ue] vocat* (with Plate XXV).

before a crucifix being embraced by the crucified Christ.³⁵ The church of the Augustinians at Nuremberg possessed an altar piece with this Cistercian motif,³⁶ where Chelidonius may have seen it. Dürer was aware of Bernardine spirituality and legend as well, as evidenced by the fact that a woodcut of the year 1503, attributed to him, shows the *Amplexus Bernardi*.³⁷ This mystical element corresponds with another devotional expression in Chelidonius' poem about Christ at the Mount of Olives: Christ is addressed as "Most sweet Jesus", a phrase found in many examples of medieval devotion and mysticism.³⁸

Elements of pagan Greek mythological terminology entered into several of his verses. *Tellus* as the personified earth and *Tartarus* as the designation for the infernal regions occur in the opening line of the 'Foot Washing'.³⁹ The personified nymphs of the springs emerge in the same poem. On the mocking of Christ, our humanist poet is reminded of the Greek furies that he mentioned as the *Erinnes* (*Erinyes*) who growl like dogs.⁴⁰ In the poem on Christ descending into hell, Chelidonius makes explicit reference to *Orcus*, the infernal region, and to the three-headed dog *Cerberus* who with open mouths guards Hades.⁴¹ However, the woodcut itself does not show *Cerberus* at all. Furthermore, in his poem on the risen Christ appearing to his mother, Chelidonius incorporates another ancient Greek idea, that of Olympus. He lets Christ say to Mary that after his three days in the grave (*lustra*), she will take her place with him on the Olympic seat.⁴² He employs the plural of the notion *lustrum* that, in Latin, has several meanings. It may mean a morass, a den of a wild beast, or even a brothel; it may thus stand for hell. *Lustrum* also means an expiatory

---

³⁵ See Franz Posset, "The Crucified Embraces Saint Bernard: The Beginnings of the *Amplexus Bernardi*", CSQ 33 (1998) 289–314.

³⁶ Attributed to Michael Wolgemut, depicted in Franz Posset, *Pater Bernhardus: Martin Luther and Bernard of Clairvaux* (Kalamazoo 1999) 246.

³⁷ The woodcut is included in the book *Salus animae*, printed by Hieronymus Hoeltzel in 1503 at Nuremberg; see its depiction in Campbell Dodgson, ed., *Holzschnitte zu zwei Nürnberger Andachtsbüchern aus dem Anfange des XVI. Jahrhunderts, 106 Abbildungen in Zinkhochätzung* (Berlin 1909) 18, no. 70.

³⁸ *Dulcissime Iesu*; see Franz Posset, "Christi Dulcedo: The 'Sweetness of Christ' in Western Christian Spirituality", CSQ 30 (1995) 245–65.

³⁹ *Quem Tellus. Mare. Tartarus.*

⁴⁰ *Turpes caetera ganniant Erinnes.*

⁴¹ *Rictu trifauci Cerberus obstrepat.*

⁴² *Sedem vna mecum . . . Post tria lustra tenebis olympicam.*

sacrifice (an ox, sheep, or sow) to be offered every five years at the close of the census on behalf of the Roman people.

Chelidonius speaks of the bread broken at Emmaus in a very humanist phrase: the heavenly 'Olympic bread' (*panis olympicus*). Another use of ancient terminology is seen in his *tartarea flamma*, the 'fire of hell' that he mentions for the Last Judgment. In the same poem, he writes of God who takes his place as the Judge in the valley of the Solymi.[43] Another hint of Greek mythology is found in the poem on Christ appearing to Mary Magdalene; in it Chelidonius describes Christ's victory in terms of a Titan recalling his *quadrigas*.

Chelidonius also made use of several concepts from the Greek New Testament: *soter* (savior), in his poem on the entombment,[44] or *pneuma* (spirit), in his verses on Pentecost.[45] Those among his readers familiar with the Latin author Cicero may have been aware of his use of the originally Greek word, *soter*,[46] for savior, and they may have actually understood it. Chelidonius, however, was not consistent in his usage of the Greek term *soter*. He also used the Vulgate word *salvator*. Remarkably, Erasmus would later use *servator* in his retranslation of the New Testament from Greek into (humanist) Latin, and occasionally, so would Luther.[47]

In *The Little Passion*, Chelidonius displays a sophisticated model of the humanist ideal of the correlation of word and image. The humanist ideal at that time apparently required the complementation of *pictura* and *eloquentia*.[48] Each woodcut/theme is accompanied by a reference to a specific type of poetry of Chelidonius' choice.[49] Six of his thirty-seven poems are heroic songs, relating in a pagan context to demigods, and in the Christian context to the God-man Jesus Christ, as in the poems on the Last Supper, Christ before Caiaphas,

---

[43] *Tum solymis deus in conuallibus arbiter sedebit*. *Solymi* may refer to the aboriginal inhabitants in Lykia, who are called *Solymi*, or to the inhabitants of Jerusalem.

[44] *En soter hominem iuste releuaret*... In his Marian poem, Chelidonius used the same Greek title again, 'Savior of the people', *hominum soter*; see Winkler, 140.

[45] *Orando sacrum pneuma*.

[46] See Casell's *New Latin Dictionary* (New York 1959).

[47] For Chelidonius' use of *salvator*, see his Marian poem no. 8; Winkler, 84. For Erasmus' use of *servator*, see August Bludau, *Die beiden ersten Erasmus-Ausgaben des Neuen Testaments und ihre Gegner* (Freiburg 1902) 470. For Luther's use, see Franz Posset, *Luther's Catholic Christology According to his Johannine Lectures of 1527* (Milwaukee 1988) 82–84, 197, 242.

[48] See Winkler, 13.

[49] For the complete overview of these correlations, see Posset, "Benedictus Chelidonius", 435–436.

Christ taken down from the cross, the resurrection, and his appearance to his mother. The poem on Adam and Eve is also called 'heroic'. Our poet opted for the designation *Elegia* for the scene on the horrors Christ endured at the Mount of Olives. Overall, he preferred the designation *Ode* which implies the poem to be of irregular metrical structure. Thirteen of his poems are *odes*, eight are *carmen* (poems of any kind), seven are elegies, five are simply called 'verses', and one is called a *hymnus* (originally a Greek term, used in the scene with Veronica).

The technical terms *anapaesta* and *satyra* he uses once each. For the temple scene Chelidonius employs the expression *satyra* which refers to satyrs (bestial creatures) who form a chorus in a drama, as he pictures the temple filled with inappropriate figures whom he labels 'contaminators' that need to be driven out. When he calls the poem on Christ bearing his cross an *anapest*,[50] he signals to the reader that this poem is written in a certain metrical foot that consists of two short or unstressed syllables followed by one long or stressed syllable. His choice reminded the humanist reader that this kind of verse was first used in early Spartan marching songs. For this reason it may have been selected for the poem on Jesus' 'Way of the Cross' on the *via dolorosa*.

His 'Pindaric Song' (*Carmen Pindaricum*) for the Pentecost woodcut refers to the lyric poet of Thebes, Pindar (c. 520–446 BC). The specification, *alcmania/alcmanium*, occurs on two occasions: for the scene with Christ before Herod he writes the *Carmen Dactylicum Alcmanium*, that is, a poem with the verse meter of one long, followed by two short syllables. With the term *Alcmanium* he alludes, in terms of content, to Herod as a maniac like the Greek Alkmaion (Alcmeon), who murdered his mother at the wish of his father, and was afterwards driven mad. For the scene after the resurrection when the risen Christ encounters doubting Thomas and the other apostles, Chelidonius chooses the poem *Ode Alcmania*. We may surmise that he is implying that Thomas was crazy for not believing in the resurrection—another 'alcmaniac'.

Glicon was Chelidonius' reference to the Greek *glycon*, meaning a wrestler or a physician, an expression that Chelidonius aptly uses for

---

[50] For these and other technical terms, see *The Hutchinson Dictionary of Difficult Words* (Helicon Publishing Ltd. 1998).

the two woodcuts 'Foot Washing' and 'Emmaus'. Both scenes involve concepts to be wrestled with, or which were puzzling to the participants: the confused Peter at first refuses to have his feet washed; the disciples at Emmaus were struggling with the insight of Christ's presence in their midst with the 'Olympic bread' (see above).

In reference to the Greek poet, Alcaeus, who invented a specific meter that was imitated by Horace, Chelidonius used alcaic verses (i.e., four-liners, each line of which has four feet) for his two poems on Christ before Annas and Christ descending into hell. When Chelidonius describes scenes involving a woman, as with the Annunciation to Mary, Veronica, and Mary Magdalene in the garden ('Do not touch me'), he prefers the poetic form of a sapphic, named after Sappho, the seventh-century BC poetess of Mytilene in Lesbos, a contemporary of the above-mentioned Alcaeus.

Our humanist writes three of the thirty-seven poems with the qualifier *Archilochius*: (a) for his *Versus Heroicus* on Christ before Caiaphas, (b) for the *Versi Heroici* on Christ after his death (deposition from the cross), and for the *Carmen* about the Last Judgment. Archilochos was a Greek satiric poet and the inventor of iambic verse. The adjective *archilochius* has the connotation of sharp pain and thus correlates to the content of the three depictions: the pain of rejection before Caiaphas, the pain of death, and the pain of eternal damnation at the Last Judgment. The woodcut of the Last Judgment shows a sharp sword issuing from Christ's mouth as the Judge. Evidently, on numerous occasions, Chelidonius made a conscious effort to correlate image and word by his choice of meters for certain contents to be described. At other times, however, he simply used a verse measurement as a specific designation for a poem, such as a *Dactylica* (used four times), without any obvious correlation to the content. His expression *Choriambica/Choriambicum* (used eight times) is the poetic notion for four syllables, the first two forming a trochee (a metrical foot of two syllables) and the second two an iambus.

Chelidonius accomplished here an impressive correlation not only of word and image, but also, in terms of evangelization, the correlation of Christ's salvific life and death with certain humanist concepts of pagan, classical antiquity. This great variety of sophisticated poetic forms was appealing to the intellectuals of his time. In other words, he told the Christian history of salvation in the classical Latin terms of Renaissance humanism. He used humanist Latin in order to reach his humanist audience. Evidently, judging by his fame at the time, he succeeded in marketing the mysteries of the faith to contemporary humanists by using humanist packaging.

At that time great interest existed not only in Passion piety, with the focus on Christ, but also in Marian piety, with the focus on Mary's role in Christ's life. During the Late Middle Ages and before the Reformation the poet and the artist capitalized on the great importance of Mary in popular Christian devotion. Indeed, Dürer's pictures tend to be folklorist, some being based on legend. Chelidonius' verses are rather sophisticated, not always so easily understood.[51] The image showing how Mary and Joseph tried to survive in Egypt perhaps demonstrates best the intent of the artist, making Mary's story appealing to the common folks. The corresponding poem describes Mary's work of weaving clothing for the child and Joseph's craftsmanship.[52] The artistic depiction of Mary and Joseph as ordinary folk does not quite correspond, however, to the poetic description of Mary as 'goddess' or of Joseph, the small-town carpenter, as the second and excellent *Daedalus*,[53] i.e., comparable to the mythical ingenious artist of the great city of Athens.

On Mary's life, Chelidonius wrote eighteen poems and introductory and closing prayers in Latin classical meter directly for Dürer's picture book on the Virgin Mary, *Excerpts from the Story of the Holy Virgin Mary Presented in Pictures by Albrecht Dürer, the Bavarian, with Annexed Verses by Chelidonius*,[54] printed by Hiernoymus Höltzel in 1511. According to the full title, the poet's verses were 'annexed'[55] to the woodcuts of Albrecht Dürer, in a joint publication. Apparently, in this case, the images ranked higher than the 'annexed' poems. Some of the pictures came into existence several years before they were published with these poems.[56] Thus, the poems appear to be later and

---

[51] See Winkler, 170.
[52] See Winkler, 129.
[53] *Alter & egregie daedalus*, see Winkler, 129.
[54] Published as *Epitome in divae parthenices Mariae historiam ab Alberto Dvrero Norico per figuras digestam cvm versibvs annexis Chelidonii*; see Winkler, 39–161; Knedlik, 294; Anna Scherbaum, "Das Marienleben", in Rainer Schoch, Matthias Mende, and Anna Scherbaum, eds., *Albrecht Dürer. Das druckgraphische Werk*, vol. 2: *Holzschnitte und Holzschnittfolgen* (Munich 2002) 214–279. The title page of the Mary book, which is dedicated to Caritas Pirckheimer, is depicted in Georg Deichstetter, ed., *Caritas Pirkheimer: Ordensfrau und Humanistin—ein Vorbild für die Ökumene. Festschrift zum 450. Todestag* (Cologne 1982) 11.
[55] *CVM VERSIBVS ANNEXIS CHELIDONII*, Winkler, 39.
[56] Most of the Marian pictures were made between 1503 and 1505; see Winkler, 16, 160f; see also Hults, 89.

may have had the function of bringing unity to the series of twenty woodcuts.[57]

However, picture and poem do not always fully correspond,[58] as is demonstrated by several examples. In picture 5, there is no showing of any stars or the moon, of which the poet speaks in the corresponding text; there are also no choirs of heaven that would sing from a star-filled sky. The poem describes Anna nursing Mary with sweet mother's milk, a scene not depicted by the artist, who has two women offering food and drink to Anna in childbed. Poem 6, on the young Mary and her parents going to the temple, speaks in verses 11 and 12 of the little girl decorated with flowers and dressed like a Roman lady in her stately outfit, called *urbana cyclade*.[59] The picture shows none of this. The Christmas poem and illustration also differ considerably. The picture already existed around 1503 and shows an old stable as the setting of the nativity scene, while the poem describes it as a cave.[60] Poem 19 eulogizes the Assumption of Mary into heaven, with audacious titles of majesty, while the artist features the coronation of Mary. Therefore, we are led to ask whether the poet simply wanted to provide descriptions of the pictures at hand, or whether his poems were written independently from the given images. The images and poems were then combined, quite successfully in most instances. Recent scholarship rightly argues that Chelidonius' verses depend primarily on Baptista Mantuan.[61]

A successful correlation may be seen, for example, in the poem and image on the Annunciation. In typical humanist manner, the Holy Spirit (in ecclesiastical Latin, *Spiritus Sanctus*) is the 'Almighty Spirit' (*Spiritus omnipotens*), shown in the very traditional image of the form of a dove hovering over Mary's head. However, here the poet does not use the Greek *pneuma* for 'spirit', as he did in the Pentecost poem of the series on Christ's Passion. Quite untraditionally, the messenger greets Mary not as being 'full of grace' in the Vulgate

---

[57] See the overview of the themes in Posset, "Benedictus Chelidonius", 438.
[58] Hults, 89, maintains a close correspondence between text and images.
[59] See Winkler, 72.
[60] See Winkler, 103.
[61] See Claudia Wiener, "Hochmittelalterliches Marienlob? Benedictus Chelidonius' Elegien in ihrem Verhältnis zu Baptista Mantuanus' *Parthenice Mariana* und Dürers *Marienleben*", in *Lateinische Lyrik der Frühen Neuzeit*, eds. Beate Czapla, Ralf Georg Czapla, and Robert Seidel (Tübingen 2003) 98–131; Scherbaum, *Albrecht Dürers* Marienleben, 122–126.

version of *Ave gratia plena*, but instead with *Chara [Cara] deo* in verse 12[62] (standing in place of 'full of grace', *gratia plena*), with the meaning: 'you are dear to God'. The humanist poet with his translation into humanist, not ecclesiastical, Latin was tuned in to Renaissance scholars' efforts to return to the original sources (*ad fontes*); he wanted to translate Luke 1:28 more closely to the Greek original which reads χαῖρε, κεχαριτωμένη ('Greetings, [you who are] dear to God').[63] A few years later, in 1516, Erasmus of Rotterdam would get into trouble with people in Louvain for trying to do the same thing; that is, to provide a translation into humanist Latin that was much closer to the Greek original,[64] disregarding or being unaware of the dogmatic implications of the traditional version which speaks of Mary 'full of grace'.

Also in typical humanist manner, Chelidonius called Mary a *diva* (saint, divine),[65] which stands for the ecclesiastical Latin *sancta* (saint).[66] In general, however, his designation of *dea* (goddess) for Mary[67] appears to be quite rare among humanists. This majestic-sounding designation does not correspond at all with the artistic depiction of Mary as a working woman, dressed in the contemporary clothing of a German housewife. The humanist Latin titles used here are simply translations of the traditional designation *sancta* in ecclesiastical Latin. A goddess would not ride a donkey. One should not, therefore, read idolatry into these humanist Latin titles of Mary. At one point he gave her other titles that would have been understood only by the elite of Renaissance humanists, titles that he says were written on the grave of her who was taken into heaven: 'Birth-giver of the king of Olympus', 'Queen of the kings', 'goddess of the stars' (literally 'starry goddess'), or 'glittering goddess' (*siderea dea*). He lets Christ himself call her the 'new goddess' to whom heaven and earth sing praises.[68] At other times, less strange or offensive to us today,

---

[62] See Winkler, 84.
[63] The Greek root verb has the meaning 'to make pleasing'.
[64] See Erika Rummel, *Erasmus' Annotations on the New Testament: From Philologist to Theologian* (Toronto 1986) 167-71.
[65] See *diva Maria nascitur* in poem no. 5, Winkler 66.
[66] On this view, I follow Stephan Beissel, *Geschichte der Verehrung Marias im 16. und 17. Jahrhundert: ein Beitrag zur Religionswissenschaft und Kunstgeschichte* (Freiburg and Saint Louis 1910) 105f; Winkler, 62.
[67] "And future generations had to call upon this goddess by her name, that is mother", poem no. 4, Winkler, 58; see also poem no. 6, Winkler, 72.
[68] See poem no. 19, Winkler 149.

Mary is the holy *parthenos* (Greek for virgin, girl), or even the 'royal *parthenos*'.[69] She is like a Vestal virgin.[70] She is the mother of Jesus Christ, the *Phoebus*, surname of Apollo, the god of light.[71] In his poem on the flight of the Holy Family into Egypt, Chelidonius makes references to the local gods, Isis, Osiris, and Anubis, who according to legend fell from their thrones at the moment when the Virgin Mary entered Egypt.[72] His use of Greek terms is quite rare. Here, in the *Life of Mary*, he mentions *parthenos* and *Sophia* ('wisdom') in poem 16 on the twelve-year-old Jesus in the temple conversing with the teachers of Israel.[73] Evidently, Christ is Wisdom personified.

The final poem is a prayer of supplication to Mary, Mother of God, the 'powerful mother', the protectress (*præsidium*) of mortals and the sick, who is asked to let the divine salvation rain down from heaven, to wash away our sins, and to reconcile us with heaven. Our poet uses here the Greek *polos* (Latin *polus*, for 'pole'),[74] which the classical Latin poets Virgil and Ovid employed metaphorically for 'sky' or 'heaven'.

The dedication text, placed at the end of the book, is written to the leader of the virgins (*virginibus ducem*) at Nuremberg, i.e., to the prioress Caritas Pirckheimer,[75] of the Poor Clares at Nuremberg, who was one of the very few known humanist nuns in Germany. She was the sister of the famous humanist Willibald Pirckheimer,[76] to whom Chelidonius had dedicated *The Little Passion*. In his dedication to the prioress Chelidonius hints at her ability to read Latin texts, as she sits by the waters of *Castalia*, the sacred spring on Mount Parnassus belonging to Apollo and the Muses; its waters were used at the oracle of Delphi.[77] Chelidonius calls her *Archimater* (arch-mother) and *antistes* (presiding priestess, prioress)[78] of the virgins at the nunnery of *diva Clara* (Saint Clare). Only a scholarly nun (and a learned readership in general) could understand this kind of humanist Latin:

---

[69] See title page, Winkler, 39; *Regia parthenice*, Winkler, 92.
[70] See poem no. 7, Winkler, 78.
[71] *Phoebis dius parens*, Winkler, 44.
[72] See Winkler, 123.
[73] *Disseruit sacra de Sophiaque puer*, Winkler, 135.
[74] See Winkler, 155.
[75] See Winkler, 155; Deichstetter, 32.
[76] See Josef Pfanner, "Caritas Pirckheimer—Biographie der Äbtissin", in Deichstetter, ed., 45–60.
[77] See Winkler, 157.
[78] This humanist expression *antistes* is otherwise used for 'bishop' or 'abbot'.

A Choriamb to Caritas Pirckheimer, the most reverend arch-mother
of the house of Saint Clare at Nuremberg.
The author.
[You are] the strong presiding priestess [prioress] of vigilant virgins...[79]

A reading of these lines without insight into the biography of Caritas would not necessarily tell us that she was the prioress of the nunnery of Saint Clare.

It seems the poet's and the artist's works can be understood independently from each other. For instance, Chelidonius' poems were applied not only to Dürer's *Little Passion*, but also to the picture book on Christ's Passion by Johannes Wechtelin.[80] And, with regard to the *Life of Mary*, we must realize that the pictures were never edited without text.[81] This would indicate that the text played a more significant role than we would normally assume today.

Published only six years before the publication of Luther's *Ninety-Five Theses* in 1517, Dürer's and Chelidonius' *Life of Mary* mirrors the contemporary Catholic version of Mary's story that was recognized by the Church both before and after the Reformation. The cycle won high praise from Catholics during the Council of Trent. It was popularly reprinted and circulated throughout the turbulent days of the Counter-Reformation. This 'Catholic' aspect of the *Life of Mary* has not always been given serious academic attention, since it was deemed to contradict Dürer's well-known sympathy for Martin Luther.[82] However, during the years of the Reformation the popularity of the *Life of Mary* gradually waned. The book was not reprinted after the 1511 edition.[83]

---

[79] *Choriambicum ad Charitatem Pirchamaeram aedis
diuae Clarae Noricoburgae Archimatrem dignissimam.*
Author.
*Antistes vigilum strenua virginum.
Nobis castalidum scripta sequentibus
Te charam latiae, quas legis impigre
Et claram faciunt, foemina, litterae.*
Winkler, 155; Scherbaum, 225.

[80] See Winkler, 13; the poem is reprinted in Ursula Hess, "Oratrix humilis. Die Frau als Briefpartnerin von Humanisten, am Beispiel der Caritas Pirckheimer" in *Der Brief im Zeitalter der Renaissance*, ed. Franz Josef Worstbrock (Bonn 1983) 173–203, here 185, note 35.

[81] See Winkler, 36.

[82] On this subject, see Junhyoung Michael Shin, *Et in picturam et in sanctitatem: Operating Albrecht Dürer's Marienleben (1502–1511)* (Berlin 2003).

[83] Scherbaum, *Albrecht Dürers* Marienleben, 215.

Regardless of the issue of how Lutheran or Catholic Dürer was, the poems by Chelidonius, both on Christ and on the Virgin Mary, as they were composed in humanist Latin, helped to market the artist's images among intellectuals in Germany and beyond. On the other hand, we cannot deny that Dürer's images helped to broadcast the religious poetry of our Benedictine humanist.[84]

Chelidonius wrote poems, religious and secular, on numerous occasions. An early poem (undated, extant only in manuscript form from the hand of the contemporaneous copyist Hartmann Schedel) describes the life of Saint Benedict, following the *Dialogues* of Gregory the Great on this subject. Chelidonius unfolded the hagiographic account in sixty-five distichs. At the end of his poem, he added a note, also in poetic form, in which he defended his poetic version of Benedict's life against competitors. One such poet was Jacob Locher (1471–1528), called Philomusus (lover of the muses), who in a similar fashion wrote his *Carmina in Vitam Sancti Benedicti*, extant in the same collection of Schedel in which Chelidonius' unpublished poetry is found.[85]

A Latin poem to Pirckheimer probably dates to the end of 1501, as it concludes with his wish for a happy New Year. The poem is a eulogy to Pirckheimer as a friend of the muses and as the one who is most knowledgeable about the ancient languages.[86] Chelidonius also composed a Latin poem in praise of Pirckheimer's Latin version of Plutarch's work on God who is slow to punish.[87] Chelidonius had helped Pirckheimer in his translation of Plutarch's work from Greek into Latin. In return, in an undated letter (December 1511?), Chelidonius asked him to correct several verses.[88]

---

[84] Another book with poetry by Chelidonius is known; it has the following title and was printed after Chelidonius' death in Cologne in 1526: *Passio Christi amarulenta, certis et primaries effigiata locis, vario carmine Benedicti Chelidonii et tandem Christiani Ischyrii illustrata*. See Knedlik, 294.

[85] See Wiener, "Chelidonius", in VL 2005.

[86] *Viro, latine graeceque doctissimo*. The poem is edited in Emil Reicke, *Willibald Pirckheimers Briefwechsel* (Munich 1940) vol. 1:144–50 (no. 45). Hereafter quoted as Reicke, vol. 1.

[87] *Fr[ater] Benedictus Chelidonius in Plutarchi de scelerum vindice Deo libellum, a magnifico et clarissimo patricio senatoreque Norico Bilibaldo Pirckheymer latinitate donatum* (1513), full text in Emil Reicke, *Willibald Pirckheimers Briefwechsel* (Munich 1956) vol. 2:250f (no. 245). Hereafter quoted as Reicke, vol. 2.

[88] See Niklas Holzberg, *Willibald Pirckheimer: Griechischer Humanismus in Deutschland* (Munich 1981) 119, 206, 210, 293; Reicke, vol. 1:151 (no. 46); Wiener, "Chelidonius", in VL 2005.

In 1506/1507 Chelidonius wrote a dedication (a sapphic ode) to the humanist Conradus Celtis, who had been crowned poet laureate in Nuremberg in 1487. The date of this poem is the earliest relatively secure date for the career of Chelidonius, and is found in a work by the composer/musician Petrus Athesinus Tritonius (1465–1525), a teacher and music director in Brixen. This work is a setting to music of the Odes of Horace and carries the title *Melopoiae sive harmoniae tetracentricae super XXII genera carminum*; it was printed at Nuremberg[89] and Augsburg in 1507 as the first German printing of music notation.[90]

After 1507, rumors spread that Abbot Georg Truchsess von Wetzhausen (1499–1530) of the Benedictine monastery of Auhausen on the Wöritz River had died during the diet of Constance in 1507. He was a sophisticated lover of the arts. Chelidonius refuted the rumor with a poetic dialogue in which the 'Poet' at first laments over the abbot's death and then enters into a dispute with 'Fama' (Rumor) over the false rumor. Finally 'Fama' discloses that his life has been spared after all. The poem is extant only in a copy by Hartmann Schedel.[91]

Johannes Cochlæus wrote a six-liner (*hexastichon*) to the readers of Chelidonius' rhymes (*modos*) and to his muses (*Chelidonia musa*). Since Cochlæus was steeped in music, his praise of Chelidonius includes the mention of a musical instrument (*lyra*) and the musical concept of *barbitos*, which means a song sung to the lyre (an expression used by Ovid).[92] Cochlæus pointed out that Chelidonius did not write these poems in the 'Theban faith' or 'Lesbian [faith]' (that is, pagan faith), but with the watchful, ever-burning devout care of a Christian. Being simultaneously mindful of the wordings of classical authors like Ovid or Virgil, and of the subject matter of Christ's Passion at hand, Cochlæus praised Chelidonius as the one who sings to the lyre, sighing about the cross of Christ, and not making a joke or game of it. He sings about the thorns, the wounds, and the bitter death of Christ who is the great trophy of God (*magna Trophaea dei*).[93]

---

[89] See Hillmann, 139.
[90] See *Die Musikdrucke der Staats- und Stadtbibliothek Augsburg 1488–1630* (Harald Fischer Verlag); Wiener, "Chelidonius", in VL 2005.
[91] See Wiener, "Chelidonius", in VL 2005.
[92] See *barbitos* in Casell's *New Latin Dictionary*.
[93] *Io. Coclei. Ad lectorem. Hexastichon*
Hos lege chare modos lector. Chelidonia musa

Around 1510 Cochlæus was the principal of the Latin school of Saint Lorenz in Nuremberg, where in 1511 his *Quadrivium Grammatices* (later repeatedly reprinted) and his *Tetrachordum Musices* for the young people of his school appeared. Master Cochlæus wrote this treatise

> with divine aid... chiefly for the instruction of the youth at the church of Saint Lorenz, but also for the more profitable and uncomplicated instruction of others who are beginners in the art of music.[94]

For Cochlæus' music manual Chelidonius wrote a poem to the reader (*ad lectorem*), which Pirckheimer introduced with an epigram. Both texts are included on the opening page:

Chelidonius Musophilus to the reader

Delius, high-priest of the Muses, intones a varied and sweet sounding song on Olympus,
And by the sea the Sirens harmoniously sing enticing melodies.
The air listens to birds with their joyous songs in vocal harmony.
Orpheus, and Linus too, play their music in Elysium;
Cochlæus, companion of the Muses, assists music with his art,
Teaching and creating poetic song.[95]

Chelidonius was also the author of the foreword for the revised cosmography of the ancient Pomponius Mela (in Spain, in the time of the Emperor Claudius or Caligula), edited by Cochlæus in 1512 and known under the abbreviated title *Brevis Germaniæ Descriptio*.[96] The author gave special consideration to Germany. Chelidonius' poetic preface was included on the title page.[97] He also wrote the post-

---

Quos cura vigili promsit & igne pio
Non Thebana fides, non lesbia, nec lyra flacci
Sed gemebunda canit Barbitos ista crucem:
Non loca, non lusus, spinas & vulnera Christi
Et mortem diram, magna Trophaea dei.
British Museum edition, Vienna copy.

[94] *Johannes Cochlaeus, Tetrachordum Musices*, Introduction, Translation and Transcription by Clement A. Miller. Musicological Studies and Documents, vol. 23 ([Dallas] American Institute of Musicology, 1970) 16.

[95] A facsimile of the title page is found in Miller, 1; English translation by Miller, 89; see also Reicke, vol. 2:79 (no. 191).

[96] *Cosmographia Pomponii Mele, authoris nitidissimi, tribus libris digesta, parvo quodam Compendio Joannis Coclei Norici adaucta, quo geographie principia generaliter comprehenduntur. Brevis quoque Germanie descriptio.* See *Johannes Cochlaeus, Brevis Germanie Descriptio (1512) mit der Deutschlandkarte des Erhard Etzlaub von 1501*, edited, translated and commented by Karl Langosch (Darmstadt 1969, 2nd ed.) 8.

[97] *Chelidonius Musophilus Ad lectore[m] Que canit historias duino carmine Clio* (Nuremberg: Johann Weissenburger, 1512); Reicke, vol. 2:122 (no. 200).

script, praising Cochlæus for providing brief geographic descriptions of the cities of "our Germany" and for taking their history into consideration (*more historico*).[98] The date of his postscript, 23 January 1512, makes possible the dating of Cochlæus' book.[99] Furthermore, Chelidonius contributed the preface in five distichs (*ad lectorem*) for Cochlæus' edition of the three books of Aristotle's *Meteorologia*, with paraphrases by the French biblical humanist, Jacobus Faber Stapulensis.[100]

1513 saw the death of Anton Kress (Cressus), a significant religious figure in Nuremberg and the chief pastor of Saint Lorenz church. Chelidonius must have known him quite well, as he wrote an elegy on the occasion of his death. The poem appeared in print together with that of his friend,[101] the teacher and humanist, Johannes Cochlæus.[102]

The study of Hebrew was not part of Chelidonius' education or interest; historiography, however, was. He wrote two pieces in verse on the history of his monastery, Saint Aegidius; one on its beginnings in 1140, the other on its abbots since 1418.[103] In 1515, Chelidonius contributed a dedicatory poem to the Emperor Maximilian for the *Gesta Friderici*, an edition of the works of the medieval chronicler, Otto of Freising (†1158, Cistercian, Bishop of Freising in Bavaria). It was edited by the poet laureate of 1493, Johannes Cuspinianus (1473–1529).[104]

---

[98] Latin edition with German translation in Langosch, 166–69.
[99] See Langosch, 25.
[100] *Meteorologica Aristotelis, eleganti Jacobi Fabri Stapulensis Paraphrasi explanata commentarioque Joannis Coclaei Norici declarata* (Nuremberg: Friedrich Peypus, 1512); Langosch, 7–8; Reicke, 2:131. On Faber as a biblical humanist, see Augustijn, *Humanismus*, 72–75.
[101] See Monique Samuel-Scheyder, *Johannes Cochlaeus: Humaniste et adversaire de Luther* (Nancy 1993); Ralph Keen, "Johannes Cochlaeus: an introduction to his life and work", in *Luther's lives. Two contemporary accounts of Martin Luther*, translated and annotated by Elizabeth Vandiver, Ralph Keen and Thomas D. Frazel (Manchester and New York 2002) 40–52.
[102] *Ioanni Cocleo, In mortem Antonii Cressi I. V. Doctoris, F. B. Chelidonii Elegia*; see Wiener, "Chelidonius", in VL 2005.
[103] *Versiculi de fundatione coenobii Aegidiani*; on the abbots, *De abbatibus nonnullis eiusdem coenobii*, printed posthumously in *Monasteriorum Germaniae Praecipuorum ac maxime illustrium: Centuria Prima* by Kaspar Bruschius in Ingolstadt in 1551; see Wiener, "Chelidonius", in VL 2005; Flachenecker, 38; Hillmann, 143f with note 10; Patrick J. Barry, "Irish Benedictines in Nuremberg. An examination of the Chronicle of the Monastery of St. Aegidius in Nuremberg", *Studies: An Irish Quarterly Review* 21 (1932) 578–97.
[104] *Ottonis Phrisingensis Episcopi, viri clarissimi, Rerum ab origine mundi ad ipsius usque tempora, Libri Octo* (Strasbourg: Matth. Schürer, 1515); see Hillmann, 144–145; Wiener, "Chelidonius", in VL 2005.

Chelidonius also wrote an epic in 'two books' (manuscript extant at the Cistercian Stift Heiligenkreuz; it did not get printed) in 1515, on the contemporary political events surrounding the gathering of the princes of the Western world in Vienna that year. In addition he wrote a play, dedicated to the imperial secretary Jacobus de Bannissis.[105] Chelidonius' morality drama dealt with "the struggle between lust and virtue".[106] It was performed in Latin by students of noble descent from his monastery school, whose names we know.[107] His drama was set to music by the Viennese composer Jacob Diamond. The performance in Vienna in 1515 was dedicated to the young Archduke of Burgundy, later Emperor Charles V, who was present, as was Queen Mary of Hungary, and the ambitious cardinal at the Hapsburg court, Matthew Lang of Wellenburg (1468–1540),[108] later prince-bishop of Salzburg.

The woodcut on the title page[109] shows the virtuous Heracles (Hercules) with a shield on which the imperial double-headed eagle of the Hapsburg monarchy is depicted. The coat of arms of the printer

---

[105] *De conventu Diui Caesaris Maximiliani, Regumque Hungariae Boemiae et Poloniae, ceterorumque sacri ordinum Imperii, Principumque, Viennae in Pannonia habito, Ad Iacobum de Bannisis. Caes. Maiestatis Secretarium, Consiliariumque conscriptum etc. F. Benedicti Chelidonii Libri duo*; see Wiener, "Chelidonius", in VL 2005.

[106] *Voluptatis cum Virtute disceptatio: Carolo Burgundiae duce Illustrissimo, Diuique Caes. Maxaemiliani Nepote, litis diremptore aequissimo. Viennae Pannoniae cora[m] MARIA Hungarorum Regina designata, Dominoque Mattheo S. angeli diac[ono] Cardinali Reuerendissimo recitata. A BEnedicto [sic] Chelidonio Heroicis lusa uersibus, per Ioannem Singrenium expensis vero Leonardi Alantee [printer]* 1515. On this, see Josef Nadler, *Literaturgeschichte Österreichs* (Salzburg 1951, 2nd ed.) 106; Heinz Kindermann, *Theatergeschichte Europas* (Salzburg 1959) vol. 2:254–57 with fig. 33 (title page); the title page is also shown in Nagl and Zeidler, *Deutsch-österreichische Literaturgeschichte*, 453; Hillmann, 144, Hedwig Gollob, "Der Herkules des Wiener Chelidonius von 1515", *Gutenberg Jahrbuch* (1966) 284–86 with reproduction of the title page; Antonio Stäuble, "Risonanze Europee della Commedia Umanistica del Quattrocento", in *The Late Middle Ages and the Dawn of Humanism Outside Italy*, Proceedings of the International Conference, Louvain May 11–13, 1970, eds. Gerard Verbeke and Jozef Ijsewijn (Louvain 1972; The Hague: Martinus Nijhoff, 1972) 182–194, here 194 (on Chelidonius' drama).

[107] See Nagl and Zeidler, *Deutsch-österreichische Literaturgeschichte*, 452.

[108] On him, see Johann Sallaberger, *Kardinal Matthäus Lang von Wellenburg (1468–1540): Staatsmann und Kirchenfürst im Zeitalter von Renaissance, Reformation und Bauernkriegen* (Salzburg 1997).

[109] The artist is unknown. The technical execution may point to an Italian graphic model or a sculpture. The composition of the woodcut has no similarity to Dürer's 'Great Heracles'. Yet, both images probably depend on the same Italian model, according to Gollob, 284–285. On this subject, see also Markus Reiterer, *Die Herkulesentscheidung von Prodikos und ihre frühhumanistische Rezeption in der 'Voluptatis cum virtute disceptatio' des Benedictus Chelidonius* (dissertation, Vienna 1955).

Voluptatis cum Virtute disceptatio:

Carolo Burgúdiæ duce Illustrisſimo, Diuiq; Cæſ. Maxæmi-
liani Nepote, litis diremptore æquiſſimo. Viennæ Pan-
noniæ corā MARIA Hungaror Regina deſignata,
Dominoq; MATTHEO S. angeli diac. Cardinali
Reuerendiſſimo recitata. A BEnedicto
Chelidonio Heroicis luſa uerſibus.

Suſtulit alcides non uno monſtra labore
Cæſar idem peragit, par gloria cedat utriq;.

Fig. 4. Title Page of Chelidonius' morality drama 'The struggle between lust and virtue' (*Voluptatis cum virtute disceptatio*). Österreichische Nationalbibliothek, Vienna.

Alantee is displayed on his chest. Heracles fights against the three-headed Geryon, who was believed to be the strongest man on earth. His kingdom was in the westernmost part of the world. The idea of a struggle between virtue and frivolous licentiousness spoke to the political, philosophical, and artistic milieu of the time and is symbolized in Heracles, who must choose between virtue and voluptuousness.[110] The Heracles figure must have been popular among Christian humanists, as around 1520 Marcus Marulus also composed a 'Dialogue about Hercules who was surpassed by those who honor Christ' (*Dialogus de Hercule a Christocolis superato*).[111]

In Part I, Venus and her allies are introduced as catchers of souls. Her dispute with Pallas Athene is monitored by Charles. In Part II, Epicurus appears on Venus' side, inspired by Satan. Hercules emerges with Pallas; he is shown as the conqueror of the vices. Part III proclaims the judgment by Charles in favor of Pallas and Hercules. As Charles is going to crown Pallas as the winner, she instead crowns him. Epicurus receives a public beating on stage.[112]

As a Latin poet Chelidonius was so famous that he was asked to provide the translations for the captions to the images for the emperor's *Triumphal Arch*, a huge frieze composed of woodcuts.[113] The original German wording had been provided by Johann Stabius († c. 1522), the imperial poet, astronomer, and historiographer. Chelidonius translated the text into Latin (according to his preface in *De sacrosancta trinitate*, see below). The *Arch* was sponsored by the emperor himself. It consisted of 192 giant woodcuts designed by Albrecht Dürer and Albrecht Altdorfer (c. 1480–1538); at least, giant if compared to the usual size of woodcuts of that time.[114] When assembled, the com-

---

[110] See Gollob, 284–285. On Geryon (Gerion), see the entry "Heracles, Labours of", X. The Cattle of Geryon, in Michael Stapleton, *The Illustrated Dictionary of Greek and Roman Mythology* (New York 1978) 100–101.

[111] See the English translation by Nikolina Jovanović in "Dossier Marko Marulić", in *Most/ The Bridge. A Journal of Croatian Literature* 1–4 (1999) 52–57; Bratislav Lučin, "Hercules and the Poets", *ibid.*, 121–126.

[112] The dramatic performance may have been influenced by the tradition of carnival plays in Nuremberg; see Wiener, "Chelidonius", in VL 2005.

[113] Its full title reads: *Porta honoris, Hoc est Descriptio Porta Honoris Qvondam Caesareae Maiestati Maximiliano Primo, anno 1515. Erecta per Ioannem Stabium Viennensem Maiestatis Illius Ibidem Historiographum* (Nuremberg: Hieronymus Andreae, 1517–1518); see Thomas Ulrich Schauerte, *Die Ehrenpforte für Kaiser Maximilian I. Dürer und Altdorfer im Dienst des Herrschers* (Munich 2001). For a brief description and depiction, see Hults, 100–101 with Fig. 2.22.

[114] Now in the Austrian National Library in Vienna.

Fig. 5: *Triumphal Arch of Emperor Maximilian* by Albrecht Dürer and others (1515–1517) with Latin texts by Benedictus Chelidonius. Österreichische Nationalbibliothek, Vienna.

position measured about 3.4 by 2.9 meters.[115] Emperor Maximilian also sponsored the *Triumphal Procession,* created between 1516 and 1518. Its completion was halted, however, by the emperor's death in 1519.[116] The *Triumphal Procession* was intended as a supplement to the slightly earlier "paper tribute",[117] the *Triumphal Arch.*

During his short term in office as abbot, Chelidonius edited in 1519 the tract *De sacrosancta trinitate,* a summary text originally made by the twelfth-century theologian Bandinus[118] of a scholastic manuscript on Peter Lombard's *Sentences,* which the controversial (later anti-Lutheran) humanist theologian from Ingolstadt, Johannes Eck (1486–1543), had discovered in Chelidonius' monastery library in Vienna. Eck encouraged Chelidonius to revise and publish it. He did so with the note that it had never been printed before.[119] Chelidonius dedicated his edition to Emperor Maximilian.

Chelidonius apparently did not write a dedication to Dr. Eck, as we might expect since Eck had made him aware of this manuscript. This disregard may be interpreted as an indirect, gradual distancing from Eck, whose opposition to Luther had quickly become widely known. Chelidonius apparently sided with his life-long friend Pirckheimer, who was credited with the coarse satire against Eck, *Eckius dedolatus* ("Eck planed down": the German word *Eck* means 'corner' or 'edge').[120] In revenge, Eck included Pirckheimer in his list of dangerous Luther-sympathizers who were to be excommunicated. Eck had been empowered by Rome to include any names he wanted in the papal bull of excommunication of 1520. In 1521 Pirckheimer succeeded in having his name removed and he was absolved, but not without painful personal humiliation. Since Chelidonius was originally

---

[115] About 11 by 9.5 feet; see Hults, 100.
[116] See Nagl and Zeidler, *Deutsch-österreichische Literaturgeschichte,* 449.
[117] Hults, 100.
[118] Bandinus, *Sententiae theologicae*; see *Patrologia Latina,* vol. 192:967–968.
[119] The work has the following title according to the copy extant in Vienna's *Schottenstift* (I use exactly the same capitalization): *BANDINI VIRI DOCTISSIMI SENTENTIARVM THEOLOGICArum libri quatuor quam diligentissime castigati, Per Reuerendum in Christo patrem, Dominum Benedictum Chelidoniu[m] Abbatem ad Scottos Viennae Vatem excellentissimu[m], antea nunq[ue] impressi* (Vienna: Joh. Singrenius, 1519). I am grateful to Magister Gerhard Schlass for providing me with copies.
[120] See *Eckius Dedolatus. Der enteckte Eck,* trans. and ed. by Niklas Holzberg (Stuttgart 1983); Eckhard Bernstein, "Humanistische Intelligenz und kirchliche Reformen", in *Die Literatur im Übergang vom Mittelalter zur Neuzeit,* 166–197, here 187–188.

a Nuremberg monk, he apparently sided with other reform-minded Nurembergers; among them was the priest Georg Spalatin with whom Chelidonius had had contact since 1512.[121] Spalatin worked for the Elector of Saxony, Frederick the Wise (1463–1525), and later became a close friend of Luther.

Up to 1525, Pirckheimer's sympathies were with the Reformation. In taking sides he apparently found support from Chelidonius, who wrote to him from Vienna in November 1519 that Eck was not worth talking about.[122] At this point, the denominational delineation between 'Roman Catholics' and 'Wittenberg Catholics' (later called Protestants or Lutherans) was not clear-cut; neither was the separation between Roman Catholic and Protestant humanists (the confessionalization of humanism).

During the first decades of the sixteenth century, controversy raged over the humanist Johann Reuchlin. He quarreled with the Jewish convert Johann Pfefferkorn (1469–1522/23) and the Cologne Dominicans over the destruction of Jewish books. The Reuchlinists dominated the debate, as they fostered the arts and the study of the humanities and favored the 'bright, renowned men' (*clari viri*). Reuchlin had published their approving letters to him (*Epistolæ clarorum virorum*) in 1514. The Cologne party was styled by their opponents as 'the obscurantists' (*viri obscuri*). The most important document of this feud was the classical satire of the humanists, *The Letters of Obscure Men* (1515).

In 1516 a papal mandate postponing the Reuchlin case was issued. Finally, in 1520, Reuchlin was condemned by Rome to keep silent on the matter and to pay the full costs involved. Despite Reuchlin's demonstrably life-long ecclesiastical loyalty, he was apparently viewed by conservatives as siding with Martin Luther. In reality he was not, and he appears ultimately to have been satisfied that Rome had cleared him of any charges of heresy.[123] Reuchlin pointed out that

---

[121] Chelidonius' letter of 10 August 1512 to Spalatin is extant, quoted in Jakob Friedrich Hekelius (Heckel), *Manipulus primus epistolarum singularium* (1695), and reprinted in Reicke vol. 2:29 (no. 177) note 9.

[122] See Chelidonius' letter of 3 November 1519 to Pirckheimer, in Helga Scheible, ed., *Willibald Pirckheimers Briefwechsel* (Munich 1997) vol. 4:107–109 (no. 628) with note 3.

[123] *Und habent heresim und ketzery fallen lassen*, Reuchlin's letter to Frederick the Wise of 3 January 1521, written from Ingolstadt, as quoted by Peter G. Bietenholz, "Erasmus und die letzten Lebensjahre Reuchlins", *Historische Zeitschrift* 240 (1985) 45–66. See Ludwig Geiger, *Johann Reuchlins Briefwechsel* (Tübingen 1875; reprint: Hildesheim 1962) 327 (no. CCXCVIII).

the reason for the Roman decision against him lay with the Dominicans who portrayed his 'Expert Opinion' on the use of Jewish books in his *Eye Mirror* as "irritating and favoring the Jews" (*ergerlich und den Juden günstig*). He added that the Dominicans were threatened with a high fine themselves if they tried to burn his *Eye Mirror*.[124] Reuchlin had to pay a fine for his excessive language against the theologians in Cologne, but this fine was a punishment for slander, not for heresy.

"Reuchlin did not keep silence and did not pay the costs".[125] Evidently nobody bothered to exact the fine from him. Yet, despite the fine, his faithfulness to the Catholic Church was beyond doubt, and, if necessary, he was ready to "suffer injustice for our Christ" as he put it repeatedly, in particular in his dedication to Pope Leo X, a text published with his *De arte cabalistica* in 1517. After Reuchlin had been acquitted of heresy by the Roman authorities, he felt that his case should now be dealt with by the civil authorities in Germany, so he asked Elector Frederick to bring his case before the emperor.[126] Obviously, the feud continued and it signaled a prelude to the Reformation. All Germany was divided into two camps. Chelidonius evidently sided with Reuchlin, the famous layman and humanist, as Chelidonius' name was included in a list of humanist theologians which Pirckheimer established on 30 August 1517 in defending Reuchlin. Pirckheimer's list also included the Augustinians Johann von Staupitz and Martin Luther himself.[127]

In conclusion, Chelidonius' poetry clearly remained in demand in later days. In 1530/1531, a decade after his death, one of his couplets accompanied four paintings with the same motif, *Venus and Cupid with a Honeycomb* by Lucas Cranach (1472–1553), another leading artist of the German Renaissance and the court painter at Wittenberg in Luther's days.[128] The verse is found (without the name of the author) in the upper left corner in three 1530–1531 paintings with

---

[124] See Reuchlin's letter to Frederick the Wise of 3 January 1521 (see previous note).
[125] Roland H. Bainton, *Erasmus of Christendom* (New York 1982) 151.
[126] See Reuchlin's letter to Frederick the Wise of 3 January 1521.
[127] *Epistola apologetica*, Helga Scheible and Dieter Wuttke, eds., *Willibald Pirckheimers Briefwechsel* (Munich 1989) vol. 3:146–72 (no. 464), here 162, line 576 (with the spelling *Chelydonius*).
[128] See Max J. Friedländer and Jakob Rosenberg, *The Paintings of Lucas Cranach* (New York 1978) nos. 244, 245, 247, 248.

the same motif.¹²⁹ Evidently, the poem came into existence first and was later incorporated into the painting. The search for the authorship of the poem caused considerable debate.¹³⁰ Until now, Chelidonius has never been considered to be Cranach's source. Chelidonius had based his couplet on the story of Cupid in Theocritus' *Idyll* 19: Cupid, pursued by angry bees, rushes to his mother, who comforts him by telling him that the wounds caused by his arrows cause far more pain than bee stings.¹³¹ The nude Venus is draped in a transparent veil. Apparently the artist included Chelidonius' text as a reminder that lust (*voluptas*) is transitory.

The accomplishments of Albrecht Dürer have rightly been praised over the centuries. However, the literary achievements of Chelidonius have been neglected, even though Chelidonius was friends with the most famous humanists of his time, poet laureates included. He deserves a place of honor in the history of humanism in general and of monastic humanism in particular. He should also be recognized as an important figure in the history of pastoral care for the intellectuals of the Renaissance on the eve of the Reformation. Chelidonius successfully used the elitist medium of humanist Latin poetry (and the Renaissance artist's images) for the purpose of 'evangelization', i.e., of making the story of Jesus Christ and his mother Mary attractive to the humanists of his time. He had such a command of classic

---

¹²⁹ See nos. 244, 247, 248. No. 245 has the text in the upper right corner. The Latin text as given in painting no. 244 in the upper left corner is: DVM PVER ALVEOLO FVRATVR MELLA CVPIDO/FVRANTI DIGITVM CVPISDE FIXIT APIS/SIC ETIAM NOBIS BREVIS ET PERITVRA VOLVPTAS/QVAM PETIMVS TRISTI MIXTA DOLORE NOCET.

¹³⁰ Previously, the couplet was attributed to Melanchthon, the Wittenberg humanist, or to his relative, the poet Georg Sabinus (a student at Wittenberg in the 1520s). Doubts were raised about Melanchthon's authorship by F. W. G. Leeman, "A Textual Source for Cranach's 'Venus with Cupid the Honey-Thief'", *The Burlington Magazine* 126 (1984) 274ff; Leeman suggested taking Ercole Strozzi's poem into consideration, published in 1513 by Aldus Manutius; Michael Bath, "Honey and Gall or: Cupid and the Bees. A Case of Iconographic Slippage", in *Andrea Alciato and the Emblem Tradition. Essays in Honor of Virginia Woods Callahan*, ed. Peter M. Daly (New York 1989) 59–94, here 65–69, opted for Sabinus. See on this Franz Matsche, "Humanistische Ethik am Beispiel der mythologischen Darstellungen von Lucas Cranach", in *Humanismus und Renaissance in Ostmitteleuropa* (1996) 58, note 112. Matsche, note 119, leaves the issue of the couplet's author undecided: *noch immer offen*. Chelidonius is not discussed as a likely possibility. I follow the source identification that assigns the poem to Chelidonius, which is given at the following internet location: www.gallery.euroweb.hu/html/c/cranach/lucas_e/2/13venus.html

¹³¹ The Latin text is, however, not a direct quotation from *Idyll* 19, as Friedländer and Rosenberg claim on p. 118.

studies that he was able to produce a marvelous correlation between ancient pagan mythological concepts and the biblical and devotional themes of salvation history, of Christ's Passion and Mary's life. On which side he would have come out during the subsequent confessionalization of humanism and the Reformation is, of course, impossible to tell. Yet, his verses on Mary and Dürer's images of her demonstrate that the Renaissance humanists in Germany on the eve of the Reformation not only had a great interest in Jerome, the scholar and Church Father,[132] but also in Mary and her mother Anna,[133] and in the ecclesiastical doctrine of the immaculate conception of Mary in Anna's womb,[134] for which the *Life of Mary* by Chelidonius and Dürer appears to have argued.[135]

---

[132] See Eugene F. Rice Jr, *Saint Jerome in the Renaissance* (Baltimore and London 1985); Berndt Hamm, "Hieronymus-Begeisterung und Augustinismus vor der Reformation. Beobachtungen zur Beziehung zwischen Humanismus und Frömmigkeitstheologie (am Beispiel Nürnbergs)", in Kenneth Hagen, ed., *Augustine, the Harvest, and Theology (1300–1650). Essays Dedicated to Heiko Augustinus Oberman in Honor of his Sixtieth Birthday* (Leiden etc. 1990) 127–235.

[133] See Marie Anne von Roten, *Die Marienverehrung bei den oberrheinischen Frühhumanisten* (unpublished dissertation, Fribourg 1940), as referred to by Scherbaum, *Albrecht Dürers Marienleben*, 230–234; Virginia Nixon, *Mary's Mother Saint Anne in Late Medieval Europe* (University Park, Penn. 2004) 72–75, 122.

[134] See Beda Kleinschmidt, *Die Heilige Anna. ihre Verehrung in Geschichte, Kunst und Volkstum* (Düsseldorf 1930) 162; Scherbaum, *Albrecht Dürers Marienleben*, 234–245.

[135] See Scherbaum, *Albrecht Dürers Marienleben*, 249.

CHAPTER THREE

A HISTORIOGRAPHER AND DISTINGUISHED
VERSE MAKER: BOLFGANGUS MARIUS,
MONK OF ALDERSBACH, BAVARIA

The Cistercian abbey of Aldersbach in Bavaria was founded in 1146.[1] By the year 1500, several Bavarian monasteries were affiliated to it.[2] One of its most famous abbots, perhaps the greatest of the Aldersbach abbots, was Wolfgang Mayr (or Mair), whose Latinized name was Bolfgangus Marius.[3] Marius' fame was based not only on his exemplary monastic attitude, his eagerness to uphold Cistercian monastic discipline, and his administrative skills, but most of all on his humanist scholarship, and on his art in poetry and history writing (historiography). In these skills he followed in the footsteps of the ancient authors, as the poets were the first historians.[4]

He was born Lukas Mayer (or Mayr, Mair) on 18 October 1469 at Dorfbach near Passau, Bavaria. His parents were poor, but teachers recognized the boy's potential and furthered his schooling at the monastic school in Fürstenzell and at the cathedral school in Passau.[5] In 1490, at the age of twenty-one, he entered the Cistercian monastery of Aldersbach and received the name *Bolfgangus*, as he himself spelled

---

[1] See Klugseder, ed., *850 Jahre Zisterzienserkloster* (Vilshofen 1996).
[2] Fürstenfeld, 1265, Fürstenzell, 1274, and Gotteszell, 1285; see Josef Oswald, "Die Gedichte des Abtes Wolfgang Marius von Aldersbach", in *Ostbairische Grenzmarken: Passauer Jahrbuch für Geschichte, Kunst und Volkskunde* 7 (Passau 1964/1965) 310–319, here 310. Hereafter quoted as Oswald, "Gedichte".
[3] See Nikolaus Paulus, "Wolfgang Mayer, ein baierischer Cistcrzienser des 16. Jahrhunderts", *Historisches Jahrbuch* 15 (1894) 575–588; Ludwig Schrott, ed., *Bayerische Kirchenfürsten* (Munich 1964) 149–59; Josef Oswald, "Abt Wolfgang Marius von Aldersbach: Leben und geschichtliche Schriften", in *Speculum historiale: Geschichte im Spiegel von Geschichtsschreibung und Geschichtsdeutung*, eds. Clemens Bauer, Laetitia Boehm, and Max Müller (Freiburg and Munich 1965) 354–74; hereafter quoted as Oswald, "Abt"; see also Oswald, "Gedichte", 311–12 (biography); Joseph Oswald, "Bayerische Humanistenfreundschaft", in Dieter Albrecht *et al.*, eds., *Festschrift für Max Spindler zum 75. Geburtstag* (Munich 1969) 401–20; Hans Göttler, "Gelehrter und Poet dazu. Vor 450 Jahren starb Abt Wolfgang Marius von Aldersbach", *Literatur in Bayern* (no. 38, 1994) 67; Claudia Schwaab, "Marius", *Lexikon der Reformationszeit*, 497.
[4] See Donald R. Kelley, *Renaissance Humanism*, 102.
[5] See Manfred Knedlik, "Marius", BBKL 24 (2005) 1059–1062.

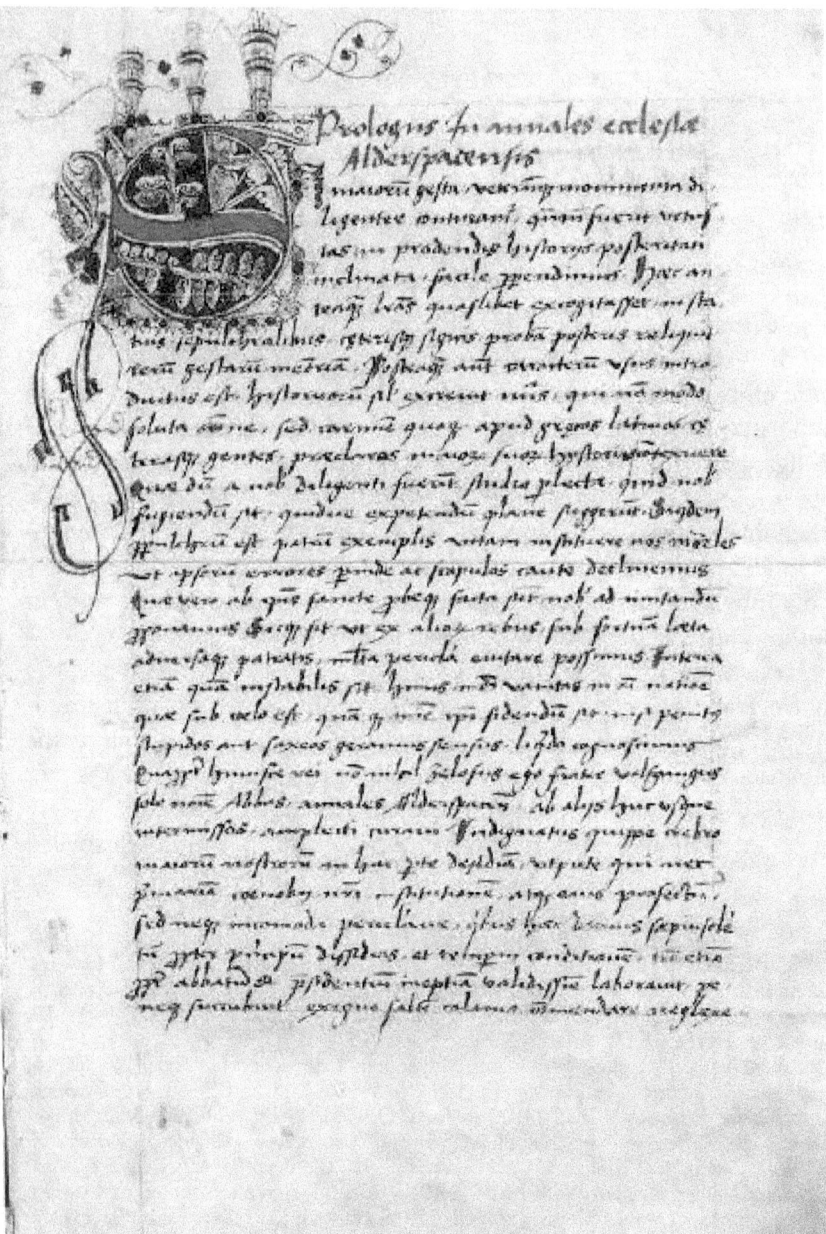

Fig. 6 Marius' *Prologus In Annales*.

his name (usually, it is spelled *Wolfgang*). His abbot, Simon Kastner (in office from 1486 to 1501), who was inclined toward humanist studies, sent him to the University of Heidelberg in 1493, where the Cistercian College of Saint Jacob had been in existence since 1368/1394.[6] For three years he studied philosophy, languages, theology, and canon law and graduated with a master's degree. His language professors may have been Rudolph Agricola and Johann Reuchlin. Jacob Wimpfeling was his history teacher. Marius never made use of his academic title due to his monastic humility. A confrère at Heidelberg was Conrad Reuter (or Reiter), later equally famous as the abbot of the Cistercian monastery of Kaisheim (in Latin, *Caesarea*) in southern Germany from 1509 to 1540.[7] Another college friend was Ulrich Molzner, abbot of the Cistercian monastery of Raitenhaslach in Bavaria from 1502 to 1506.[8]

In 1497, Marius was ordained to the priesthood at Passau. In 1498 he became the parish vicar at Saint Peter Parish in Aldersbach and the secretary and chaplain to his abbot. After the abbot's death, Marius was transferred to the preacher's position at the shrine of Kößlarn (Lower Bavaria), and in 1504 he became the parish vicar at Rotthalmünster, to which the shrine belonged at the time. He worked in parish ministry for about a decade (up to 1514), a period that included war in 1504/1505, between the heirs of Duke George the Rich of Bavaria (†1503) over the Landshut inheritance. His parish suffered much damage from that war. He described the experience of these trying times in the lengthy hexameter poem *Carmen de bello Norico* (Song about the Bavarian War); *Noricum* is a medieval designation for Bavaria. On 2 June 1514 Marius was elected abbot of Aldersbach and ordained to this position by the supervising abbot of the mother abbey of Ebrach in Franconia. Marius was abbot for thirty years until his death at the age of seventy-five, on 11 October 1544.

He was concerned about the inner reforms of his monastery after the lax reign of his predecessor, who had often been absent from the abbey. Consequently, monastic discipline had not been enforced.

---

[6] About 600 Cistercians studied there between 1368–1522; see Marian Gloning, "Konrad Reuter, Abt von Kaisheim 1509–1540", StM 32 (1912) 450–92.

[7] See Gloning, "Konrad Reuter", 454.

[8] See Marian Gloning, "Aus der Gedichtesammlung des Abtes Marius von Aldersbach", StM 33 (1912) 76–89, here 84–87; F. Hacker, "Abt Ulrich Moltzner von Raitenhaslach (1502–1506)", StM 35 (1914) 347–350.

He was also concerned about the education of the young monks. Some of them he sent to the universities at Ingolstadt and Vienna, both of which were centers of humanism. They studied philosophy, theology, and also the natural sciences. Marius himself became known as the learned (*eruditus*) abbot who sponsored scholarly fellow monks (*doctos apud se coenobitas*), as the contemporary humanist poet and historian Caspar Bruschius (1518–1559) observed. Bruschius gave Marius the honorific title 'Distinguished Verse Maker' (*versificator insignis*).[9]

We need to see this Cistercian monk and abbot in the context of Christian poets who wrote in humanist Latin on Christ and other religious themes, a phenomenon that was not at all uncommon at the time. For example, Nicolaus Salicetus (†1494), the Swiss humanist, physician, and Cistercian abbot, edited the Pseudo-Bernardine *Oratio rhythmica* (Strasbourg: Johann Grüninger, 1489)[10] in his prayer book called *Antidotarius animae*,[11] which contains meditations and prayers that serve as antidotes for the soul. More than twenty editions of this book are known from 1489 to 1513. Salicetus pointed out that prayers which aim at meditation on Christ's Passion are to be considered the most efficient antidotes.[12] Further, in 1501/1502 the Venetian printer Aldus Manutius printed an anthology of ancient and modern Christian poems, *Poetae Christiani veteres*, which included, for instance, the poem on Christ's Passion attributed[13] to Lactantius.[14]

At that time, we find several monastic humanists who were poets. In southern Germany and Austria there were Benedictus Chelidonius

---

[9] See Oswald, "Gedichte", 312.

[10] *Patrologia Latina*, vol. 184:1319ff; see Franz Posset, "The Crucified Embraces Saint Bernard; The Beginnings of the *Amplexus Bernardi*", CSQ 33 (1998) 289–314, here 295–296.; Sheryl Frances Chen provided an English translation in "Bernard's Prayer Before the Crucifix that Embraced Him: Cistercians and Devotion to the Wounds of Christ", CSQ 29 (1994) 23–54, here 25–40.

[11] Full title: *Liber meditationum ac orationum devotatum qui anthidotarius animae dicitur*. See Luzian Pfleger, "Nicolaus Salicetus, ein gelehrter elsässischer Cistercienserabt des 15. Jahrhunderts", StM 22 (1901) 588–597.

[12] See Pfleger, 594–595.

[13] See *Patrologia Latina*, vol. 7:283–86; J. Denk, "Pseudo-Laktanz' 'Carmen de passione Domini'—das Machwerk eines italienischen Humanisten aus dem 15. Jahrhundert?", *Theologische Revue* 5 (1906) 382–383.

[14] Lactantius: *De passione Domini*; on this, see Charles Béné's book with the trilingual title: *Sudbina jedne pjesme. Destin d'un poème. Destiny of a poem: Carmen de Doctrina Domini Nostri Iesu Christi Pendentis in Cruce Marci Maruli* (Zagreb and Split 1994) 92. I am grateful to Tinka Katic, Zagreb, for providing me with this book. The *Poetae Christiani veteres* also included works by Homer, Vergil, Sedulius, and for example the *Opusculum ad Annuntiationem beatissimae Virginis* (in a Greek-Latin version).

(see Chapter 2) and Angelus Rumpler (c. 1460–1513), the Benedictine abbot of Vornbach in Bavaria. He wrote the *Carmen de passione Christi* (a fragment), probably shortly before his death.[15] In Croatia, the layman Marcus Marulus composed a *Carmen* on the crucified Christ as part of a larger work. The poem was re-edited in booklet form at Erfurt in a "veritable de luxe edition" by the Cistercian Henricus Urbanus[16] (see Chapter 4). The poem celebrated the Passion of Christ, as the full title indicates: "M. Marulus' poem about the teaching of our Lord Jesus Christ as he is hanging on the cross by way of a dialog between Christ and a Christian" (*M. Maruli Carme[n] de doctrina domini nostri Jesu Christi pende[n]tis in Cruce p[er] modu[m] dialogissmi Christi & Christiani*). It is a "very beautiful booklet"[17] of only seven pages, including the woodcut by an anonymous craftsman.

Monks at the Benedictine abbey of Maria-Laach in western Germany composed Christian poems which were never published. For example, their prior, Johannes Butzbach (1477–1516), wrote a song of praise of sacred scriptures: *Carmen de laudibus sacre scripture*, hymns to Mary, Anna, and Benedict.[18] Another, little-known Rhenish humanist, Johannes Curvello, of the monastery of Johannesberg, near Bingen, wrote a prayer to the incarnate and crucified Christ: *Decastychon— ad ymaginem [imaginem] crucifixi*.[19] These hints may suffice for a review of the literary-historical context of Christian poetry to which Marius belonged.

In 1514, the same year in which Marulus' *Carmen* was reprinted at Erfurt, Marius, while a preacher at Rotthalmünster, recreated the life of Christ in the literary form of a hero's epic, in his booklet titled *Christi Fasciculus florido heroyci poematis charactere digestus* ("A fascicle on Christ in the flourishing style of a heroic epic"). It was dedicated to his former college friend, Abbot Conrad Reuter of the Cistercian abbey of Kaisheim, dated 3 May 1514. In his dedication he reveals that, at a sudden, happy hour, he was inspired to write this song

---

[15] Worstbrock, "Aus Gedichtsammlungen des Wolfgang Marius", 493 and 497; Abbot Rumpler also wrote poems on Christ's birth and on his Resurrection; Kurt Rumpler, "Angelus Rumpler", BBKL 24 (2005) 1250–1264.

[16] See Franz Posset, "A Cistercian Monk as Editor of the *Carmen* of the Croatian Humanist Marcus Marulus (died 1524): The German Humanist Henricus Urbanus O.Cist. (died 1538)", CSQ 39 (2004) 399–419.

[17] Béné, 99.

[18] See Richter, "Die Schriftsteller der Benediktinerabtei Maria-Laach", 277–340.

[19] See F. W. E. Roth, "Johannes Curvello O.S.B.: Ein vergessener Humanist des XVI. Jahrhunderts", *Annalen des Historischen Vereins für den Niederrhein* 62 (1896) 209–210.

on the life and death of Christ, and since it is so short (about sixteen pages), he called it a "fascicle on Christ".[20] The explicit mention of a sudden inspiration for the coming into existence of his poem is linked to the classical conviction that poetry is the product of divine inspiration (i.e., according to Virgil's *De rerum inventoribus*, 1.8).[21]

The poem was printed at Landshut in 1515 by Johannes Weyssenburger († c. 1536).[22] Marius included the *Christi Fasciculus* in his 1526 collection of poems. He sent a copy to the student Wolfgang Seidel (1492–1562), who later became known as the Benedictine humanist Sedelius at the monastery of Tegernsee. Sedelius may have been instrumental in the printing of this work.[23] Later, in 1580, a German translation was produced at the monastery of Tegernsee, titled "The Passion of Jesus Christ collated from the four Gospels presented in verse form".[24] In a similar way to the Benedictine Chelidonius, our Cistercian abbot articulated the Passion of Christ in a style and form that was appealing to contemporary humanists. We can see his efforts as a sophisticated type of evangelization of humanists by the linguistic means to which they were accustomed. This heroic epic demonstrates not only the author's rhetorical skills, but also his deep Christian spirituality. The *Christi Fasciculus* shows that its author was a Christ-centered biblical humanist and theologian.

In return, Marius himself received a poem from his friend Conrad Reuter, the abbot of Kaisheim.[25] Between 1501 and 1526 Marius

---

[20] The Latin text of the dedication to his friend is printed in Gloning, "Konrad Reuter", 489–490.

[21] See Donald R. Kelley, *Renaissance Humanism*, 102 with note 59.

[22] Also in 1515, this printer edited a book of woodcuts on the lives of the saints; see Hans Bleibrunner, ed., *Das Leben des heiligen Wolfgang nach dem Holzschnittbuch des Johann Weyssenburger aus dem Jahre 1515* (Regensburg 1967). Also known from this printing press is the *Ars moriendi: ex variis sententiis collecta cum figuris ad resistendum in mortis agone dyabolice suggestioni valens cuilibet Christifideli utilis ac multum necessaria* (Landshut: Weyssenburger, 1514).

[23] *Fratris Wolfgangi Mayer Abbatis Alderspacensis, liberalium arcium Magistri divine cultoris Sophieque studiosissimi: Christi Fasciculus Florido Heroyci poematis charactere digestus. Impressum Landshut per venerabilem virum Joannem Weyssenburger caleographum sacerdocii professorem accuratissimum. Anno M. D. VX* (printing mistake for the correct XV, *i.e.*, 1515); see Oswald, "Gedichte", note 52.

[24] *Passio Jesu Christi aus den vier Evangelien zusammengezogen und in Gesangsweise dargestellt.* See Paulus, 579; Oswald, "Abt", 364.

[25] Partly edited in Gloning, "Konrad Reuter", 489. The poem is included in Reuter's *Mortilogus F. Conradi Reitterii Nordlingensis, Prioris Monasterii Caesariensis, Epigrammata ad eruditissimos vaticolas* (Augsburg: Erhard Owglin and Georg Nadler, 1508; with woodcuts); the title *Mortilogus* may mean something like 'the dance of death', *dance macabre*; see Gloning, "Konrad Reuter", 487–489.

composed about eighty poems.[26] He also collected poems by other humanists,[27] such as those by the Carmelite Baptist Mantuan,[28] who was considered by contemporaries to be the "modern Virgil" (*Vergilius neotericus*). Marius composed a prayer to the glorious Virgin Mary for the prosperity of his monastery, *Alma dei genitrix et praestantissima virgo*, that she might hold her shield (*clypeus* = *clipeus*) over her servants and preserve peace for that place.[29]

In addition, Marius created a prayer in the poetic form of a Sapphic ode to honor the two patron saints of the monastery infirmary: to Mary, who was to be venerated as the mother of the eternal king, and to John the Baptist. They could both be asked to intercede for protection from infection by "the painful poisons of the threefold foe" (*triplicis nos ne inficiant venena hostis acerba*).[30] Significantly, the so-called Isenheim altarpiece of Matthias Grünewald (†1528) that was painted for another monastic infirmary (the hospital of the order of Saint Anthony, an order of doctors and nurses who specialized in infectious diseases) shows both these saints under the cross: Mary fainting and John the Baptist with his elongated finger pointing to the crucified Christ.[31] That Mary and John the Baptist were the

---

[26] See Oswald, "Abt", 364; and "Gedichte".
[27] See Worstbrock, 491–504.
[28] *F[ratris] Baptiste Mantuani Carmelite Theolog[i] Contra poetas Impudice loquentes carmen*, Worstbrock, 495. This poem may have been written in Rome in 1487; see Wilfred P. Mustard, *The Eclogues of Baptista Mantuanus* (Baltimore 1911) 14.
[29] *Alma dei genitrix et praestantissima virgo*
 Laus immensa soli, gloria luxque poli.
 Dignior es cunctis coeli terraeque creatis,
 Et speciale dei summitonantis opus.
 Religio patrum, quos hac collegit in aede
 Sub clypeo famulos suscipe virgo tuos.
 Pelle procul nocumenta hostis, mala scandala perde,
 Ac subeas votis nos vigilare datis.
 Coenobii semper pereutis sit tibi cura et
 Hunccine sub grata pace tuere locum.
Gloning, "Gedichtesammlung", 78.
[30] *Regis aeterni veneranda mater,*
 Lux poli, et clarum decus angelorum,
 Sanctior baptista deique Joannes
 Dulcis et abba.

 Supplices vestris famulos sub alis
 Jugiter seruate pii patroni,
 Triplicis nos ne inficiant venena
 Hostis acerba.
Gloning, "Gedichtesammlung", 80.
[31] See the numerous internet examples of Grünewald's *Crucifixion*.

patrons of the infirmary at Aldersbach and that they both featured in the hospital painting at Isenheim (Alsace) may have something to do with their function in medieval piety as intercessors for the sinners at the Last Judgment (the iconographic motif of *deësis*), of which the patients were reminded when they looked at it. Although it is not clear what Marius meant in his concluding verses by the "threefold foe" and infectious diseases, we can assume that he was referring to three major dangers of the time: pestilence, cholera, and 'Saint Anthony's Fire' (or Holy Fire, a disease similar to leprosy),[32] or perhaps simply to epidemics, death, and the devil.

Besides poetic prayers to saints, Marius wrote poems for friends like Abbot Conrad Reuter, including a poem in which he alludes to mythic figures and pagan gods and goddesses (Apollo, Diana, Orpheus, Phoebus, Amor, Clio, and Minerva) and to the muse of poetry, Calliope.[33] Marius also wrote three poems for Abbot Ulrich Molzner of Raitenhaslach (dated to 1504, due to an allusion to the Landshut War in one of them).[34] For the funeral of his fatherly friend, Abbot Wolfgang Simon, who died on 11 September 1501, he composed a poem and the words for his gravestone.[35]

Marius not only wrote poetry but collected poems written by others,[36] such as his Benedictine friend, Abbot Angelus Rumpler, author of a hymn on the Passion of Christ and other works.[37] Marius' collection further included three poems by Adam Werner von Themar, the Heidelberg humanist, who had dedicated them to the Cistercian humanist Conradus Leontorius, secretary to the Cistercian Abbot General, Jean de Cirey.[38]

---

[32] See Adalbert Mischlewski, "Die Antoniter und Isenheim", in Max Seidel, *Mathis Gothart Nithart Grünewald, Der Isenheimer Altar* (Stuttgart 1973) 256.

[33] See Gloning, "Gedichtesammlung", 81–84.

[34] See Gloning, "Gedichtesammlung", 85–86.

[35] See Gloning, "Gedichtesammlung", 87.

[36] Worstbrock provides an overview of the poems which Marius collected.

[37] *Carmen fratris angeli [Rumpler] in passionem Christi Inuocatio*, also known as the *Carmen de passione Christi heroicum* (fragment); Worstbrock, 497 and 503; Rumpler was also the author of a poem (*epistola*) of 28 stanzas dedicated to Conradus Celtis: *Ad Conradum Celtis fratris Angeli* [Rumpler] *Sapphica epistola*; see Rupprich, ed., *Der Briefwechsel des Konrad Celtis*, 599–603. Each stanza ends with *plaudite, Musae!* (Applaud, you Muses!). On Rumpler as historiographer, see Erika S. Dorrer, *Angelus Rumpler Abt von Formbach (1501–1513) als Geschichtsschreiber. Ein Beitrag zur klösterlichen Geschichtsschreibung in Bayern am Ausgang des Mittelalters* (Munich 1965).

[38] *Aliud Carmen Ade ad commissarium Cisterciensem*, Worstbrock, 500 (nos. 2–4); Wolff, "Conradus Leontorius. Biobibliographie", 407, has edited some of the verses in his note 91.

Like other monastic humanists Marius not only composed poetry but was also interested in historiography. He copied older authors' historical works, such as the "Life of the Holy Bishop Otto of Bamberg" in three books by the Benedictine Herbord (†1168), of the monastery of Michelsberg near Bamberg, Germany. He was also well-versed in the art of book illumination. In 1508 he wrote the above-mentioned *Carmen de bello Norico* from personal experience of the war over the Landshut inheritance.[39] In five parts, comprising one hundred pages written in hexameters, this is his longest work. As an eyewitness, Marius' work is esteemed as a source for local historiography.[40]

In 1518 he compiled a list of all the possessions of his abbey, as he was working on a history of his monastery in sixty-two chapters, which was then continued with five more chapters covering the years up to 1542: *Annales sive Cronicon domus Alderspacensis*[41] (see Fig. 6). He

---

[39] A transcript of the manuscript, part 2, is given here, following the internet version at www.mgfuerstenzell.de:
Secundus de bello Norico Liber
Principio postquam bellonae semina dirae
Boiugenumque annos odii fervore calentes
Lusimus et martis dedimus primordia saevi
Ordiar hinc rerum seriem[,] aspirate canenti
Pierides, plectris animam Gaiorgius umbris
Ut vacuis princeps animam Gaiorgius umbris
Miscuit[,] et regni cupidos finivit honores[,]
Funus Lanzhutam deducit non sine pompa
Militis egregii processio[,] claraque turba
Heroum[,] qui duo comitantur in ordine tristi
Abbates[,] de more mitraque stolaque superbi.
Et populus non parvus adest, martyrum qui caterva.
Nobile subsequitur non aequa mente cadaver.
Triste mi[ni]sterium peragunt, nam fletibus altis
15 Ora pudica madent volitant in pectora pugni.
Sunt ibi claustra sacris quondam fundata puellis,
Dulcesonant ubi, Christe, tuas quae iugiter odas,
Foelix vallis habent nomine, nam rite beato
Vivitur hic voto[,] et sub virginitatis amore,
Illic egregius parvam dux suscipit urnam.
Nec non clara premunt patrum monumenta priorum.
Quis per acerba ducis non ploret fata subortis
Nunc lachrymis sancta qui foedera super alebat.
[40] See Oswald, "Gedichte", 314.
[41] Michael Hartig, ed., "Die Annales ecclesiae Alderspacensis des Abtes Wolfgang Marius", *Verhandlungen des Historischen Vereins für Niederbayern* 42 (1906) 1–112; 43 (1907) 1–113; translated into contemporary German by Alois Kapsner and edited in Klugseder, ed., *850 Jahre Zisterzienserkloster*, 51–165 (based on the manuscript in Munich, Clm 1012); Alois Kapsner, "'De bello Norico'. Ein unveröffentlichtes Epos

was convinced of the usefulness of historical studies, and wrote in his preface to the *Annales* about the moral insights that one gains from the study of history.⁴² He occasionally connected the local history of his abbey to world political and ecclesiastical events, as his references to the Bohemian reformer John Hus (c. 1370–1415) and the Councils of Constance and Basel show.⁴³ Marius also mentioned the persecutions of the Jews in Passau and their expulsion in 1477/78.⁴⁴

The influence of Saint Bernard of Clairvaux on Marius and his work is evident at two places. In Chapter 45 of the *Annales*, he writes about the decadence of his abbey around the first half of the fifteenth century, and he deplores that prelates in general do not heed Saint Bernard's words in Book 2, *On Consideration*:

> It is a monstrous thing: the highest position [is filled with] the lowest disposition, the first seat with the lowest low life, a big mouth and a lazy hand, all talk and no fruitful results, stern face and behavior capricious, mighty authority and wavering stability.⁴⁵

In Chapter 47, on the Council of Basel, Marius quotes Bernard's Epistle 42, section 36, to the Bishop of Sens, that abbots should not try to act like bishops. Abbots remain monks, listening to the teaching given on the steps of humility.⁴⁶

In Chapters 62 to 67 Marius describes his activities and the events of his own abbacy. About his contemporary Martin Luther, he says that of all these events it was Luther's teaching that shook the earth most and caused unrest. He briefly lists Luther's writings on faith and good works, Christian freedom, against the sacraments of the Church, the Mass, and monastic vows. Luther's doctrine was accepted, Marius wrote, as if it had fallen straight from heaven. His poison was spread throughout Germany. His message would have won victory, had God himself not aroused discord among Luther's follow-

---

des Abtes Wolfgang Marius von Aldersbach über den Landshuter Erfolgekrieg", in *Ostbairische Grenzmarken: Passauer Jahrbuch für Geschichte, Kunst und Volkskunde* 44 (Passau 2002) 39–56.

⁴² See Klugseder, ed., *850 Jahre Zisterzienserkloster*, 51.
⁴³ See chp. 42, Klugseder, ed., *850 Jahre Zisterzienserkloster*, 115.
⁴⁴ See chp. 55, Klugseder, ed., *850 Jahre Zisterzienserkloster*, 138–139.
⁴⁵ *De consideratione* II.14 in J. Leclercq and H. Rochais, eds., *Sancti Bernardi Opera*, 8 vols. (Rome 1957–1977), vol. 3:422,3–5; hereafter quoted as SBO. Martin Luther made use in a similar way of Bernard's *On Consideration*, see Franz Posset, *Pater Bernhardus: Martin Luther and Bernard of Clairvaux* (Kalamazoo 1999) 353–65.
⁴⁶ Ep 42.36; SBO, vol. 7:130, 9–20. This letter was also quoted by another humanist priest, Wimpfeling; see Chapter One above, 45.

ers, who differed among themselves on the interpretation of the Scriptures. At this point Marius mentioned two booklets of his own,[47] one on the defense of monastic vows and one on the contradictions in Luther's teachings: *Votorum monasticorum tutor* (1526, never printed) and *In aliquot Lutherana paradoxa Dialogus*, a dialogue between an abbot and a monk (1528, but never printed during his lifetime). The latter incorporates numerous ideas of Erasmus of Rotterdam.[48] Defensive about his monastic position, Marius may have been driven in 1534 to translate *The Rule of Saint Benedict* into German, *Sanct Benedikten-Regel*, and to write a prologue and an appendix for the Latin version, *Regula s. Benedicti cum prologo et appendice*.[49] With these works Marius became one of Luther's significant theological humanist opponents. Marius continued his annals with a review of the Peasants' War, the so-called revolution of 1525,[50] which Marius, like other, non-monastic, but more famous humanists,[51] saw as the direct result of Luther's teaching:

> When finally the people everywhere claimed the evangelical freedom for themselves, they banded together and rose up against the princes of the lands, the leaders, and the prelates of the Church. Within a short time they pillaged Franconia, Swabia, and other territories in the southwest of Germany where they burned more than two hundred fortresses and sixty monasteries... It is said that more than 100,000 people died. The other monasteries bribed them with large sums of money. We [at Aldersbach] paid 1,200 Gulden... in 1525.[52]

In Chapter 65 (covering the year 1529/1530) Marius pointed out that as a result of Luther's (alleged) stirring-up of unrest, the universities were deserted and no-one wanted to study the sciences and literature any more. In addition, priests and monks were held in low esteem, with few wanting to follow the monastic way of life.[53] On

---

[47] See chp. 64, Klugseder, ed., *850 Jahre Zisterzienserkloster*, 153–154; Marius' anti-Lutheran writings are edited in part by S. Wiest, *De Wolfgango Mario... scriptore*, 4 vols. (Ingolstadt 1788–92), here in vol. 4 according to Schwaab (see note 3 above).
[48] See Paulus, 584–586.
[49] See Oswald, "Abt", 364; "Gedichte", 312 with note 20.
[50] Peter Blickle, *The Revolution of 1525: The German Peasants' War from a New Perspective*, translated by Thomas A. Brady, Jr., and H. C. Erik Midelfort from the 2nd edition (Baltimore 1981 and 1985).
[51] Erasmus, Mutianus, Beatus Rhenanus, and Ulrich Zasius; see Eckhard Bernstein, "Humanistische Intelligenz und kirchliche Reformen", in *Die Literatur im Übergang vom Mittelalter zur Neuzeit*, 166–197, here 183.
[52] See chp. 64, Klugseder, ed., *850 Jahre Zisterzienserkloster*, 154.
[53] See Klugseder, ed., *850 Jahre Zisterzienserkloster*, 157.

the occasion of the diet of Augsburg in 1530, many disputations on the "Lutheran split" were held as the participants tried to come to an agreement. Since no compromise was reached, Emperor Charles abruptly departed. In Switzerland the discord ended in war. About 18,000 people of Zwingli's party were killed.[54] The Turkish threat became very real. However, Marius continued, these external perils meant little compared to the spiritual ones brought about by "this evil schism" that had already lasted for so many years, killing souls and throwing them into hell. "One heresy after another surfaces; and one sect creates another".[55] He called the discord a "pestilence". The Lutheran sect kept spreading; its representatives gathered at Schmalkalden in 1539 and formed a federation, which, in his opinion, should rather be called a "conspiracy" against the pope in Rome.[56] Marius noted that a general Church council was to convene at Trent in 1542, but added that he had no hope that it would convene in a proper fashion.[57] He concluded his book with a comment on the local wine of that year, namely, that it was sour, while aged wines were very expensive. Throughout that year in Bavaria, they drank good old wines imported from the Rhine and the Neckar Valleys.[58]

In 1542 Marius finished his research on the local history of the diocese of Passau with Lorch and its bishops.[59] For this project he relied on a work of 1462 written by the Viennese theologian and historian, Thomas Ebendorfer (1388–1464).[60] Marius, the reform-minded abbot, was rather critical in his book of the contemporary administrator of the diocese of Passau, Duke Ernest of Bavaria (1500–1560), who obtained the post as a teenager and held it from 1516 to 1540. Yet, Johann von Staupitz met Duke Ernest once and came away with the impression that the duke was on the side of Catholic reformers like himself.[61] In 1540 Ernest became archbishop of Salzburg, a position that his family had wanted for him as early as 1513, when he was only thirteen years old. As prince-bishop of

---

[54] See Klugseder, ed., *850 Jahre Zisterzienserkloster*, 159.
[55] See Klugseder, ed., *850 Jahre Zisterzienserkloster*, 161.
[56] See Klugseder, ed., *850 Jahre Zisterzienserkloster*, 163.
[57] See Klugseder, ed., *850 Jahre Zisterzienserkloster*, 164.
[58] See Klugseder, ed., *850 Jahre Zisterzienserkloster*, 165.
[59] He called his work *Pontificum et Archipraesulum Laureacensis et Patauiensis Ecclesiarum Cathalogus, ab incerto autore editus, per me fratrem Bolfgangum [sic] Abbatem in Alderspach nonnihil castigatus atque abbreviatus.*
[60] See Oswald, "Abt", 370.
[61] On Staupitz and Duke Ernest, see Posset, *The Front-Runner*, 277.

Salzburg he held one of the highest ecclesiastical offices in the German lands, which he resigned in 1554. Marius complained that Duke Ernest was never ordained to the priesthood during his entire reign of twenty-three years as a bishop at Passau, and that he was more interested in things secular than in things spiritual.[62]

Around 1542 Marius compiled a list of popes and emperors, *Ordo et numerus summorum pontificum et imperatorum Romanorum*, and a list of the monks of Aldersbach from 1460 to 1541. His works on the history of his monastery (*Annales*, 1518–1542) and on the history of the bishops of Passau (*Cathalogus*, 1542) are considered to be competent historiography, even by modern criteria.[63]

The Protestant reformers' challenges to monasticism were felt at his abbey. During his time as abbot only seventeen new members entered, and five of them left again. Renewal of monastic life was on Marius' mind, but also on the agenda of the political leaders of Bavaria. The Dukes of Bavaria, William IV and Ludwig, apparently consulted with other territorial lords on this matter. Duke William was advised by the Elector of Saxony, Frederick the Wise, to use Staupitz's services for the reform of the Premonstratensian monasteries within his realm.[64] Abbot Marius was summoned, on the recommendation of Pope Hadrian VI, to the reform committee of August 1522 that was in charge of the visitations of the Bavarian monasteries and also of any counter-actions against Lutheran infiltration. Marius had already written several recommendations on this subject for the synod of the bishops of the ecclesiastical province of Salzburg, held in May 1522 at Mühldorf, a Salzburg enclave. At this synod he was the only monastic representative from the diocese of Passau; Cardinal Matthew Lang was the prince-bishop of Salzburg and Johann von Staupitz the abbot of Saint Peter's Benedictine monastery in Salzburg. Staupitz had been Martin Luther's superior in the Augustinian order, but had switched to the Benedictines. These prelates were involved in both ecclesiastical reforms and the advancement of humanist studies. Staupitz was more interested in spiritual reform,[65] while Duke William focused on ecclesiastical personnel. He

---

[62] See Oswald, "Abt", 373.
[63] See Oswald, "Abt", 365.
[64] Posset, *The Front-Runner*, 259.
[65] For instance, Staupitz purchased for his monastic library in Salzburg Erasmus' Greek edition of the New Testament, Oecolampadius' *Grammatica Graeca*, Melanchthon's *Loci Communes*, and Lorenzo Valla's *Elegantiae*; see Theodor Kolde, *Die deutsche Augustiner-*

delivered a "sharp speech on the reformation of the clergy" at a meeting on ecclesiastical reforms in Regensburg in 1524.[66]

The Nestor of Bavarian historiographers, Johannes Aventinus (1477–1534), praised Marius in a poem as a religious who was filled with wisdom and dedicated to the higher things in heaven as he adorned the cross of the Lord with his verses. This was a hint at Marius' *Christi Fasciculus*. Aventinus prayed to God that Marius, as a leader, would preserve his priests (*mystas*) for the holy life.[67]

Marius decided to write his own obituary and had the text of one of the four drafts carved to frame the red marble slab that covers his grave, and on which he is depicted with staff and rule in his hand. His epitaph[68] (see Fig. 7) reads as follows:

> I, Abbot Bolfgangus Marius, according to God's will have decayed under this marble, and I have become food for the worms. O Christ, my salvation, you have freely given me so much in my life, give now [eternal] rest to [me] the deceased.

Congregation und Johann von Staupitz. Ein Beitrag zur Ordens- und Reformationsgeschichte nach meist ungedruckten Quellen (Gotha 1879) 335, note 1.

[66] *Ein scharffe red auff di Reformation der Geistlichen*; W. Hauthaler, "Cardinal Mattäus Lang und die religiös-sociale Bewegung seiner Zeit. Zumeist nach Salzburger Archivalien. II. Theil", *Mitteilungen der Gesellschaft für Salzburger Landeskunde* 36 (1896) 317–402, here 387; Posset, *The Front-Runner*, 322.

[67] *Tu catus rerum meliora sectans*
Spernis insani populi tumultus.
Tu studes foelix superos, supremam et
  Noscere causam.
Tu bonis cantas avibus, deumque
Concinis vates meliora plectro,
Tu crucem nostril domini deique
  Versibus ornas.
Maximus rerum pater optimusque
Te precor servet duce te sequentes
Servet et mystas meliora vitae
  Vota beatae.

Gloning, "Gedichtesammlung", 77–78. On Aventinus, see Alois Schmid, entry "Aventinus" in *Lexikon der Reformationszeit*, 51–52.

[68] *Abbas Bolfgangus Marius post fata sub isto*
Marmore computrui, et vermibus esca fui,
Munera viuenti tua, que mihi sponte dedisti,
Defuncto requiem, da, mea Christe salus.

Paulus, 588; Gloning, "Gedichtesammlung", 89.

Fig. 7. Tombstone of Bolfgangus Marius, Abbot of Aldersbach, Bavaria. Parish Archive Aldersbach. From: *850 Jahre Zisterzienserkloster Aldersbach 1996* (Vilshofen 1996), 47.

CHAPTER FOUR

A LATINIST, SUPPORTER OF REUCHLIN, AND EDITOR OF CHRIST-CENTERED POETRY: HENRICUS URBANUS, MONK OF GEORGENTHAL, THURINGIA

Urbanus is listed among the contemporaries of Erasmus of Rotterdam, is mentioned in one of the *Letters of Obscure Men*[1] and was a close friend of the famous priest and humanist Conradus Mutianus Rufus, who from 1503 was a canon at Saint Mary's in Gotha. Mutianus was the leader of the humanists in the Erfurt/Gotha region; after 1505 they became a quite radical group of poets and scholars.[2] Mutianus went to study at Erfurt in 1486, earned his master's degree in the liberal arts in 1492, and continued his studies at Bologna, Rome, and Ferrara, where in 1501 he earned a doctor's degree in canon law.[3] At Gotha, he became an independent scholar, spending most of his time on humanist studies. Until about 1515, Mutianus was recognized as the leader of the Erfurt humanists. The correspondence between Canon Mutianus and the Cistercian monk Urbanus

---

[1] See Erich Kleineidam, "Henricus Urbanus" in Peter G. Bietenholz and Thomas B. Deutscher, eds., *Contemporaries of Erasmus: a biographical register of the Renaissance and Reformation*, 3 vols. (Toronto and Buffalo 1985–1987) vol. 3:355–356. His name is found together with those of Eobanus Hessus, Georg Spalatin, Ulrich von Hutten, and others, in the letter of "Petermann Kachelofen, Licentiate, to Magister Ortwin Gratius" in: *On the Eve of the Reformation. "Letters of Obscure Men"*, translated by Francis Griffin Stokes. New introduction by Hajo Holborn (New York etc., 1964), 79 (I.38).

[2] According to Erich Kleineidam, *Universitas Studii Erffordensis* (Leipzig 1969, 2nd ed. 1992) vol. 2:223, the following men were members: Crotus Rubeanus, Peter Eberbach (Petreius), Eobanus Hessus, Euricius Cordus, Ulrich von Hutten, Johannes Lang, Justus Jonas, Adam Krafft (Crato), Justus Menius, and Johannes Camerarius. Urbanus is not included in this list, although he was always in close contact with the leader Mutianus, as their correspondence shows. On Mutianus' correspondence see now Fidel Rädle, "Mutians Briefwechsel und der Erfurter Humanismus", in Gerlinde Huber-Rebenich and Walther Ludwig, eds., *Humanismus in Erfurt* (Erfurt 2002) 111–129.

[3] See Peter Walter, "Mutianus Rufus", *Lexikon der Reformationszeit* (2002) 535; Eckhard Bernstein, "Humanistische Standeskultur", in *Die Literatur im Übergang vom Mittelalter zur Neuzeit*, 97–129, here 125–126.

Fig. 8. Crotus' Rectorate Page with Urbanus' emblem in the center of the bottom row, c.1521. Stadtarchiv Erfurt, Germany.

began on 29 June 1505.[4] On 14 November 1513 Mutianus called him a master, perfected in every kind of humanist erudition.[5]

The reasons we still know of this Cistercian monk are as follows: (1) his name is mentioned in the correspondence between Mutianus and Erasmus (Erasmus, Ep. 1425);[6] (2) he collected much of the correspondence of his more famous friend Mutianus[7] that would otherwise have been lost. Mutianus repeatedly requested that Urbanus destroy his letters, which, fortunately, Urbanus ignored; (3) Urbanus' name is associated with the edition of a poem on Christ Crucified by Marcus Marulus (see below). Apparently, Urbanus did not write or publish anything of his own. Yet, he recognized the significance of works by Marulus, who became an admirer of Erasmus.[8]

Remarkably, we find the Cistercian Urbanus in the illustrious company of seventeen humanists on the beautifully decorated page of the rector of the University of Erfurt of 1521, Crotus Rubeanus (c. 1480–1545), a document that marks the end of his term in office in 1521. The humanists are represented by their emblems which make up the frame of the page. Four major figures of the time are represented and their emblems placed in the four corners: Erasmus of Rotterdam, Johann Reuchlin, Mutianus Rufus, and Martin Luther. Urbanus' emblem is located at the center of the bottom row of emblems.[9]

Urbanus was probably younger than Mutianus, who in 1494 was Urbanus' teacher.[10] Urbanus became his "best and greatest friend".[11]

---

[4] See Mutianus' letter of 29 June 1505 to Urbanus, in Krause, *Der Briefwechsel des Mutianus Rufus*, 13 (no. 11); hereafter quoted as Krause. The other edition, *Der Briefwechsel des Conradus Mutianus*, ed. Karl Gillert, 2 vols. (Halle 1890) was not available to me.

[5] *Henrico Urbano magistro in omni genere humanitatis perfecto*, according to Junghans, *Der junge Luther*, 229.

[6] Mutianus to Erasmus in February or March 1524.

[7] See the description of the codex at Frankfurt with its 522 letters collected by Urbanus, RBW 2, XXXV.

[8] See Bratislav Lučin, "Erasmus and the Croats in the Fifteenth and Sixteenth Centuries" in: *Erasmus of Rotterdam Society Yearbook* 24 (2004) 89–114, here 100–101.

[9] See Bernstein, "Der Erfurter Humanistenkreis", 137–165; Posset, "Polyglot Humanism in Germany Around 1520" (see note 17 in Introduction).

[10] See Martin Burgdorf, *Der Einfluß der Erfurter Humanisten auf Luthers Entwicklung bis 1510* (Leipzig [n.d.] c. 1925) 32.

[11] *Vale, mi Urbane, amicorum optime, maxime* (Letter of spring 1506), Krause, 65 (no. 60).

The monk once received a silver signet-ring from him. Mutianus appears to have assigned certain insignia to his younger admirers and friends: to Crotus Rubeanus the hunter's horn, to Spalatin the stork as the symbol of *pietas* and dedication to the education of offspring according to Pliny,[12] and to Urbanus one half of a carriage (*rotae dimidium*)[13] (i.e., two wheels of a four-wheeled wagon; the two wheels are shown with the emblem on Rector Crotus' page of 1521). Mutianus gives a witty reason for his gift: Urbanus did not yet have his own seal, and he (Mutianus) wanted to assist him in finding one, at least one half of a wagon. He would now have his own permanent seal so that he would no longer be forced when signing letters to use a coin (*nomisma*). Furthermore, he weighed carefully several other reasons for it: the two wheels were a reminder that the city in which he lived belonged to two bishops, of Mainz and of Osnabrück, who both claimed the entire four-wheeled wagon. Mutianus explains further that he read in the books of Saint Bernard (*divus Bernardus*) that this most holy father (i.e., of the Cistercians, the order to which Urbanus belonged) had lost his own seal. And, as a humanist, he had to quote one of the ancient authors, Hesiod, who once said that half is better than the whole, that is, he preferred the moderate to the immoderate.[14] For all these reasons, Urbanus' seal shows only two of a normally four-wheeled wagon.

Urbanus' emblem also reflects his religious background, as it includes the abbreviation C. M. T., for the slogan *Christus mundum transigit* ("Christ overcomes the world"), entered on a golden background.[15] However, a discrepancy exists between Urbanus' emblem and the name that was ascribed to it in a handwritten, abbreviated addendum of a later date (i.e., *Urbanus Rhegius*, who has no con-

---

[12] *Spalatinum officio pietatis insignem donavi ciconia, cujus pietatem Plinius et Graeci celebrant* (Pliny X, 2332), Mutianus' letter of 11 November 1512 to Urbanus; Krause, 261–262 (no. 207). On the iconography of the stork as a symbol of *pietas*, see James D. Garrison, *Pietas from Vergil to Dryden* (University Park, Penn. 1992) 49–60 with illustrations 2–4.

[13] *Rotae dimidium* does not mean half a wheel, as Krause, 261, assumes, but half a wagon.

[14] See Letter of 11 November 1512; Krause, 262 (no. 207).

[15] See August Emil Frey, a researcher in the nineteenth century and an Evangelical-Lutheran pastor at Saint Marcus in Brooklyn, NY, *Luther und seine Freunde. Erster Theil. Die Freunde Luthers bis zum Beginne der Reformation* (Saint Louis 1884) 67. Bernstein, however, interpreted the abbreviations as German words, for *Christus mein Trost* (Christ is my comfort), "Der Erfurter Humanistenkreis", 153.

nection to the Erfurt humanists around Crotus).[16] The confusion of the names of these two humanists is understandable.[17] Today it is clear, however, that the later entry of the name Urbanus Rhegius was a mistake.

What is known of the monk Henricus Urbanus? His original name was Heinrich (Henric[h]us) Fastnacht from Orb (*Urba*, in Latin), a town near Gelnhausen. According to a document in the archives of Gotha, he was known as *Henricus Fastnacht*, with the designation of his profession as *Hoffemeister* (i.e., *Hofmeister*) at Erfurt; this was an office within the ecclesiastical feudal system meaning 'steward'.[18] He belonged to the Cistercian monastery of Georgenthal,[19] near Gotha in Thuringia, where he also held the position of steward.[20] His priest-friend, Canon Mutianus, called Urbanus' vowed life in the Cistercian order the "piety with the haircut", or the "piety of the tonsure" (*attonita pietas*),[21] referring to the distinct monastic haircut. The dates of his birth and death are not known.[22]

To gain more information on this humanist monk, it is necessary to study his correspondence. Most of the letters that we have are those that were exchanged between Urbanus and Mutianus, particularly those collected by Urbanus as he received them.[23] Mutianus was a scholar of Latin and Greek without attachment to a university in his later years. During the period 1499–1503, before Mutianus traveled to Italy where, among others, he visited the famous monastic humanist, the Carmelite Baptista Mantuan at Mantua,[24] Urbanus had the chance to get to know Mutianus as his teacher in Erfurt.[25]

---

[16] See Frey, *Luther und seine Freunde*, 67.
[17] Martin Lehmann in his biography of Justus Jonas still has it for Urbanus Rhegius: *Justus Jonas: Loyal Reformer* (Minneapolis 1963) 27.
[18] See Krause, VIII, note 1 with reference to the research by K. Gillert. For further clarification of the designation *Hofmeister*, I am grateful to Gerhard Winkler.
[19] Cistercian since 1143, a filiation of Morimond.
[20] Urbanus is addressed as *H. Urbano oeconomo et patri familias coenobitarum* in Mutianus' letter of August or September 1505 to Urbanus; Krause, 22 (no. 21), note 1.
[21] *Oh miseram conditionem attonsae pietatis!* Krause, 108 (no. 92).
[22] The last trace of his life suggests the time of his death as October 1538, after his monastery of Georgenthal had been devastated in the 1520s during the Peasants' War; see Krause, X; the same date of death is given in RBW 2, 403, note 2.
[23] See Krause, in his Introduction, X.
[24] See Krause, 52, note 2.
[25] This information is provided by Irmgard Höss, *Georg Spalatin 1484–1545. Ein Leben in der Zeit des Humanismus und der Reformation* (Weimar 1989; 2nd ed.) 20.

114   CHAPTER FOUR

Fig. 9. Granary of the monastery of Georgenthal, the only building that survived the Peasants' War in 1525. Photo from c. 1902 in the private possession of the author.

Whether Urbanus learned Greek at that time (or how much) is hard to determine. We do not know whether he knew of and studied the *Orthographia*, a book on the correct spelling of Latin and Greek edited by Nikolaus Marschalk (c. 1470–1525) at Erfurt in 1501.[26] We do not know the date of his ordination to the priesthood. However, by August 1505 he was a priest, as he is called at that time "a priest of Saint Bernard",[27] a "specimen of Bernard's family",[28] "a true Israelite, and the most humanist presbyter",[29] "patron of the muses".[30] However, he does not appear to have had a formal university degree at this time.

His job as steward was not restricted to the monastery at Georgenthal, as his monastery had other possessions in the surrounding areas, including at Gotha and Erfurt. By about 1505, Urbanus and Mutianus had had a chance to meet and to become friends, as one learns from their correspondence.[31] Mutianus offered to help him with his humanist studies[32] and also gave him a copy of the book *De integritate* by Jacob Wimpfeling, published in January 1505. Mutianus must have liked this book.[33] In *De integritate* Wimpfeling was critical of monks and friars and of the value of the monastic life in general. It makes one wonder why Mutianus gave it to Urbanus, a Cistercian monk, at all.

Apparently, Urbanus had the task of preaching, at least occasionally, because for the feast day of Mary's birth on 8 September 1505, Mutianus promised to send him a sermon text to be used at his monastery.[34] Also in that year, 1505, Urbanus' and Mutianus' mutual friendship expanded to include the twenty-one-year-old Georg

---

[26] See Junghans, *Der junge Luther*, 35. Marschalk's book was the first Greek textbook edited in Germany.

[27] *H. Urbano divi Bernardi sacerdoti*, Mutianus' letter of about 1505 to Urbanus; Krause, 3 (no. 3); *presbyter Bernardi*, Mutianus' letter of about 1505 to Urbanus; Krause, 5 (no. 5).

[28] *Vale tu feliciter, mi Urbane, decus et specimen Bernardianae familiae*. Mutianus' letter of 1506/07 to Urbanus; Krause, 67 (no. 62).

[29] *Henrico Urbano, vero Israelitae, prebyterorum humanissimo*, Mutianus' letter of 1505 (?) to Urbanus; Krause, 33 (no. 27).

[30] *Musarum patronus*, Mutianus' letter of the summer of 1505 to Urbanus; Krause, 16 (no. 15).

[31] See Krause, VIII.

[32] See Mutianus' letter of 29 June 1505 to Urbanus; Krause, 13 (no. 11); this fact is mentioned also by Junghans, *Der junge Luther*, 73.

[33] See Burgdorf, 82–83.

[34] See the letter dated prior to 8 September 1505; Krause, 22 (no. 20).

Spalatin, who had been the amanuensis (assistant) of Nikolaus Marschalk.[35] Spalatin would later become an influential Lutheran reformer. Mutianus called their triangular relationship a "triumvir of our friendship".[36] Mutianus recommended Spalatin for a teaching position at Urbanus' monastery, i.e., as a teacher of the novices.[37] From a remark by Mutianus at that time, teaching novices Latin was part of his assignment.[38] With Spalatin working there, Mutianus claimed that Urbanus' monastery would soon become famous among the monasteries of Germany.[39] Spalatin stayed at Georgenthal from 1505 to 1508, not only as a teacher but also as the director of the monastic library.[40]

The three men, Mutianus, Spalatin, and Urbanus were known to the public as "the poets", which was a derogatory designation at that time. Urbanus recalled having heard a Benedictine monk say that "poets ruin the universities",[41] reflecting a conservative's fear of anti-scholastic humanism. Everything they said sounded Greek to outsiders: "They speak Greek in contrast to the tradition and they think like atheists", according to contemporary public opinion cited by Mutianus.[42] In reality, they were spiritual men, who liked to read Saint Bernard and the Carmelite Baptista Mantuan. In a letter of January 1506 to Spalatin, Mutianus indicates that he warms himself with reading the books from the Cistercian library, including Baptista Mantuan; and, since Spalatin was at the (Cistercian) monastery all day long together with their mutual friend Urbanus, he should make sure that he loved Saint Benedict and his Rule (by which the Cistercians lived) no less than Saint Bernard himself. Mutianus thanked God for Saint Benedict and the "sect" (*secta*) of the Cistercians (who followed the *Regula monasticorum*). Mutianus expressed fondness for the

---

[35] We know of his position from a note on the back of the title page of a book printed in 1501, *Laus musarum ex Hesiodi. Ascraei Theogonia*... (ed. Spalatin); see Höss, 12 and 442; Junghans, *Der junge Luther*, 40.

[36] *Triumviratum amicitiae nostrae*, letter to Urbanus in 1505; Krause, 34 (no. 27).

[37] See Mutianus' letter of 1505 to Urbanus; Krause, 8 (no. 8). What subject(s) Spalatin had to teach is not specified in the otherwise rather elaborate biography by Irmgard Höss.

[38] See Höss, 38.

[39] See Mutianus' letter of the summer of 1515 to Urbanus; Krause, 16 (no. 15); see Höss, 27.

[40] See Höss, 27–41.

[41] *Poeten verderben die Universitäten*, as quoted by Burgdorf, 28.

[42] *Urbanus, Spalatinus, Mutianus poetae sunt, graece loquuntur; de rebus divinis impie sentiunt*; Mutianus' letter of about 1506 to Urbanus; Krause, 52 (no. 46).

Cistercians mainly because, through Urbanus, they supplied him with the necessities of life and books. He called the Cistercians of Georgenthal the "most benign fathers of the order of the Cistercians". Mutianus confessed that he was moved to tears when he read the praise of the Cistercians under Father Benedict in a book[43] which he had borrowed from the library of Georgenthal. About Saint Bernard he (Spalatin) could learn from monastic hearsay that he was a "very sweet and most affable man", and Spalatin should sharpen his pen so that he could become the public defender and eulogist of both these fathers, Benedict and Bernard.[44] In Mutianus' letter of 1505, Saint Bernard's words on patience and humility had already been recommended to Urbanus: "Your Bernard lifts up patience with wonderful praises".[45] Bernard was esteemed so highly in these circles that Mutianus asked Urbanus to write a biography of Saint Bernard.[46] This suggestion is somewhat surprising, since numerous vernacular booklets on Bernard's life had already been published by that time (c. 1475).[47] To the Erfurt/Gotha humanists, Saint Bernard was the leader of "Christ's militia".[48] Monastic life in the Cistercian order with the admirable example of Bernard was preferred over the others.[49] In an earlier letter, Mutianus had written that he did not care for those who followed the rules of Saint Augustine and Saint Francis[50] (i.e., of the mendicant friars, not monks like Urbanus).

---

[43] It was a book (with woodcuts) about the monastic rules of Benedict, Basil, Augustine, and Francis, printed at Venice in 1500. From it Mutianus quoted and commented on his tears: *Ex Benedicti schola novem clariores sectae provenerunt. Inter quos Cistercienses non sunt infimi. Mirum in modum delectavit me picture cum his verborum illectationibus: "Venite benedicti patris mei, benedicti vos a domino, qui fecit coelum et terram. Respice de coelo et vide et visita vineam istam, memor esto congregationis tuae, pater sanctissimae". Mi Spalatine, nun demum sentio me pii et religiosi cordis esse. Ita haec verba movent et paene lacrimas excitant. Pergo legere: invenio commentarium Joannis Turris Crematae Cardinalis* [†1468]; Krause, 59 (no. 53).

[44] See Krause, 58–60 (no. 53). In this letter Mutianus added that he did not care for the rule und teachings of Augustine and Francis: *Nam Augustini et Francisci dogmata nihil moror* (Krause, 60).

[45] Krause, 51 (no. 48).

[46] *Cur non scribes vitam divi Bernardi?* Letter of 15 May 1507; Krause, 75–76 (no. 70).

[47] See Franz Posset, "Saint Bernard of Clairvaux in the Devotion, Theology, and Art of the Sixteenth Century", *Lutheran Quarterly* 11 (1997) 308-52, here note 9 with a review of editions of the "Life of Saint Bernard" (*Leben sant Bernharts*).

[48] See Mutianus' letter of 21 December 1507 (?); Krause, 88 (no. 82).

[49] *Miramur in divo Bernardo, monasticae vitae celebri auctore...*, Mutianus' letter of 13 April 1508 to Urbanus; Krause, 91–94 (no. 85). See Mutianus' letter of c. 1508 to Urbanus; Krause, 106 (no. 91).

[50] See Krause, 60 (no. 53).

Evidently, these humanists enjoyed the great popularity of Saint Bernard at that time, which culminated in what may be called the "Bernard Renaissance"[51] of the fifteenth century.

In the correspondence of these men, humanist Latin was used. It may at times have sounded confusing, especially when Mutianus wrote to Urbanus that he had the "grace of Jupiter". He applied the names of ancient pagan gods to notions of the Christian religion. At one point Mutianus had to clarify his meaning:

> There is only one god and one goddess; but there are many forms and many names—Jupiter, Sol, Apollo, Moses, Christ, Luna, Ceres, Proserpina, Tellus, Mary... In religious matters we must employ fables and enigmas as a veil. You [in speaking to Urbanus] who have the grace of Jupiter, the best and greatest God, should in secret despise the little gods. When I say Jupiter, I mean Christ and the true God. But enough of these things which are too high for us.[52]

Supposedly, these humanists spoke Greek. It is, however, hard to determine how much Greek Urbanus actually knew. In one of the early letters of Mutianus to Urbanus (1505), we find he assumes that his correspondent knew some Greek, using a Greek word for "fish eaters" (but with its Latin translation).[53]

The study of Greek was definitely on the rise in the Erfurt circle at this time. In 1499 the printer Wolfgang Schenck produced the first Greek texts in Erfurt, investing his money on the cutting of Greek letters for his printing press. Two years earlier, Anton Koberger had begun using Greek letters in his workshop at Nuremberg.[54]

While we are uncertain about his expertise in Greek, Urbanus' outstanding knowledge of classical Latin is beyond doubt. Mutianus addresses him occasionally as an "ingenious and Latin man".[55] In Mutianus' letter to Urbanus (dated prior to 1505) the Cistercian monk is honored with a poem that calls him an eager user of Latin.[56]

---

[51] Berndt Hamm, *Frömmigkeitstheologie am Anfang des 16. Jahrhunderts* (Tübingen 1982) 193.

[52] Krause, 94 (no. 85); quoted also in Bernard M. G. Reardon, *Religious thought in the Reformation* (London and New York 1981) 21; Reardon commented that Mutianus later curbed his paganizing fancy, but his contempt both for scholasticism and for ecclesiastical officialdom persisted (p. 22).

[53] See Krause, 8 (no. 8).

[54] See Junghans, *Der junge Luther*, 34, note 130.

[55] Letter of 1505; Krause, 36 (no. 20).

[56] *Et prodesse studet latinitati*; Krause, 1 (no. 1).

Nothing is known about Urbanus' knowledge of Hebrew, the third of the three sacred languages that Renaissance humanists ideally aimed to master (*vir trilinguis*).

In 1505/1506, Urbanus was in contact with the printer Aldus Manutius (c. 1450–1515) in Venice, for the purchase of books. On this occasion he asked for his friendship.[57] Apparently, the monastery librarian, Spalatin, used Aldus as his supplier of books. The best editions of Greek and Latin works came from Italian printers, in pocketbook format.[58] Spalatin and Urbanus ordered the following books for their cloister library:[59] *Magnum Etymologicum*,[60] *Vocabularium Iulii Pollucis*,[61] *Epistolae Merulae*,[62] and the works of the Greek Cardinal Bessarion (1403–1472).[63] Aldus was probably very happy that the Germans bought these books, as they were considered highly priced.[64] In response, Aldus wrote to Urbanus about the latter and his two friends, Mutianus and Spalatin, as follows:

> I most highly esteem Mutianus Rufus because of his learning and humanity and confess myself to be very much in his debt, on the one hand because he constantly speaks well of me, and on the other because he kindly procured for me the friendship of a man decked out with learning and holy ways like you. And therefore if I did not only completely esteem you and Mutianus and Spalatinus as men both learned and well-disposed towards me, but also love you so very much in return, I would be the most ungrateful man of all.[65]

Other books of interest to these German humanists became available at the Frankfurt Book Fair in 1506. They included *Athanasius* and Reuchlin's *Rudimenta hebraica* (edited in March 1506) and a book

---

[57] Urbanus' letter of 20 November 1505 to Aldus Manutius; Krause, 46f (no. 40).
[58] See Höss, 28; on Aldus, see Wilson, *From Byzantium to Italy*, 127–148.
[59] See Höss, 29, note 7.
[60] A later edition is known: *Mega etymologicon = magnum etymologicum Graecae linguae, nunc recens summa adhibita diligentia excusum & innumerabilibus pene dictionibus locupletatum* (Venice 1549).
[61] Presumably, Pollux, 'the Grammarian' (2nd century A.D.), Greek lexicographer and rhetorician.
[62] Presumably, Georgius Merula (c. 1430–1494), Italian humanist and classical scholar.
[63] No book titles were specified. On him, see Ludwig Mohler, *Kardinal Bessarion als Theologe, Humanist und Staatsmann* (Paderborn 1923–1942; reprint: Aalen 1967). Bessarion's Latin version of *Xenophon* may have been one of the books they bought.
[64] On Aldus' book prices, see Wilson, *From Byzantium to Italy*, 128 and 133. For example, the five volumes of Aristotle cost eleven gold pieces.
[65] Letter of 22 February 1506; Krause, 48 (no. 43).

on "Christ's Passion with very beautiful and incomparable pictures".[66] Perhaps this was the *Passio Iesu Christi Saluatoris mundi vario Carminum genere F. Benedicti Chelidonij Musophili doctissime descripta* (if printed in 1506) with woodcuts by Wechtelin and lyrics by Chelidonius,[67] or (even more likely) it may have been the *Passio Christi* by Geiler von Kaisersberg (see below).

The friendly gatherings of Urbanus, Spalatin, and Mutianus lasted for about three years. Then all of a sudden, in the summer of 1508, Urbanus was sent into exile to Leipzig. The monk was accused of, or may actually have had, an inappropriate relationship with a nun, who was evidently his friend, a member of the Cistercian convent of the Holy Cross in Gotha, supervised by the monastery of Georgenthal.[68] She had fled the community and was pregnant. Urbanus had to leave[69] in order to avoid a public scandal. We can presume that he lost his job as steward at Georgenthal, but he was not dismissed from the Cistercian order. His abbot, Johannes III (called Duronius, abbot from 1503 to 1525),[70] sent him for further education to the Cistercian college of Saint Bernard at the University of Leipzig, where he was enlisted as *frater sacerdos Henricus de monasterio vallis sancti Georgii* (Georgenthal).[71] There he received his bachelor's degree in 1508.[72] His name is not found in the list of the masters of arts of Leipzig. Yet, he may have received his graduate degree in 1509/1510, as he was addressed at one point as *Urbano magistro Lipsensi* ("to Urbanus, Master of Leipzig").[73]

Urbanus was not happy about this compulsory relocation. His friend Mutianus, who at first appears not to have known the reason

---

[66] See Mutianus' letter of 15 April 1506 to Urbanus; Krause, 64f. (no. 59). The book on 'Christ's Passion' cannot be definitively identified.

[67] On Chelidonius and Wechtelin, see Franz Posset, "Benedictus Chelidonius O.S.B. (C.1460–1521), A Forgotten Monastic Humanist of the Renaissance", ABR 53 (2002) 426–52, here 429.

[68] See Krause, 5, note 1, on Abbot Johannes III of Georgenthal and his patronage of the convent in Gotha.

[69] See Krause, IX; Horst Rudolf Abe, *Der Erfurter Humanismus und seine Zeit: die Geschichte des Erfurter Humanismus bis zum Jahre 1516* (dissertation, Jena 1953) 219, as referred to by Junghans, *Der junge Luther*, 46. Bernstein, "Der Erfurter Humanistenkreis" 148, has Urbanus dismissed from the order altogether, which is probably incorrect.

[70] See Höss, 21.

[71] See Krause, 107 (no. 92), note 1.

[72] See Krause, 117 (no. 99).

[73] Mutianus' letter of 1513/1514 to Urbanus; Krause, 399 (no. 328); Kleineidam, "Urbanus", in *Contemporaries of Erasmus*, vol. 3:355–356.

for his sudden transfer to Leipzig, had to console him in his exile.[74] At that time, Spalatin, too, must have left Georgenthal, as he sent Urbanus a poem for a happy new year, from Torgau in Saxony, probably in January 1509.[75] Urbanus at Leipzig did not continue his correspondence, as Mutianus complained about his silence, and in doing so also mentioned in passing the low quality of education he would receive at Leipzig.[76] Unaware of the reason for Urbanus' relocation, Mutianus wrote to him that he was not sure whether he should congratulate him or feel sorry for him on his transfer to Leipzig, being an innocent man who had suddenly been thrown into an exile where a learned monk would have to endure inferior teachers. Such a situation was due to living under the monastic vow of obedience, as Mutianus exclaimed: "O what a miserable condition, to live under the tonsured way of life!" (*attonsa pietatis*). However, Mutianus consoled him that on his return with a graduate degree he might have a chance, some day, to become an abbot. He concluded his letter with a reference to the monastic humanist Baptista Manutan, whose book on patience he should read (*De patientia*).[77]

It appears that Mutianus became aware of the circumstances of Urbanus' transfer only in late summer of 1510. From a letter (dated after 11 July 1510) that Mutianus wrote to Urbanus, we know that Mutianus now knew of the sex scandal in which Urbanus was involved. In this letter Mutianus mentions the abbot who had interrogated him when he was called to Georgenthal in order to be interviewed about Urbanus' alleged sexual relations. Mutianus persuaded the abbot that silence should be observed so that a scandal could be avoided. The abbot decided that the crime was to be denied.[78] In doing this, the abbot did the right thing, Mutianus opined, who in turn pointed out that he told the abbot that he did not believe that Urbanus was the perpetrator. Urbanus wrote to him[79] that he was innocent and that he called upon God as his witness.[80] In another letter of that same period, Mutianus wrote to Urbanus that if he

---

[74] See Mutianus' letter of the summer of 1508; Krause, 107–108 (no. 92).
[75] See Krause, 129 (no. 108).
[76] See letter of 19 October 1508; Krause, 117–119 (no. 99).
[77] See letter of the summer of 1508; Krause, 107f. (no. 92).
[78] *Crimen infitiatur*, Krause, 181 (no. 140).
[79] The letter is lost.
[80] *[Urbanus] scripsit et mihi se innocentem esse deum testem advocando*, letter of 11 July or later, 1510; Krause, 181 (no. 140).

did not rape his lover, he should not be concerned, and he should wash the whole affair down with a glass of good wine, as the ancient adage says: "Evius [Bacchus] dissipates destructive worries".[81] Around Easter 1509, Urbanus was appointed to an administrative post at another house (*Hof*) that the Cistercians owned at Erfurt, which was called *Georgenthaler Hof*.[82] This assignment appears to have marked the end of the affair at Gotha.

Mutianus wished Urbanus to continue his studies of Greek and he recommended the learned physician Christophorus Sonfeld at Leipzig as a potential teacher.[83] However, Urbanus' Greek instructor was someone else, namely a master from Crete (*sub magistro Cretense*) whose name is not known.[84] In later letters mention is made of several teachers from Crete who were to be consulted about the pronunciation of Greek words.[85] Apparently scholars in Germany at that time hired native speakers of Greek to teach them this language.[86]

In the fall of 1509, Urbanus started his new job at Erfurt. He still had time for visiting Georgenthal, and also for visiting Spalatin in Torgau.[87] Urbanus hoped not to have to return to Georgenthal permanently, as may be inferred from Mutianus' letter to him in June 1510.[88] He stayed at Erfurt, from where he got involved in helping Spalatin, who was illegitimate, to obtain papal dispensation from this 'defect' in order to qualify for higher-paid ecclesiastical positions. Sometime in 1512, Spalatin sent his request to Rome for the necessary diploma of dispensation. The first hint about this action can be found in a letter that Urbanus received from Mutianus.[89]

---

[81] *Sin autem non rapuisti amatam, mitte consternationem et bibe bonum vinum. "Dissipat curas Evius edaces"*, see Krause, 188 (no. 141). The adage quoted by Mutianus is that of Horace.

[82] See Mutianus' letters of that time, Krause, 134–39 (nos. 111, 112, 113). See Walter Schmid-Ewald, "Der Georgenthaler Hof in Erfurt", *Mitteilungen des Vereins für Geschichte und Altertumskunde von Erfurt* 46 (1930) 94–106.

[83] See Mutianus' letter of the beginning of June 1509 to Urbanus; Krause, 146–147 (no. 117). A letter of Urbanus to Sonfeld is extant, Krause, 264 (no. 209).

[84] See Krause, 136 (no. 111).

[85] See Mutianus' letter of 21 April 1517 to Johannes Lang, Krause, 616 (no. 548). *Quid tui Cretenses?* Mutianus' letter of 15 May 1517 to Lang; Krause, 619 (no. 550).

[86] The editor Krause speaks of Cretan monks (in the plural), Krause, 616 (no. 548), note 4.

[87] See Krause, 169 (no. 133), note.

[88] See Krause, 172–173 (no. 136).

[89] See letter of 30 September 1512; Krause, 248f (no. 195); Höss, 57.

Urbanus, who as chief financial officer of the monastery had access to funds, had to lend the impoverished Spalatin the required sum of money (15 gold *gulden*) in order to pay the fee to the papal authorities.[90] Finally, on 3 October 1513 Mutianus could report to Urbanus that Spalatin had found in him (Urbanus) his "unique savior", whom he would repay what he owed.[91]

In 1513, Urbanus was encouraged by Mutianus to write a letter of support to their embattled humanist colleague, Johann Reuchlin, who was involved in one of the greatest controversies of the sixteenth century and which carries his name (the 'Reuchlin Controversy' or 'Affair').[92] Reuchlin had dared to defend the use of Jewish books against Johannes Pfefferkorn. Around 20 August 1513 Urbanus complied with Mutianus' wish. In his letter he addresses Reuchlin as a "philosopher, lawyer and theologian, and as his most sweet teacher".[93] With great joy, Urbanus wrote, did he observe how he (Reuchlin) stood up to the so-called theologians (*theologista*) at Cologne in defense of the ancient theology (*prisca theologia*, an expression coined by Marsilio Ficino [1433–1499], with a neo-platonic connotation)[94] and in defense of his Hebrew clients (*Hebrais clientibus*), the Jews. Apparently Urbanus viewed Reuchlin's defense of the Jews in a positive light, compared to Mutianus who criticized Reuchlin for doing damage to Christians by favoring the Jews.[95] Perhaps Mutianus' unfavorable opinion was the real reason for his urging Urbanus to write a letter to Reuchlin rather than writing one himself. Urbanus included a poem against Reuchlin's enemies.[96] In his response of 22 August 1513, Reuchlin praised Urbanus for his careful reading of his *Defensio* and, addressing him as a priest of the Cistercian order at Erfurt, called him his most learned and beloved friend who defended his innocence against slanderers.[97]

---

[90] See Mutianus' letter of 1513 (?) to Urbanus; Krause, 286 (no. 231); Höss dated this letter for the period between 29 August and 3 October 1513.
[91] *Spalatini tu unicus es salvator. Gratiam referet et solvet debita. Vale*, Krause, 380 (no. 307); Höss, 58–60.
[92] See Erika Rummel, *The Case against Johann Reuchlin: Religious and Social Controversy in Sixteenth-Century Germany* (Toronto etc. 2002).
[93] ... *praeceptori suo dulciss[imo]*, Urbanus' letter to Reuchlin; Krause, 357–358 (no. 291); RBW 2, 401–402 (no. 223).
[94] See RBW 2, 403, note 5.
[95] See RBW 2, 403, note 4.
[96] The poem, however, may not be from Urbanus' pen, but from that of Mutianus; see note 17 in RBW 2, 405.
[97] See RBW 2, 414 (no. 225).

On 15 October 1513, Urbanus again took up his correspondence with Reuchlin. He excused Mutianus for not writing to him (Reuchlin) because he was busy with the grape harvest (*vindemia*), which must have meant that Mutianus was supervising the harvest. Urbanus reported that the students of literature (*iuventus literaria*) at the University (*gymnasium*) of Erfurt sided with him (Reuchlin) and esteemed him, while the *theologistae* of the faculty of Erfurt (with their so-called 'expert opinion' on the *Eye Mirror* of 3 September 1513) only followed in the footsteps of the theologians of Cologne, displaying their *ignorancia*.[98]

Mutianus also instigated Urbanus to write to their friend Spalatin, now at the court of Frederick the Wise, to explain to him their position on the 'Reuchlin Controversy'. Spalatin brought this matter to the attention of Elector Frederick, who then wrote a letter of support to Reuchlin.[99] He in turn mentioned the elector's support and expressed his gratitude to Mutianus in a letter of 22 August 1513.[100] Years later, when the elector asked for a recommendation of a suitable candidate to teach Greek at the new University of Wittenberg, Reuchlin recommended his twenty-one-year-old grand-nephew, Philip Melanchthon.[101] He was offered the job and accepted it.

From another letter that Urbanus received we learn that the theologians should have been more concerned about a certain Dr. Faustus than about Reuchlin. His full name was Georgius Faustus Helmitheus Hedelbergensis. In this letter of 3 October 1513, we find an unflattering characterization of the legendary Dr. Faustus, who apparently surfaced as a magician in Erfurt at this time. Mutianus, like his humanist friend Johannes Trithemius, simply regarded Dr. Faustus as a charlatan, who eight days ago blew into town. Mutianus called him an idiot (*fatuus*). However, it seems the simple folks admired him. In Mutianus' opinion, the theologians should have been standing up against Faustus rather than against the philosopher Reuchlin (*philosophus Capnio*).[102]

In May 1515, Urbanus sought the friendship of Master Johann Lang of the Augustinian order in Erfurt. At that time an Augustinian

---

[98] *Amat juventus literaria totius hujus gymnasii...*, Krause, 387 (no. 315); RBW 2, 449 (no. 230). On the 'Reuchlin Controversy', see Chapter 6 (Ellenbog).
[99] See Höss, 77.
[100] See Krause, 637 (no. 601).
[101] See Reuchlin's letter to Mutianus of 22 June 1518; Krause, 646–647 (no. 626).
[102] *Capnio* is the humanist name for Reuchlin; Mutianus' letter to Urbanus; Krause, 380 (no. 307).

trio of like-minded friars (i.e. Johann von Staupitz as the head of the Augustinian reformed congregation in Germany, Martin Luther, and Johann Lang) was scheduled to arrive in Gotha for their chapter meeting.[103] In his letter of introduction, Urbanus inserted a quotation in Greek letters from Homer, evidently in order to impress the Augustinians, and in particular Friar Lang, who was an expert in Greek.[104] Clearly Urbanus' Greek studies had borne fruit.

In July 1515 plans were made to attend the Frankfurt Book Fair, and Mutianus asked Urbanus to buy books for him.[105] At that time, Urbanus' position as steward (*oeconomus*) at the Cistercian house in Erfurt seems not to have been very secure. When it became clear, however, that Urbanus was indeed to remain in his position, Mutianus sent him a letter of congratulation.[106]

Evidently Georgenthal had become a rich and powerful monastery, owning large estates. It reached its peak at the beginning of the sixteenth century, perhaps due to its able manager, Urbanus. However, being known for its wealth, the monastery was looted during the Peasants' War of 1525,[107] perhaps by the former Cistercian and now rebel leader Heinrich Pfeiffer, originally from another monastery. Most of its buildings were destroyed, so that the monks of Georgenthal had to flee to Erfurt where they possessed property (i.e., *Georgenthaler Hof*). Evidently it was not advisable at that time to wear the monastic habit outside the monastery. It is said that Urbanus ceased to wear the cowl during the year 1525. His monastery was never rebuilt, but somehow he kept his job in Erfurt as steward at the *Georgenthaler Hof*, in which he was confirmed by the territorial prince (elector) as late as 1534/1535, although apparently the monastery had ceased to exist. It is difficult to say whether Urbanus was now an ex-monk due to the circumstances of the destruction of his monastery or due to the now-fashionable reformational trend of monks and nuns leaving their cloisters. During these early years of the Reformation Urbanus developed a personal friendship with Melanchthon at Wittenberg, but he never seems to have adopted Luther's teachings.[108]

---

[103] On this and on the relationship between Mutianus and Staupitz, see Franz Posset, *The Front-Runner of the Catholic Reformation: The Life and Works of Johann von Staupitz* (Aldershot, Great Britain 2003) 163, 201–204.
[104] See Urbanus' letter of 4 May 1515 to Lang; Krause, 540–541 (no. 475).
[105] See his letter to Urbanus of 19 July 1515; Krause, 569–570 (no. 506).
[106] See Mutianus' letter of September 1515; Krause, 586–587 (no. 523).
[107] See Blickle, *The Revolution of 1525*.
[108] See Kleineidam, "Henricus Urbanus" (see note 1 above).

Urbanus did not leave any written works of his own to posterity. However, he achieved some minor fame as the promoter and editor of a *Carmen* on Christ Crucified which was the work of the then-renowned Croatian humanist Marcus Marulus.[109] Urbanus' success in this regard needs to be seen within the contemporary context of the popularity of Christian verse making.[110]

Occasionally, the *Carmen* was ascribed to Urbanus himself; his friend Mutianus may have given the impression that he thought it was written by Urbanus, to whom he wrote in this regard on 28 May 1513.[111] The editor of Mutianus' correspondence took the words *Vidi Marulum tuum* to mean Urbanus' own work ("I have seen your Marulus").[112] However, Mutianus really may only have meant: "I have seen the book by Marulus which you possess" or "which you lent to me". Mutianus mentioned the poem and the *exempla* again in his letter of 15 June 1513 to Urbanus, who, he said, really should arrange the reprint of this work.[113] He had the entire work of Marulus in mind: *Instruction on How to Lead a Virtuous Life Based on the Example of Saints (Institutio bene vivendi per exempla sanctorum)*. The *Carmen* formed its conclusion.[114] Since this poem was the epilogue to Marulus' *Institutio*, it is definitely not Urbanus' own work. Marulus' *Institutio* was published for the first time in Venice in 1506. It was standard practice with humanist writers and poets to conclude a book with a poem.[115]

Since Mutianus called this text "wholly Christian" in May 1513,[116] he could not have been referring to the 1514 edition, but only to the 1506 or 1509 editions, both of which were edited by Franciscus Lucensis, a priest in Venice.[117] Mutianus evidently meant the main part with the examples of the saints, explaining that he read it "in

---

[109] See Franz Posset, "A Cistercian Monk as Editor of the *Carmen* of the Croatian Humanist Marcus Marulus (died 1524): the German Humanist Henricus Urbanus O.Cist. (died 1538)", CSQ 39 (2004) 399–419.

[110] See Chapter on Marius.

[111] *Nunc ad hilariora veniamus, ut dulce amarumque una misceatur. Vidi Marulum tuum. Carptim legi. Totus est christianus?* Krause, 308–309 (no. 250).

[112] The editor Krause in his note 5 of letter 250 took it as Urbanus' work.

[113] *Paucis ante diebus admonui, ut opus novum exemplorum investires*, Krause, 314 (no. 255).

[114] For excerpts in English, see Bratislav Lučin, ed., "Dossier: Marko Marulić" in *Most / The Bridge. A Journal of the Association of Croatian Writers* 1–4 (1999) 3–171, here 58–63; bibliography on Marulus, 13–14.

[115] See Béné, *Sudbina jedne pjesme. Destin d'un poème. Destiny of a poem*, 91.

[116] *Totus est christianus*, Mutianus' letter of 28 May 1513 to Urbanus, Krause, 309 (no. 250).

[117] See Béné, 98.

pieces" (*carptim*). He obviously selected certain sections from it at different times, that is, from the many pious stories which, as he wrote, the author spouts up. Mutianus thought this collection of stories of the saints would also be beneficial to Urbanus as a preacher.[118]

Marulus' Venetian edition of his *Institutio* with the *Carmen* (1506 and 1509) was evidently so much in demand that it was reprinted in Basel in 1513 and 1518.[119] Perhaps Mutianus did not know, when he urged Urbanus to arrange for a reprint at Erfurt, that a new edition was coming out in Basel in that same year. But since the Basel edition did appear in 1513, at least the *Carmen* by itself should be printed, as it was judged by the two humanists at Erfurt to be worthy of a reprint in a separate booklet. This edition could not have been too costly as it comprises only seven pages. It was printed in 1514 with large, beautifully formed lettering provided by the press of Joannes Canappus (Hans Knappe the Elder) at Erfurt.[120]

Obviously, Mutianus wished that Urbanus' discovery of Marulus' work, including the *Carmen*, should be made more widely known and better promoted from among the many new books that came out of Venice into their part of Germany. The full title of the Latin *Carmen* reads: *M. Maruli Carme[n] de doctrina domini nostri Jesu Christi pende[n]tis in Cruce p[er] modu[m] dialogissmi Christi et Christiani* ("M. Marulus' Song About the Teaching of Our Lord Jesus Christ Hanging on the Cross, by way of a dialogue between Christ and a Christian"). For marketing purposes, Mutianus suggested in his letter of 15 April 1506 (Letter 59) that Urbanus' edition of the *Carmen* should be graced with at least one illustration (the plan of re-publishing Marulus' entire work at Erfurt had apparently been dropped). Publications of Christ-centered poetry by humanists, especially when illustrations were included, were very popular at that time. Mutianus and Urbanus rode on this wave of popularity. Mutianus recommended "dressing the prints of Marulus well from the feet to the hip, yes all the way from head to feet".[121] He may have meant that some eye-catching illustrations should be added to the text, or he may have been alluding to the possibly offensive wording in the *Carmen* on Christ's naked

---

[118] *Vidi Marulum tuum. Carptim legi. Totus est christianus. Piis fabulis et quidem mulijugis scatet, utilis tibi contionaturo*, Krause, 308–309 (no. 250).

[119] Basel: Adamus Petrus de Langendorff, 1513 and 1518; Béné, 98–99.

[120] See the facsimile reprint in Béné, I.1.3.1–7.

[121] Mutianus' letter of June 1513 to Urbanus; Krause, 313 (no. 254).

Fig. 10. Title page of Marulus' *Carmen*, edited by Urbanus (Erfurt: Canappus, 1514), probably patterned after the woodcut of Urs Graf (see Fig. 11). From: Charles Béné, *Sudbina Jedne Pjesme. Destin d'un Poème. Destiny of a Poem. Carmen de Doctrina Domini Nostri Iesu Christi Pendentis in Cruce Marci Maruli* (Split 1994), 1:1.3.2.

Fig. 11. Urs Graf, woodcut in *Passio Christi* by Johann Geiler von Kaisersberg (Strasbourg: Knobloch, 1506). From: Anna Scherbaum, *Albrecht Dürers* Marienleben (Wiesbaden 2004), 311.

body (the Christian in the poem asks Christ: "Why is your body naked?"), a text that would thus require to be "dressed".

Indeed, Urbanus' edition was published with an illustration by an anonymous, less skilled, craftsman who used as his pattern the woodcut of the Swiss goldsmith and graphic designer, Vrs Graf (or Urs, †1527/1528). A comparison of the two pictures leaves no doubt about the anonymous copyist using Graf's woodcut. Graf had marked his woodcut with his initials VG at the bottom of the print, directly under Christ's cross.[122] Graf's woodcut was first used in 1506 for the *Passio Christi* by Johannes Geiler von Kaisersberg, cathedral preacher at Strasbourg. Geiler compiled this book as a gospel harmony and published it through the local printer, Johann Knobloch. Graf's picture is one of twenty-six woodcuts incorporated in the *Passio Christi* of 1506, which was also published in several vernacular versions up to 1509.[123] Urbanus and the printer Canappus, therefore, could have used any of these editions to pattern the title page of their edition of Marulus' *Carmen*.

Christ crucified dominates the center of the picture as he hangs on the *tau* cross. He is shown with a huge crown of thorns and a small loincloth, flanked by the crosses of the two criminals whose bodies are twisted around the beams. The souls of the two criminals are depicted in the form of little naked persons above their heads as they depart from their bodies. The soul of the good thief on Christ's right side is received by an angel of heaven, while the soul of the criminal on the left is grabbed by the hairs by a devil. Soldiers on foot and one on horseback mock Jesus. The horseman, on the left, points his finger to his forehead as he looks at Christ, as if he wants to indicate to Christ by this gesture: "You are crazy!"[124]

The *Carmen* has become a "very beautiful booklet"[125] of only seven pages. The added woodcut makes the Erfurt *Carmen* the first to include a full-page illustration.[126] Urbanus' edition is also the first for

---

[122] See Fig. 79 in Scherbaum, *Albrecht Dürers* Marienleben, 311 (see Chapter 2).
[123] See Scherbaum, *Albrecht Dürers* Marienleben, 179–180. This *Passio Christi* is also known as *Ringmannsche Passion*, after the humanist Matthias Ringmann (1482–1511) who worked for Knobloch as a corrector.
[124] The horseman's gesture is still understood today; see Figs. 10 and 11.
[125] Béné, 99.
[126] See Béné, 99.

north-central Germany, and thus this monk contributed to the further spreading of the fame of its author, the Croatian layman and humanist Marcus Marulus, in these central and northern German lands.[127]

---

[127] Later 16thC editions came out in Cologne in 1530 and 1531 and in Solingen (north of Cologne) in 1540; see Béné, 97; he suspects that the Erfurt edition of 1514 may have been an "impetus for adaptations and translations in Luther's Germany, which remain to be discovered" (Béné, 99). Still later editions of the *Carmen* were published in Antwerp (1577, 1584, 1593, 1601), in Paris (1586), and again in Cologne (1609 and 1686). However, there was never a German translation of it. The *Carmen* was translated into English in the second half of the 16thC by Philip Howard, Earl of Arundel (1557–1595) while he was imprisoned at the Tower of London from 1585 to 1587: *A Dialogue Betwixt a Christian, and Christ Hanging on the Crosse. Written into Latine by Marcus Marulus, & Translated into English*; Béné, II.3.1. A contemporary English version is now (1999) provided by Graham McMaster: *The Song About the Teaching of our Lord Jesus Christ Hanging on the Cross (The Christian Asks, Christ Replies)* in Lučin, ed., "Dossier: Marko Marulić", 75–76; reprinted in Posset, "A Cistercian Monk", 415–419.

CHAPTER FIVE

JACK-OF-ALL-TRADES: VITUS BILD ACROPOLITANUS,
MONK OF SAINTS ULRICH AND AFRA IN AUGSBURG

Vitus Bild was an open-minded monk of the Benedictine monastery of Saints Ulrich and Afra in Augsburg, who usually signed his letters with 'Acropolitanus' in humanist fashion. He was born on 14 April 1481 in Höchstädt, on the Danube, in Bavaria. His humanist name, composed of *acro* and *politanus*, is a reference to his birthplace. He is the most significant representative of monastic humanism in Augsburg.[1] His biography shows impressively how 'monasticism', 'humanism', and 'reformation' came together in a monk's life and work during the Renaissance. We will see him as he copes with the trends and signs of his time in those early years of the Protestant Reformation.

Certainly, for most people today, Bild is an obscure monk. This makes it all the more inspiring to study his life as a monk and how he, as a relatively insignificant scholar and Latin instructor at his monastery school, dealt with the religious and ecclesiastical challenges of his time, without abandoning either his beliefs or his monastery. By the end of Bild's life, circumstances had changed so dramatically that many people could only see the incompatibility of monasticism and the Reformation, as by then a "confessionalization of humanism"[2] and of monasticism had developed. Monks often felt compelled either to stay or to leave their communities dependent on their personal

---

This Chapter is the expanded version of my article "The Benedictine Humanist Vitus Bild (1480–1529): Sundial Producer, Mathematician, Linguist, Poet, Historiographer, Music Expert, Pro-Lutheran, Anti-Zwinglian", ABR 55 (2004) 372–394, based on my entry "Vitus Bild", in BBKL 21 (2003) 116–21.

[1] See Alfred Schröder, "Der Humanist Veit Bild, Mönch bei St. Ulrich: Sein Leben und sein Briefwechsel", *Zeitschrift des Historischen Vereins für Schwaben und Neuburg* 20 (1893) 173–227; Josef Bellot, "Das Benediktinerstift St. Ulrich und Afra in Augsburg und der Humanismus", StM 84 (1973) 394–406; Harald Müller and Anne-Katrin Ziesak, "Der Augsburger Benediktiner Veit Bild und der Humanismus. Eine Projektskizze", *Zeitschrift des historischen Vereins für Schwaben* 95 (2002) 28–51; Klaus Kipf, "Bild", VL (2005).

[2] See Erika Rummel, *The confessionalization of humanism in Reformation Germany* (Oxford and New York 2000). Vitus Bild is not included in Rummel's study.

Fig. 12. Title page of pamphlet on the Creed, *Grund vnnd Schriftliche anzaygungen*, attributed to Vitus (Veit) Bild Acropolitanus (Augsburg: Philipp Ulhart the Elder, 1525). University of Wisconsin Memorial Library, Madison, Wisconsin, 3352 Nr. 1605. From Sixteenth Century Pamphlets on microfiche, pt. 1 (1501–1530) (Leiden: IDC Publishers, 1981), fiche 621, nr. 1605.

adherence to Martin Luther's teaching after 1521 concerning monastic vows.³

Vitus Bild's monastery was an imperial abbey, affected by the reform movement within the order of Saint Benedict that issued from the monastery at Melk in Austria, and influenced also by Renaissance humanism.⁴ Pressured by the local bishop, the Benedictines of Saints Ulrich and Afra opened up to the Melk reforms around 1440. These brought new guidelines for their monastic life and prayer, with a return to a strict observance of the Rule of Saint Benedict. In this reform context, their library was enlarged, and the scribes and copyists were told to concentrate on theological works. Teaching Latin to the novices became a priority.⁵ This work appears to have been Bild's main task.

Bild's life and work is accessible to us chiefly through his correspondence. He collected about 550 letters, beginning in 1506, including 380 letters of his own which he copied and kept. To them he added those letters that he received from 1517 onwards, of which about 170 are still extant. He corresponded with almost forty people, mostly humanists.⁶ On 1 June 1516, for example, he approached Heinrich Bebel, a humanist at Tübingen and a professor of rhetoric and poetry, whose work *Facetarium* (funny stories) he liked. He had just finished the third volume when he sent Bebel six of his own funny tales that he wanted to be added to Bebel's future fourth volume. Bild's stories deal with the blindness of the Jews (*de obstinata perfidorum caecitate Judaeorum*), a dumb and haughty priest (*de presbytero superbo et indocto*), a poor but humble priest (*de presbytero paupere sed humili*), a bold little foot-soldier (*de pedite audaculo*), the curiosity or

---

³ On the impact of Luther's *On Monastic Vows*, see Hans-Christoph Rublack, "Zur Rezeption von Luthers De votis monasticis iudicium", in Rainer Postel and Franklin Kopitsch, eds., *Reformation und Revolution. Beiträge zum politischen Wandel und den sozialen Kräften am Beginn der Neuzeit. Festschrift für Rainer Wohlfeil zum 60. Geburtstag* (Stuttgart 1989) 224–237; Heiko A. Oberman, "Martin Luther Contra Medieval Monasticism: A Friar in the Lion's Den", in Timothy Maschke, Franz Posset, and Joan Skocir, eds., *Ad fontes Lutheri: Toward the Recovery of the Real Luther. Essays in Honor of Kenneth Hagen's Sixty-Fifth Birthday* (Milwaukee 2001) 183–213.
⁴ See Rolf Schmidt, *Reichenau und St. Gallen. Ihre literarische Überlieferung zur Zeit des Klosterhumanismus in St. Ulrich und Afra zu Augsburg um 1500* (Sigmaringen 1985) 56; Klaus Graf, "Ordensreform und Literatur in Augsburg während des 15. Jahrhunderts", in Johannes Janota and Werner Williams-Krapp, eds. *Literarisches Leben in Augsburg während des 15. Jahrhunderts* (Tübingen 1995) 100–59.
⁵ See Bellot, 396–397.
⁶ See Müller and Ziesak, 45; Bellot, 401.

rather perversity of women (*de mulierum curiositate potius perversitate*), and finally with a very bad tradition that should be abolished (*de pessima abolenda consuetudine melius dissuetudine*),⁷ namely, refusing to give up old familiar, but faulty lines in traditional texts. For this last issue he records the tale of a smart monastic novice who discovers a mistake in a missal and wants to correct it. The elder monks object, saying that what they have read for all these years cannot possibly be wrong. With this, the sixth story, Bild was apparently aiming at problems that humanist linguists encountered in his day when criticizing old familiar text versions and the lack of Latin erudition and motivation to correct them. The friendship between Bild and Bebel apparently did not develop because Bebel did not live long enough to cultivate it.

Bild also offered his friendship to the twenty-year-old Johannes Denck (1500–1527), later a famous dissenter from Lutheranism and an Anabaptist, to whom he sent, as his initial gift of friendship, a poetic greeting in Greek and Latin.⁸ We can assume that he was also in contact with Johannes Trithemius, as Bild apparently helped in copying Trithemius' *Polygraphia* (cryptology) for his monastery.⁹

Bild was educated at the University of Ingolstadt, where two teachers impressed him. One was the humanist and poet laureate Jacob Locher, a disciple of Conradus Celtis and the first poet laureate crowned by Emperor Maximilian I.¹⁰ He was an expert in the ancient classics and asserted the value of poetry independent of theology. Jacob Wimpfeling disliked this trend and countered with his *Contra turpem libellum Philomusi defensio theologiae scholasticae et neotericorum* (Oppenheim 1510). Wimpfeling probably followed in the footsteps of Bapista Mantuan with his *Carmen contra poetas impudice loquentes* (Strasbourg 1501).¹¹ Locher had transferred to Ingolstadt after his dismissal from the Freiburg chair of poetry.

---

⁷ See Schröder, 202 (no. 112).
⁸ See Schröder, 206 (nos. 154–156, 161, 164); on Denck, see M. Gockel, "A reformer's dissent from Lutheranism. Reconsidering the theology of Hans Denck", *Archive for Reformation History* 91 (2000) 127–48.
⁹ Codex 136; Kipf, "Bild", VL (2005).
¹⁰ See Anthony Levi, *Renaissance and Reformation. The Intellectual Genesis* (New Haven 2002) 268.
¹¹ See Anna Morisi, "Traditionalism, Humanism, and Mystical Experience in Northern Europe and in the Germanic Areas in the Fifteenth and Sixteenth Centuries", in D'Onofrio, *History of Theology. III*, 346 with note 33.

Bild's other teacher at Ingolstadt was the mathematician and imperial historiographer, Johann Stabius.[12] Bild kept in touch with him over the years.[13] After Bild left Ingolstadt in 1500, at the age of nineteen and probably without a degree, he took on the job of parish secretary (*scriptor parochiae; Pfarrschreiber*) with the monastery of Saints Ulrich and Afra in Augsburg. He held this position until June 1502. It required proficiency in letter writing and participation in liturgical singing, and it was preferable that the office holder should be ordained at least to the lower rank of sub-deacon, which then happened on 1 February 1503.[14]

His free time he spent with poetry. In humanist fashion, he sent some of his poems to known humanists in order to become better connected. For instance, he corresponded with Conrad Peutinger (1465–1547), who was the learned city clerk and imperial councilor of Augsburg. Peutinger was the center of the literary sodality of Augsburg (*sodalitas literaria Augustana*).[15] Bild borrowed his copy of Horace in order to make corrections in his own copy. Eventually, Bild's humanist connections landed him a better-paid job of the same kind at the bishop's court in Augsburg, and a still better one (with a benefice) at Wiesensteig, where he arrived as a newly-ordained sub-deacon. Wiesensteig was connected to the bishopric of Augsburg.[16]

As a humanist poet, following in the footsteps of his licentious teacher Jacob Locher Philomusus, Bild too lived an easy-going life until he fell ill and had a terrifying dream-vision that caused his moral conversion. He then entered the Benedictine monastery at Augsburg on 1 April 1503. A year later, he made his final monastic profession (2 February 1504) and was subsequently ordained to the priesthood.[17] He was fully aware that a change of location and a dress code alone would not be sufficient. He wrote in 1506 that the perfect life does not consist in wearing the monastic habit, but

---

[12] On Stabius' influence on Bild, see Christoph Schöner, *Mathematik und Astronomie an der Universität Ingolstadt im 15. und 16. Jahrhundert* (Berlin 1994).
[13] See Bellot, 400.
[14] See Andreas Bigelmair, "Der Briefwechsel von Oekolampadius mit Veit Bild", *Reformationsgeschichtliche Studien und Texte* 40 (1922) 117–135, here 118.
[15] See Bellot, 399; Schöner, 277 with note 26.
[16] See Müller and Ziesak, 42; on the connection between Augsburg and Wiesensteig, see Siegfried Hermle, *Reformation und Gegenreformation in der Herrschaft Wiesensteig: unter besonderer Berücksichtigung des Beitrags von Jakob Andreae* (Stuttgart 1996) 19–20.
[17] See Bigelmair, 118.

in eradicating one's passions. Not the poverty of the cowl, but purity of heart is pleasing to God.

Bild was not always in good health, and because of that he may have spent much time with the muses.[18] The reason, we may assume, that he opted for the Benedictine monastery of Augsburg in the first place was the personal connection he had to the prior of this cloister, with whom he shared the same place of birth.[19] Bild entered the order as a humanist. He brought with him twelve typically humanist books (incunabula) including an edition of *M. Tullius Cicero: Pro Archia poëta oratio. Pro M. Marcello oratio*, which had been edited by his teacher Jacob Locher Philomusus (printed in Reutlingen by Johann Otmar in 1494) and four volumes of Baptista Mantuan's works, printed in 1499: *De suorum temporum calamitatibus; Parthenice prima, sive Mariana; Parthenice secunda, sive Catharinaria; Contra poetas impudice loquentes*.[20] The other books that he brought with him into the monastery were texts on rhetorics. Each of the twelve books carries Bild's entry to the effect that he conferred ownership of these books on the monastery of Saints Ulrich and Afra.[21]

As a Renaissance monk, he was eager to attain the humanist ideal of a tri-lingual scholar, knowledgeable in the sacred languages of Latin, Greek, and Hebrew. How close he came to this ideal is difficult to determine as he never graduated with a formal degree and did not have the opportunity to continue his studies at universities which would have allowed him to study the biblical languages thoroughly. The only major journey that he undertook was to the monastery of Melk, where he stayed for about a year in 1511.[22]

---

[18] See Schröder, 174–77.

[19] His name was Wilhelm Wittwer from Höchstädt; see Bigelmair, 118.

[20] See Ilona Hubay, *Incunabula der Staats- und Stadtbibliothek Augsburg* (Wiesbaden 1974) no. 571 (Cicero); nos. 263, 267, 269, 272 (Mantuan); see Müller and Ziesak, 47, note 78.

[21] *Ego fr. Vitus bild höchstetensis loci huius presbiter* [sic] *et professus sanctorum vdalrici et aphrae* [Ulrich and Afra] *anno 1504 hunc eidem contuli librum*. The other incunabula are: no. 15: [Pseudo] *Aegidius Suchtelensis, Elegantiarum viginti praecepta* (Cologne: Heinrich Quentell, 1488?); no. 203: *Auctoritates Aristotelis et aliorum philosophorum* (Paris: Georgius Wolff, 1490, or Leipzig: Wolfgang Stoeckel, 1503?); no. 314: *Beda, Repertorium Auctoritatum Aristotelis et aliorum philosophorum*, together with *Auctoritates Ciceronis* (c. 1491); no. 680: *Agostino Dati* [1420–1470], *Elegantiolae* (Illerdae: Henricus Botel, 1488, or Venice: Johannes Tacuinus de Tridino, 1492, or an edition of 1496?); no. 1313: *Michael Lindelbach, Praecepta latinitatis* (1486); no. 1521: Pescennio Francesco Negro [born 1452] i.e., *Franciscus Niger, Modus epistolandi* (Augsburg: Schoensperger, 1499); no. 2145: *Jacobus Wimpfeling: Elegantiarum medulla oratoriaque praecepta* (1493).

[22] See Schröder, 177.

Bild's favorite study remained mathematics, astronomy, and astrology (then seen as linked subjects).[23] He became an expert in this field, like his professor, Stabius, at Ingolstadt, or like the Franciscan Paul Scriptoris (c. 1460–1505) at Tübingen.[24] He constructed sundials, which were in great demand. His manuscripts on these subjects, including manual-like texts on how to make sundials, are extant. However, it seems impossible to distinguish between Bild's own treatises (if he wrote any at all) and excerpts that he made from books on astronomy by the humanists Johannes of Gmunden (c. 1380–1442) and Regiomontanus (1436–1476).[25] In 1510, Bild got into arguments about numbers with his fellow Benedictine and humanist, Nikolaus Ellenbog (Chapter Six). They disagreed on the meaning of the Latin *sesquimillesimus* ('one half more' of 'thousand') which Ellenbog interpreted as '1500', while Bild thought (mistakenly) it meant '1000'.[26] Many years later, Bild renewed his friendship with Ellenbog with his letter of 14 March 1522. At that time Bild also asked Ellenbog whether, through him, he could obtain a globe that he had wanted for a long time.[27]

On the occasion of the imperial diet at Augsburg in 1518, when the elector of Saxony, Frederick the Wise, was in town, Bild received an order for sixteen sundials from him. He was paid three *gulden* and a coin with the image of the elector. The craftsmen whom Bild employed for this task received another ten *gulden*.

At that time the study of geography was connected with the study of mathematics, and interest in it increased with the discovery of the New World. Bild was able to make corrections in the map of Europe. For more than eight years he had tried to obtain a globe until, at the end of 1526, he finally received the *globus cosmographicus*. Linked with his interest in these sciences was the superstition that comes

---

[23] See Schöner, 275–278.
[24] Paul Scriptoris was an influential Renaissance friar in southwestern Germany; see Wolfgang Urban, "Vom Astrolabium, dem Vacuum und der Vielzahl der Welten. Paul Scriptoris und Konrad Summenhart: Zwei Gelehrte zwischen Scholastik und Humanismus", *Attempto* 69 (1983) 49–55.
[25] See Kipf, "Bild", VL (2005).
[26] See Ellenbog's letter of 1 September 1510 to Bild, Bigelmair, I:63–64 (no. 90) and Bild's letter of 30 November 1510 to Ellenbog, Bigelmair I:64 (no. 92a); Schröder, 195 (no. 34); Müller and Ziesak, 51. They renewed their correspondence in March 1522 with Bild writing to Ellenbog, Bigelmair, III:174–175 (no. 80); and again on 20 September 155, Bigelmair, III:176 (no. 85); Ellenbog to Bild on 16 October 1522, Bigelmair III:176–177 (no. 86).
[27] See Schröder, 209 (no. 197).

with astrology and horoscopes. Well-known humanists and churchmen alike asked Bild to provide horoscope information for them and their relatives. He gave in to these fads, even though his conscience appears to have troubled him over this dubious service that he provided.[28] Bild also figured out the Easter dates and produced liturgical calendars for his ecclesiastical customers and friends.[29]

As a typical Renaissance man, Bild ventured into all these fields of study—including music, connected to the study of mathematics—as part of the seven liberal arts. Music was taught along with arithmetic, geometry, and astronomy; the main objective in studying it was the demonstration of proportions. Bild possessed a handwritten copy of the *Musica figurata* (1501) by Melchior Schanppecher (†1505).[30] In 1507 Bild worked on a practice-oriented textbook for choirboys. It was published in 1508 by Erhard Öglin and Jeorius Nadler under the title *Stella musicae*.[31] No more than a simple introduction was expected of him, as his monastery conformed to the Melk Union, in which polyphony was to be discouraged and plainsong to be pursued.[32] Bild's expertise probably did not go far beyond that.

For a more sophisticated project, such as the song parts in his liturgical *Historia horarum canonicarum de S. Hieronymo vario carminum genere contexta*,[33] Bild needed to ask other experts for help. This *Historia* was Bild's first attempt at hagiography. It was a liturgy-oriented biography of the Church Father Jerome, in which he utilized antiphons, hymns, and response-songs. This work was commissioned by his abbot, Conrad Mörlin (1496–1510), who, like other humanists,[34] was a great admirer of Saint Jerome. Bild's efforts were crowned by the fact that his work was used in the monastic liturgy on the feast day of Saint Jerome in 1508. He wrote a similar liturgical *vita* for the

---

[28] See Schröder, 181–83.
[29] See Schröder, 182.
[30] See Kipf, "Bild", VL (2005).
[31] See Bellot, 401 (who gives the printer's name as Johann Oeglin); see Thomas Röder and Theodor Wohnhaas, "Die *Stella musicae* des Benediktiners Veit Bild. Eine spätmittelalterliche Musiklehre aus Augsburg", *Jahrbuch des Vereins für Augsburger Bistumsgeschichte e. V.* 32 (1998) 305–325.
[32] See *ibid.*, 309.
[33] Printed by Erhart Ratdolt, Augsburg, 1512; see Bellot, 401.
[34] See Berndt Hamm, "Hieronymus-Begeisterung und Augustinismus vor der Reformation. Beobachtungen zur Beziehung zwischen Humanismus und Frömmigkeitstheologie (am Beispiel Nürnbergs)", in Kenneth Hagen, ed., *Augustine, the Harvest, and Theology (1300–1650). Essays Dedicated to Heiko Augustinus Oberman in Honor of his Sixtieth Birthday* (Leiden etc. 1990) 127–235.

feast of Saint Dionysius, whose celebration was ordered by the bishop of Augsburg in 1506. Legend had it that Dionysius was the first bishop of Augsburg.[35]

In 1516 his monastery sponsored the edition of a sort of memorial book of its patron saints, the bishops Ulrich and Simprecht (or Simpert), and the martyr Afra, in both Latin and the local Swabian dialect of German.[36] It contained the legends of these saints. Bild may have been the monk who compiled the Latin prefaces, poems, postscripts, and certain passages of the descriptive texts, namely the entire section on Bishop Simprecht and the stories about the miracles of Saint Afra. A Latin and a vernacular version were printed by Silvan Otmar in 1516.[37] For the Ulrich legend the editor used the text of Berno Augiensis (Bern von Reichenau), an eleventh-century abbot of Reichenau.[38] Through this 1516 edition, the medieval texts about the life of Saint Ulrich appeared for the first time in print, including the canonization document of the year 993. The second part of the memorial book contained the liturgical texts (in verse form, without the melodies) used for the feast days of these local patron saints, Ulrich, Afra, and Simprecht.[39]

Bild was also the redactor of the history of Augsburg and its monastery, i.e., the *Chronographia Augustana* (or *Augustensium*), by the early humanist historiographer and German patriot Sigismund Meisterlin (written in 1456–1457). Meisterlin was one of the first historians with a touch of humanist scholarship. Interest in local and patriotic studies was typical of the Renaissance humanists.[40] In 1516 Bild added the chapters on the two contemporary abbots, Conrad

---

[35] See Schröder, 184–185.
[36] Also known in German as *Ehrenbuch* (literally, Honors Book), a hagiographic and liturgical desk copy of sorts. The Latin version is dated 14 April 1516, the German a bit later, 6 October 1516; Kipf, "Bild", VL (2005).
[37] *Glorioso|rum christi confessorum Vdalri|ci et Symperti: necnon beatissi|m[a]e martyris Afr[a]e/Augustan[a]e sedis patronorum . . .* This print is kept at the Staats- und Stadtbibliothek Augsburg (4 H 623); see Schröder, 185; Bellot, 401. The title of the German version is given as *Das leben: verdienen:|vnd wunderwerck der hailigen|Augspur|ger Bistumbsbischoffen/ sant Vlrichs|und Symprechts/auch der s[e]ligen mar|trerin sant Aphre.*
[38] See Röder and Wohnhaas, 307, note 8.
[39] See Kipf, "Bild", VL (2005).
[40] See Schröder, 186; Bigelmair, 119. In this context, K. Graf prefers to speak of the concept of 'monastic historism' (instead of *Klosterhumanismus*) at the Benedictine abbey in Augsburg, in his "Ordensreform" (see note 4 above) and in his "Reich und Land in der südwestdeutschen Historiographie um 1500", in Franz Brendle, Dieter Mertens, Anton Schilling and Walter Ziegler, eds., *Deutsche Landesgeschichtsschreibung im Zeichen des Humanismus* (Stuttgart 2001) 201–211, here 209, note 41.

Mörlin and Johannes Schrott (in office from 1510 to 1527). Meisterlin himself may have translated his *Chronographia Augustana* into German for the benefit of the city council. This translation was published, perhaps with Bild's assistance, in 1522.[41] The anonymous writer of the preface and the postscript identifies himself only as a "lover of old and divine, also of evangelical truth".[42] The writer could very well be Bild, as a sympathizer with Luther's 'evangelical truth'.

Bild was not the only humanist in his monastery. His confrère, Leonhard Wagner (1453/53–1521), was a known calligrapher and scholar of medieval manuscript types, as his 1510 collection of 100 great samples of various styles of writing shows: *Proba centum scripturarum*. He was able to differentiate the writings of the early Middle Ages from later periods. Each style received its own label and a brief description. These *Proba* were dedicated to Emperor Maximilian.[43] Bild helped Wagner with any problems that arose with the Latin language, and he had the honor of composing verses for the dedication of this work.[44] It was probably also Bild who helped Wagner to find appropriate names for the various styles of handwriting that he had discovered.[45]

Bild's main task in the monastery, however, appears to have been the teaching of Latin to boys in the cloister school. For that purpose he wrote his own Latin grammar in 1519. It was never printed, but a number of people borrowed it to have it copied, including the abbot of Donauwörth.[46] As for his Greek studies, he may have been a pioneer in the city of Augsburg, where at that time hardly anyone had mastered this language. The two leading humanists of Augsburg, the above-mentioned Conrad Peutinger and Canon Bernhard Adelmann (1457/1459–1523), readily admitted that they did not know Greek. Bild had a friend in Ingolstadt who obtained Greek textbooks for him. He also purchased Greek dictionaries and

---

[41] I am grateful to Dr. Klaus Kipf (Munich) for this information. A copy is extant at the library of Michigan State University (Special collections, DD801.W92M4): *Ein schöne Cronick vn Hystoria wye nach der Syndtfluß Noe die teutschen das stretpar volck jren anfang enfangen haben . . . auch dar bey von der kayserlichen stat Augspurg . . .* (Augsburg: Melchior Ramminger, 1522); Bellot, 401, note 14.
[42] *Liebhaber altter vnnd götlicher/ auch Euangelischer warhait*, Kipf, "Bild", VL (2005).
[43] See Bellot, 400.
[44] See Bigelmair, 119.
[45] See Schmidt, 153–56.
[46] See Schröder, 178.

a Greek-Latin edition of Lucian. Traces of Bild's knowledge of Greek are found in his correspondence, as Greek words are occasionally interspersed in the Latin letters, as in a letter to Georg Spalatin that includes the macaronic Latin/Greek expression *dulcissimus* συναδελφός[47] ("sweetest confrère") or the letter of Otmar Nachtigall (Luscinius, c. 1478–1536) of 10 June 1515 with three more Greek expressions.[48] Nachtigall was also widely known as a music expert after publishing his *Institutiones musicae, a nemine umquam prius pari felicitate tentatae* (Strasbourg 1515), for which the Gotha humanist Mutianus saluted him with an epigram of praise which he sent to Johannes Lang, then prior of the Augustinian friary at Erfurt.[49]

In December 1518 Spalatin wrote to Bild that he deplored the fact that Bild was unable to meet Martin Luther in person when he was in Augsburg. In the same letter, he reported to Bild on the status of the study of biblical languages at Wittenberg University: Philip Melanchthon had been hired as a teacher of Greek and was attracting about 400 students. Johannes Boeschenstein (1472–c. 1540), the professor of Hebrew, was also attracting "not a few hearers" (*auditores non pauci*). In sum, Spalatin wrote, one could call Wittenberg the 'second Athens'.[50]

Like all linguists among the Renaissance humanists, Bild too was interested in the original meaning of the Holy Scriptures. This was termed an investigation into the Greek truth (*graeca veritas*) of the New Testament. On this subject Bild received a progress report in 1522 from Spalatin in Wittenberg that their "common Father Martin Luther" (*pater communis doctor M. L.*), "the most Christian evangelist" (*Evangelista christianissimus*), had recently finished the translation of the New Testament from the Greek truth.[51]

When on 2 November 1518 the Graecian Johannes Oecolampadius arrived from Basel to start his job as a preacher at the cathedral in

---

[47] Dated 22 August 1522; Schröder, 223 (no. 215).
[48] See Schröder, 219 (no. 93); see also no. 191 (Oecolampadius to Bild); no. 214 (Spalatin to Bild); no. 266 (Oecolampadius to Bild); Schröder, 219–226. On Nachtigall (Luscinius), see Klaus Wolfgang Niemöller, "Otmar Luscinius, Musiker und Humanist", *Archiv für Musikwissenschaft* 15 (1958) 41ff.
[49] Mutianus may have sent this poem to Johannes Lang on 13 June 1515 (?); Krause, 599 (no. 534).
[50] Dated 10 December 1518; Schröder, 221 (no. 142).
[51] *Nuper novum testamentum a se ex Graeca veritate translatum edidit*, dated 16 October 1522; Schröder, 224 (no. 226).

Augsburg, he sent a brief letter to Bild saying that he, Augsburg's preacher, was writing from his "little peasant's hut",[52] apparently disappointed about the lodging he had been given. They became friends and Bild learned more elementary Greek from him. However, Bild was once more on his own in this endeavor when Oecolampadius left Augsburg in the spring of 1520 to enter the Brigittine monastery (*Brigittenkloster*) of Altomünster on 23 April 1520. As a monk he hoped to find time for studies.[53] However, Oecolampadius left that monastery in the fall of 1524.[54]

In the summer of 1520 Bild had asked Oecolampadius to send him Luther's *Resolutions* of 1518 for his Luther collection.[55] In December 1520, Bild must have received Oecolampadius' *Lucubrationes*, as he thanked him for the shipment.[56] In the fall of 1524 they corresponded on the questions of the real presence of Christ in the Eucharist and on purgatory. According to Oecolampadius' letter of 23 October 1524 to Bild about the *mysterio corporis Christi*, there was "much blindness in the world". The bread and wine of the Eucharist are symbols that serve as spiritual food (*spirituali autem pabulo serviunt sacrosancta symbola*), and no genuflections are required before them, as Christ does not teach homage (*adorationes*) of them. The old Fathers soundly prohibited any genuflections, which he spelled in Greek letters, ζονυκλισίας.[57] After the correspondence on this subject, relations cooled off considerably as it became apparent to Bild that Oecolampadius had joined the camp of Ulrich Zwingli (1484–1531) in Basel on the issue of Christ's real presence in the Lord's Supper. In a letter of 15 March 1527, Bild told him that he had erred on this issue.[58] Bild preferred (with Pirckheimer and Erasmus) the traditional Catholic understanding of the Eucharist.[59]

---

[52] *Ex tuguriolo meo tuus Ecolampadius concionator Augustanus*, Schröder, 220 (no. 141); in his letter of 1519 Oecolampadius spoke only of his "peasant's hut" (*ex tugurio meo*), Schröder, 221 (no. 145).
[53] See his letter to Bild of 23 July 1520, as edited by Bigelmair, 126–127.
[54] See Bigelmair, 122.
[55] See his letter to Bild of July/September 1520; Bigelmair, 124–125.
[56] See his letter of 9 December to Oecolampadius; Bigelmair, 127–128.
[57] Oecolampadius to Bild on 23 October 1524; Bigelmair, 131–134, as his response to Bild's letter of 13 September 1524; Oecolampadius' letter of 23 October 1524 was also edited by Schröder, 225–225 (no. 266).
[58] See Bigelmair, 123.
[59] See Augustijn, *Humanismus*, 116.

As the above-mentioned letter to Bild of 10 June 1515 demonstrates, the Strasbourg humanist Otmar Nachtigall (Luscinius) wanted to become friends with Bild,[60] a friendship that must have blossomed when, in 1523, Luscinius moved from Strasbourg to Augsburg. Probably with Bild's recommendation, Luscinius was employed as a Greek instructor for the monks at their monastery by Abbot Johannes Schrott.[61] He also lectured on the Psalms from the Hebrew text (not from the Vulgate, as had been done in the past). In 1524 he published his commentary on the Psalms in Latin and German.[62] "Luscinius was a talented and versatile man: theologian, jurist, musician, and a widely known scholar in 'the three languages'".[63] Luscinius certainly met Willibald Pirckheimer's criteria for what makes a good humanist theologian.[64] Bild praised him, in his letter of 28 January 1524 to the Benedictine confrère Nikolaus Ellenbog in Ottobeuren, as a man well-versed in Greek and Latin.[65] However, Luscinius stayed for only two years. How much of the sacred languages Bild learned from him is impossible to tell.

As for Bild's attempts to learn Hebrew, we do not really know how successful he was over the years. By 1513/1514 he had already received what, in his correspondence, was called "An Introduction to the Hebrew Letters".[66] Again, it was his friend in Ingolstadt who provided him with Hebrew books. At that time Johannes Boeschenstein was the professor of Hebrew there. Among Boeschenstein's students was Caspar Amman (c. 1450–1524) of Lauingen, the Augustinian friar and biblical humanist who became a leading Hebraist.[67] Amman and Bild became friends, as their correspondence shows. In 1521 Bild procured a Greek dictionary for Amman, possibly the *dictionarium graecum* of Ambrosius Calpinus (or Calepin, †1510), of the Augustinian friary in Bergamo, Italy.[68] In his letter of 15 December

---

[60] See Schröder, 218–219 (no. 93).
[61] See Niemöller, "Otmar Luscinius" (as in note 48 above); Bellot, 402.
[62] *Allegoriae psalmorum* (Augsburg: Sipert Ruf, 1524); Schmidt, 139.
[63] Klemens Löffler, "Ottmar Luscinius (Nachtigall)", *Catholic Encyclopedia* (internet edition).
[64] See *Willibald Pirckheimers Briefwechsel*, vol. 3:160–562.
[65] See Schröder, 224 (no. 250).
[66] *Introductorium in hebraeas literas*; correspondence with Pinician and Johann Kaiser; Schröder, 199 (no. 80).
[67] On Amman, see Franz Posset, "Amman, Caspar", BBKL 16 (2000) 49–52.
[68] See the correspondence between them in August and September 1521, Schröder, 207 (nos. 171–177). On Calpinus, see Junghans, *Der junge Luther*, 25, note 75.

1521, Amman expressed his joy over Bild's intention to learn Hebrew; he should let him know what books in Hebrew he already possessed. For starters, Amman sent him the Hebrew alphabet.[69] Two days later Bild responded to Amman's question and gave him a list of Hebrew books he had had for a long time: Reuchlin's works and a book called *Elementale Lipsiensium parabolis Salomonis annexum*.[70] From the books by Reuchlin in his possession, we may assume that Bild sided with this leading Hebraist in the 'Reuchlin Controversy'.

On Bild's request of 12 April 1522 to send explanations of the Hebrew alphabet, Amman promised on 31 May 1522 to send Bild a copy of the manuscript of his Hebrew grammar. He also informed him that he was staying temporarily in Dillingen, where he was tutoring the local preacher Kaspar Haslach.[71] Bild's notes on the Hebrew alphabet and its pronunciation are extant, but do not seem to be identical with Amman's text.[72] Bild may have collected whatever he could find on the subject. We do not know to what degree he became an expert in this language. All we know is that manuscripts from the monastery are extant that contain Bild's notes on the Hebrew grammar.[73]

Both the Benedictine Bild and the Augustinian Amman were sympathetic to Martin Luther.[74] Bild, residing at Augsburg, had easy access to the book market of this imperial city and, therefore, was in a position to get the latest books by Luther and other reformers for Amman, who lived at the relatively remote friary in Lauingen. Bild provided a service of book purchase and lay-away for numerous other humanists who lived out of town. No wonder then that

---

[69] See Schröder, 208 (no. 192).

[70] Reuchlin's books are listed in this letter as follows: *Dictionarius, orthographia, grammatica, psalterium cum eruditione parvula literarum hebr Capitonis* [sic]; the name is spelled wrong; it should be Capnio, which is the humanist name for Reuchlin; letter of 17 December 1521, Schröder, 209 (no. 193).

[71] See Schröder, 209 (no. 205). On the reform-minded preacher Haslach at Dillingen, see Ludwig Duncker, "Die Stellung des Prädikanten Kaspar Haslach zur Reformation", *Zeitschrift für Bayerische Kirchengeschichte* 14 (1939) 129–159.

[72] See Kipf, "Bild", VL (2005).

[73] See Schmidt, 140.

[74] See Franz Posset, "'Rock' and 'Recognition': Martin Luther's Catholic Interpretation of 'You are Peter and on this rock I will build my Church' (Matthew 16:18) and the Friendly Criticism from the Point of View of the 'Hebrew Truth' by his Confrère, Caspar Amman, 'Doctor of the Sacred Page'", in *Ad fontes Lutheri*, 214–252.

he was praised as early as 1515 for his helpfulness and friendliness (*comitas* and *humanitas*).[75]

As his correspondence with Amman indicates, Bild was not interested in books by the humanist Johannes Eck (Luther's arch-rival), such as his work on the papacy.[76] He and Amman, although they both liked Luther and his reform efforts, did not become Lutherans. Bild acknowledged, though, in his letter of 2 July 1522, that Amman himself was a preacher of the "evangelical truth",[77] which almost amounted to being Lutheran in contemporary parlance. Luther met great admiration among the people of Augsburg, including Bild's humanist friends. Bild himself compiled a still-extant list of texts by Luther. It comprises about 150 titles.

Bild deeply regretted not having been able to meet Luther on the occasion of his summons before Cardinal Thomas Cajetan (1468–1534) during the imperial diet of 1518 in his city. When, in the fall of 1518, Bild came to read Luther's defense of his *Ninety-Five Theses* on indulgences (i.e., his resolutions on the disputations about the power of indulgences, *Resolutiones disputationum de indulgentiarum virtute*), he found them to be excellent.[78] Bild solicited a copy of the *Resolutiones* from Oecolampadius, as he wanted to collect and bind Luther's texts.[79] Twice Bild tried to approach Luther with letters that he sent via Georg Spalatin, the Saxon elector's secretary. Bild would have been overjoyed if he could have received but a few lines from Luther's pen.[80] However, Luther at first seems not to have reacted to his Benedictine fan, if indeed his words "I did not respond nor will I respond to this Swabian"[81] refer to the Swabian Vitus Bild in Augsburg. This may not be Bild, as Luther actually did send a letter to Bild on 5 May 1520 via Spalatin, whom he asked to forward his letter.[82]

---

[75] See Schröder, 189 (no. 94).
[76] See Schröder, 209–210 (no. 205).
[77] *Evangelica veritas*; see Schröder, 210 (no. 209); see also Bild's letter to Amman of 16 June 1523 (no. 242); Posset, "Amman" (see note 67 above).
[78] See Junghans, *Der junge Luther*, 293.
[79] See Bild's letter to Oecolampadius of July or September 1519, edited by Bigelmair, 124–125.
[80] See Schröder, 187. Bild's letters are dated 21 September 1518 and 16 April 1520, edited in the appendix of Schröder's study, 219–222. See also the critical edition of Luther's letters, WA *Briefe*, vol. 1:206–207 (letter of 21 September 1518); vol. 2:84 (letter of 16 April 1520).
[81] *Nihil respondi nec respondebo sueuo illi*, WA *Briefe*, vol. 3:426, 6.
[82] *Mitto literas ad Vitum Bildum*, WA *Briefe*, vol. 2:98, 4.

This letter, unfortunately, is lost. It may have been Luther's response to Bild's letter of 16 April 1520.

Bild was a friend of Canon Bernhard Adelmann of Augsburg, who first approached him in 1507. Adelmann sought Bild's friendship and later occasionally helped him procure the latest books. In 1518 Adelmann promised to lend him Erasmus' commentary on the Letter to the Romans, which Adelmann esteemed more highly than gold and silver. He would send it to him as soon as he had finished reading the work.[83] Also in 1518, Bild received two of Luther's printed sermons from Adelmann, who wanted Bild to read and return them as soon as possible.[84] Bild was equally fond of these sermons and wanted to buy them for himself if they were not too expensive. His personal opinions on Luther, however, he preferred not to put in writing, but to communicate orally on another occasion.[85] Bild was privileged to read Adelmann's correspondence with Luther. Adelmann shared other Lutheran works with Bild, such as Luther's edition of the *Theologia Germanica*.[86] Bild had asked for it in the name of his sub-prior, Sigmund Zimmermann, who also showed great interest in Luther's edition.[87] In exchange, Adelmann asked Bild for the favor of letting him read the patristic literature in his monastery library, in particular the works of Saint Basil.[88] Adelmann also asked him for *Aesopus* and Jean Gerson's *De consolatione theologiae*, part 3. Besides books, Bild was able to give Adelmann some of his astronomical instruments.[89]

As Bild's correspondence shows, he and his correspondents considered Luther to be theirs, as they referred to him as "our Luther".[90] Bild's evangelical (Lutheran) spirituality is beyond doubt and is best mirrored in the lines that he wrote on 22 August 1522 to Spalatin:

---

[83] See Schröder, 203 (no. 120).
[84] See Schröder, 202–203 (no. 118).
[85] See Schröder, 203 (no. 119).
[86] The American edition is edited by Bengt Hoffman, *The Theologica Germanica of Martin Luther*. The Classics of Western Spirituality (New York, Ramsey, Toronto 1980).
[87] See Schröder, 203 (no. 121).
[88] See their correspondence of the spring of 1519; Schröder, 205 (no. 150).
[89] On Bild and Adelmann, see Franz Xaver Thurnhofer, "Bernhard Adelmann von Adelmannsfelden, Humanist und Luthers Freund (1457–1523): Ein Lebensbild aus der Zeit der beginnenden Kirchenspaltung in Deutschland", *Erläuterungen und Ergänzungen zu Janssens Geschichte des deutschen Volkes* (Freiburg 1900) vol. 2:1–153, here 100–104.
[90] See Schröder, 203 (no. 123).

The Gospel in which God instructed me through Martin [Luther], the most faithful servant of his vineyard, is so deeply rooted in my heart that I despise everything else with which I uselessly spent my earlier days; and nothing will be able to separate me from the word of Christ, with the help of God.[91]

Being a sympathizer of Luther was not without risks. When he wrote about Luther, Bild was careful in his correspondence, even with friends. Sometime in December 1522, he wrote to Sigmund Grimm about the Reformer, but he only used Martin Luther's initials, and those in Greek, M. Λ., as he calls the Reformer the "Savior of our Germany", again partly in Greek and Latin letters.[92] When in 1524 Father Christof at Ettal asked his friend Bild about his opinion of this crazy man Luther and his adherents in the city, Bild responded diplomatically that certain questions are better not answered in writing. He hoped to be able to talk with him in person about Luther. In the meantime Christof should eagerly read the New Testament.[93]

Soon afterwards, in the 1520s—particularly after the disastrous consequences of the Peasants' War in 1525,[94] for which the reformers were blamed—Bild's interest in Luther and in religious reforms seems to have decreased. He no longer sought contacts with the Wittenberg theologians. He also distanced himself completely from Oecolampadius because of his Zwinglian-sounding doctrine on the Lord's Supper. Bild, however, found Pirckheimer's[95] and Peutinger's teachings on this subject congenial and suggested (without success) that they be translated into German. Bild was a regular guest at Peutinger's table and became the father confessor of Peutinger's son, Karl.[96] He remained in contact with Pirckheimer in the 1520s, especially on issues of geography and cartography.[97] In 1528, Bild received a complimentary copy of Pirckheimer's translation of speeches by

---

[91] Schröder, 223 (no. 215).
[92] γερμανίας nostrae ιατρός (Bild has mistakenly written ίαπος for ιατρός); Schröder, 212.
[93] See Schröder, 214 (no. 259).
[94] See Blickle, *The Revolution of 1525* (see Chapter on Marius, note 50).
[95] On Pirckheimer's opposition to Oecolampadius' doctrine, see Helmut Böhme, "Willibald Pirckheimer und Nürnberg", in Andreas Mehl and Wolfgang Christian Schneider, eds., *Reformatio et Reformationes: Festschrift für Lothar Graf zu Dohna zum 65. Geburtstag* (Darmstadt 1989) 195–247, here 231–234.
[96] See Schröder, 188.
[97] See Niklas Holzberg, *Willibald Pirckheimer: Griechischer Humanismus in Deutschland* (Munich 1981) 264, 330–332. Thirteen letters by Bild to Pirckheimer, and six from Pirckheimer to him, are known; see *ibid.*, 266.

Gregory of Nazianz against Emperor Julian.[98] Bild was also proud to suffer from the gout, just like Pirckheimer. It was comforting to him to be Pirckheimer's brother in suffering, having the same brother gout (*confrater podagricus*).[99]

In 1525 an anonymous German pamphlet on the Creed of the Church, concerning the line about Christ descending into hell, was printed at Augsburg (see Fig. 12). It is attributed to Bild. In it, the author defends the relevant line in the Apostles' Creed against contemporary doubters, with arguments from the Scriptures.[100] The title page is adorned with a woodcut showing the risen Christ pulling naked human figures up from hell. Under the picture, Psalm 29:6 is quoted in Latin: "At nightfall, weeping enters in, but with the dawn, rejoicing". The twelve-page text appears to be a sermon or talk to fellow brothers who requested comments on the issue. Evidently they had compared the Nicene Creed with the Apostles' Creed and saw that the Greek Church with its Nicene Creed does not explicitly include the line on the descent into hell. Therefore, they assumed that the Greek Church and the Church Fathers did not believe in this article of faith.[101] In defending the line in the Latin version of the Apostles' Creed, the author refers to a letter of the Greek Athanasius to Epitectus (sic) which says that when Christ's body was laid in the tomb, Christ went down to the spirits in the prison of hell and preached to them. The author draws support from the Old and New Testaments, especially from 1 Peter 3:18–19, according to which Christ "went to preach to the spirits in prison" (*descensus*). In a marginal note printed along the text of page three, we find the note that Luther commented on this issue in his *Operationes* [*in Psalmos*], i.e., on Psalm 15:10. The reader can also consult the book of Pomeranus (i.e., Johannes Bugenhagen [1485–1558], Luther's father confessor and the pastor at Wittenberg) and his interpretation of the

---

[98] See Holzberg, 347.
[99] See Thurnhofer, 103.
[100] *Grund vnnd Schrifftliche anzaygungen auß hailiger geschrifft des aynigen Artickel halber vnnsers glaubens, Nemlich Christum zun hellen hynunder gestygen vnd gefaren seyn, Wider etliche Naßweyß vnserer zeyt die an dem Artickel fast Schwancken* (Augsburg: Philipp Ulhart d. Ä., 1525). I am grateful to the Archive of the Diocese of Augsburg for providing me with a copy of this print.
[101] ... *werffen mir nur die Kriechische kirchen vn[d] die vater für, die halten disen Artickel auch nicht* (opening paragraph).

Psalms, which he published in 1524 under the title *Interpretatio in librum Psalmorum*.[102] In the margin of the fifth page of the pamphlet, another reference to Luther is printed, noting that this locus is most difficult according to Luther (*Difficilissimum hunc esse locum inquit Lutherus*).

The pamphlet can be understood as a contribution to the discussions that were going on at that time. Shortly before its publication in 1525, Erasmus had edited a revised version of his *Colloquia*, in March 1524, which includes a dialogue between a Lutheran and a Catholic on the subject of the Creed. During the course of the dialogue, the Lutheran adheres completely to the Apostles' Creed, a fact that is noted positively by the Catholic dialogue partner. With this, Erasmus intended to show the Lutheran position to be essentially orthodox.[103]

In the postscript of the anonymous pamphlet attributed to Bild, the author declares that he will refrain from writing his own book on the twelve articles of the Apostles' Creed, which he had originally promised. The reason is that Dr. Urbanus Rhegius has already accomplished this very well in a recent book, in which the Creed is interpreted with references to its scriptural foundation. Rhegius held the position of chief preacher at the cathedral of Augsburg after earning his doctoral degree at Basel in 1520. By 1521 he had become known as a supporter of Luther and was forced to resign his post. The book to which the postscript refers may be either "The Twelve Articles of Our Christian Faith with Reference to the Scriptures on Which They Are Based",[104] or "An Explanation of the Twelve Articles of the Christian Faith, including the main pieces and eminent points, that are useful and necessary for all Christians to know".[105]

---

[102] See H. H. Holfelder, *Tentatio et consolatio. Studien zu Bugenhagens Interpretatio in librum Psalmorum* (Berlin 1974).

[103] See Cornelis Augustijn, *Erasmus von Rotterdam: Leben—Werk—Wirkung* (Munich 1986) 119 and 150.

[104] *Die zwolff artickel unsers Christlichen glaubens mit anzaigung der hailigen geschrifft darinen sie gegründt seind* (Augsburg: Sigmund Grimm, 1523). On Rhegius, see Scott Hendrix, "Urbanus Rhegius (1489–1541)", in Carter Lindberg, ed., *The Reformation Theologians: An Introduction to Theology in the Early Modern Period* (Malden 2002) 109–123, here 112 with note 17; Scott Hendrix, *Preaching the Reformation: The homiletical handbook of Urbanus Rhegius* (Milwaukee 2003).

[105] *Erklerung der Zwelff Artickel Christlichs glawbens. Mit den heubtstucken vnd fürnemsten puncten, allen christen nützlich vnd nötig* (Wittenberg: Hans Lufft, 1525).

Also attributed to Bild is a monastic humanist curio, the revision of the cloister's library catalogue in verse form![106] As bookshelves at that time were filled somewhat haphazardly, without any obvious method, by the whim of acquisition,[107] so were the library catalogues. Bild's catalogue in verse has four lines in Latin (with one German exception) for each letter in the alphabet, as descriptions of the library books. For example, under the letter B one reads the verses on the *Biblia*. Under C the books of the Church Fathers are listed. Under D one finds Bernard of Clairvaux as *Doctor Bernhardus*, along with *Dionisius, Rabanus, Chrisostomus, Lactancius, Bonauentura, Eusebius, Origenes*. Under E the names of Scotus and Thomas appear. Under L the poem switches to German; the verses start with *Lustig, hüpsch, schoen vil teutscher biecher ligent hie dar*, i.e., "many fine, nice, beautiful German books lie here". The strophe in German ends with the admonition that the reader should return the books after their use.[108] Under Q the user is informed that one can also find here the medical authorities *Hippocrates* and *Galenus*. The twenty strophes summarize the content of the twenty bookcases of the library.

Here is a sample of the verses for the first five bookcases:

> Metra secundum alphabetum
> in bibliotheca super arcas
> A.
> Aspice confertos, quos bibliotheca profundit,
>   Auctorum libros dictaque multiuaga.
> Abstrusum quid habet si biblia, protinus istic
>   Sanctorum reserant scripta diserta patrum.
> B.
> Biblia subsequitur, visuntur et historiarum
>   Sacrarum auctores, gesta quoque ecclesie.
> Bella et Romulidum annales hec teca reseruat.
>   Stemmata a pulchra virum teque Iosephe gerit.
> C.
> Conspice doctores hic quatuor agmine facto
>   Illustrant dictis qui loca nostra suis:
> Candidus Augustinus et Ambrosiusque seuerus,
>   Iheronimus morum precoque Gregorius.

---

[106] See Schmidt, 70. The poem about the content of the library catalogue is edited by Schmidt, 67–70.

[107] See Guy-Marie Oury, "The Monks of the Renaissance at the Heart of the Revolution of the Printed Book", CSQ 36 (2001) 163–74, here 169.

[108] *So er das gebraucht hat, legs wider an seine stat*; Schmidt, 68.

D.
Doctus Bernhardus, Dionisius atque Rabanus
　Et Chrisostomus hic lactea dicta dabunt.
Deprimit errores Lactancius ore prophanos,
　Hic Bonauentura, Eusebius, Origenes.
E.
Eloquij diui (quod non est dicere versu)
　Hoc latere occluso scripta quatema vides.
Edita sunt commenta, quibus sentencia claret
　Obscura: hic Scotus prenitet atque Thomas.[109]

Our Benedictine humanist died at the age of forty-eight, on 19 July 1529.[110] He was a monk eager to become an expert in the three sacred languages, which was the ideal of a Renaissance theologian, and he was apparently not too much afraid of being labeled a heretic. By that time, just about every scholar who wanted to keep abreast of the times was eager to learn these languages.

Why did Bild not become a Lutheran? The answer depends in part on what 'Lutheran' meant in his day. At first this label was used by opponents of Luther. It would probably never have entered Bild's mind to call himself a 'Lutheran'. In addition, we cannot simply equate Lutheranism with anti-monasticism. Bild's biography clearly demonstrates that not all humanists became anti-monastic, Protestant reformers. Bild was sympathetic to Luther's theological concerns, but he remained a Benedictine monk to the end of his life. He did not succumb to the protesters' trend of leaving behind the monastic way of life, as many of Luther's sympathizers did. One such of Bild's acquaintances, the prior of the Carmelites at Augsburg, Johannes Frosch (c. 1480–1533), got married even before Luther did. Bild—just like Luther's fatherly friend Johann von Staupitz who had joined the Benedictines at Salzburg—apparently separated the Catholic-theological concerns of Luther from the question of monastic vows and of living them. Evidently he did not appreciate (or simply ignored?) the interpretations and rejection of the monastic vows by Luther and others. The Protestant reformers' abolition of the vows marks a watershed in Europe's religious and cultural life.[111] Furthermore,

---

[109] Schmidt, 67.
[110] See Bigelmair, 118; Schröder, 177.
[111] See Oberman, "Martin Luther Contra Medieval Monasticism: A Friar in the Lion's Den", in *Ad fontes Lutheri*, 188. Incidentally, Luther himself did not get married until 1525.

the denominational fronts in those days were not at all as clear-cut as they appear to us today. Even much later in the sixteenth century, it was still not always clear what the designation 'Lutheran' could or should imply. But, most of all, Bild was already dead when in 1530 the diet took place in his city. This diet of Augsburg produced the *Augsburg Confession*, that is, the attempt of the Wittenberg Catholics ('Lutherans') to prove themselves as the true 'Catholics' (not necessarily 'Roman Catholics'). This diet signaled the definite parting of the ways for the Wittenberg Catholics and the Roman Catholics. By 1537, eight years after Bild's death, the monks of Bild's own monastery were split into 'Lutherans' and 'Catholics'.[112] There was thus not only a 'confessionalization of humanism' under way, but also a 'confessionalization of monasticism'. We will never know whether Bild would have approved of the *Augsburg Confession* of 1530, or on which side he would have stood within his monastery had he still been alive in 1537. It appears that he was a Benedictine monk and a Lutheran at heart, which to him was evidently no contradiction. In other words, he was an evangelical Catholic monk. All we can definitively say is to repeat Bild's own words from his letter of 22 August 1522 to Luther's friend Spalatin, about his own evangelical spirituality as he saw it shaped by Luther's concerns: "The Gospel in which God instructed me through Martin [Luther], the most faithful servant of his vineyard, is so deeply rooted in my heart that I despise everything else".

---

[112] See Friedrich Roth, "Die Spaltung des Convents der Mönche von St. Ulrich in Augsburg im Jahre 1537 und deren Folgen", *Zeitschrift des Historischen Vereins für Schwaben* 30 (1903) 1–41; Bellot, 402–03.

CHAPTER SIX

WHEN MONKS WERE EAGER TO STUDY THE SACRED LANGUAGES: NIKOLAUS ELLENBOG, MONK OF OTTOBEUREN, SWABIA

Nikolaus Ellenbog called himself, or was called by other humanists, *Cubitensis* or *Cubitus* after the Latin word for 'elbow', *cubitum*, in translation of his German family name *Ellenbog*. He was born on 18 March 1481 in Biberach in southwestern Germany. He died on 6 June 1543. His father Ulrich was a physician and a humanist at Memmingen where Nikolaus grew up, went to school, and where he learned Latin. He entered the University of Heidelberg on 12 July 1497. He continued his studies at the University of Cracow in Poland, on 15 November 1501, which was then known for its courses in astronomy and astrology. He also studied at Montpellier in 1502/03, most likely at the college of medicine as Montpellier was then the best-known medical school, and must have been recommended to him by his father.

However, in March 1504 he joined the Benedictines at Ottobeuren (Latin name: *Ottinpurra; Ottenbura*), the monastery closest to his hometown Memmingen, where he perhaps entered in compliance with a vow he had made during a severe illness.[1] He was ordained to the priesthood on 15 March 1506, probably at Augsburg. At his abbey he held the office of prior (1508–1512) and of novice master. He also was managing director of operations (*cellerarius*, 1512–1522) and of the printing press that his abbey established as early as 1509. He was one of the monastic humanists "at the heart of the revolution of the printed book".[2] The first book that came off this press was *Alcuinus de Sancta Trinitate*, with a preface by Ellenbog. Only ten books can be traced to this abbey press.

---

[1] The entry date may be December 1504, as Karl Schottenloher has it in "Der Benediktiner und Humanist Nikolaus Ellenbog in Ottobeuren und sein Briefwechsel (1504–1543)", *Zeitschrift für Bayerische Landesgeschichte* 11 (1938) 468–70; available on the internet.

[2] As Guy-Marie Oury put it (without mention of Ellenbog, though): "The Monks of the Renaissance"; see Chapter Five, note 107.

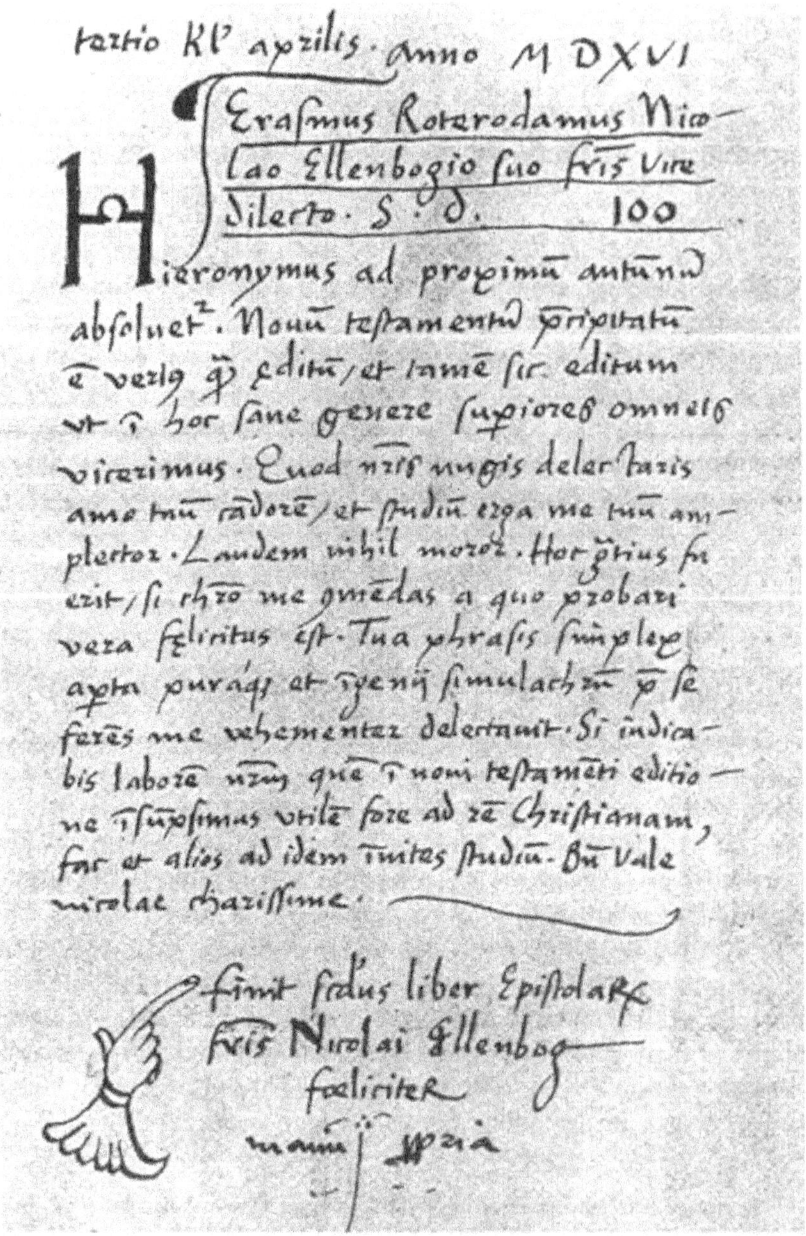

CHAPTER SIX

tertio kl' aprilis. anno MDXVI

Erasmus Roterodamus Nicolao Ellenbogio suo fris vire dilecto. S. d.   100

Hieronymus ad proximū autumnū absoluet. Nouū testamentū pręcipitatū ē verius qp editū, et tamē sic editum vt p̄ hoc sane genere superiores omneis vicerimus. Quod nr̄is uugis delectaris amo tuū cādorē, et studiū erga me tuū amplector. Laudem nihil moror. Hoc gr̄ius sē erit, si p̄ me me gmēdas a quo probari vera felicitas est. Tua phrasis simplex apta puraq; et ingenij simulachrū p̄ se ferens me vehementer delectauit. Si indicabis laborē urūz que p̄ noui testamēti editione īsupōsimus vtilē fore ad rē Christianam, far et alios ad idem īnitas studiū. Bn̄ vale nicolae charissime.

finit sc̄dus liber Epistolaru fris Nicolai Ellenbog foeliciter
manu jp̄ia

Fig. 13. Erasmus' letter to Ellenbog of April 1516. From: *Nikolaus Ellenbog: Briefwechsel*, eds. Andreas Bigelmair and Friedrich Zoepfl (Münster 1938), II:100.

One of his sisters, Barbara (or, Barbe), became a Cistercian nun at the then quite important imperial abbey of Heggbach in southwestern Germany, where she was the abbess from 1515 to 1526 (styled Abbess Barbe I Ellenbögin).[3] As abbess of Heggbach she was an imperial abbess (*Reichsäbtissin* or *Fürstäbtissin*) and, as such, a member of the diet of the Holy Roman Empire; she was also without an overlord, except for the emperor.[4] Ellenbog recommended to her that her nuns should start studying Hebrew, following the example of Paula in the time of Saint Jerome. Ellenbog also corresponded with one of the nuns at Heggbach, Ursula Wespechin.[5] His extant correspondence comprises almost 900 letters, mostly with other humanists. Especially noteworthy are Erasmus of Rotterdam[6] (see Fig. 13), Johann Eck who grew up in the territory that belonged to the abbey of Ottobeuren,[7] Bernhard Adelmann von Adelmannsfelden,[8] Conrad Peutinger,[9] and Vitus Bild.[10] The latter three lived at Augsburg. In addition he corresponded with the humanist physician at Ulm, Wolfgang Reichart (1486–1547).[11] Also known is Ellenbog's correspondence with the Franciscan Hebraist Conrad Pellican from Alsace, which began in 1514.[12]

Nikolaus inherited his father's medical library. He also remained interested in language studies, in astrology and astronomy. Like the other Benedictine, Vitus Bild at Augsburg, he produced sundials and

---

[3] See the list of the abbesses of Heggbach in *Dictionnaire d'histoire et de géographie ecclésiastiques*, ed. R. Aubert, vol. 23 (Paris 1990) 773–774.
[4] For further clarification on this issue, I am indebted to Gerhard Winkler.
[5] See Andreas Bigelmair and Friedrich Zoepfl, eds., *Nikolaus Ellenbog: Briefwechsel* (Münster 1938), vol. 2:71–72 (no. 6); hereafter quoted as *Ellenbog Briefwechsel*.
[6] See *The Correspondence of Erasmus: Letters 298 to 445. 1514 to 1516*. Translated by R. A. B. Mynors and D. F. S. Thomson. Annotated by Wallace K. Ferguson. (Toronto and Buffalo 1976) vol. 3:252 and 273 (nos. 395 and 402); R. J. Schoeck, "Nikolaus Ellenbog", in Bietenholz and Deutscher, eds., *Contemporaries of Erasmus*, vol. 1:428.
[7] See Bigelmair, "Nikolaus Ellenbog (1481–1543)" in *Lebensbilder*, 130; their correspondence after 1515 comprises 37 letters.
[8] On him, see Friedrich Zoepfl in *Lebensbilder aus dem Bayerischen Schwaben*, vol. 11 (1976) 39–45; Herbert Immenkötter, "Adelmann", *Lexikon der Reformationszeit*, 8–10.
[9] See Heinrich Lutz, *Conrad Peutinger: Beiträge zu einer politischen Biographie* (Augsburg 2001).
[10] See Chapter 5.
[11] See Walther Ludwig, ed., *Vater und Sohn im 16. Jahrhundert. Der Briefwechsel des Wolfgang Reichart, genannt Rychardus, mit seinem Sohn Zeno (1520–1543)* (Hildesheim 1999).
[12] See *Ellenbog Briefwechsel* (8 October 1514?). On Pellikan, see E. Silberstein, *Conrad Pellikan: Ein Beitrag zur Geschichte der Studien der hebräischen Sprache im 16. Jahrhundert* (Berlin 1900).

other instruments.[13] In contrast to the Rhenish monks at Maria Laach (close to Cologne), who hesitated to side with Johann Reuchlin[14] in his battle with the theologians of Cologne as supporters of his rival Johann Pfefferkorn, the south German Ellenbog cultivated a friendship with Reuchlin, the famous lawyer and 'independent scholar'[15] of biblical linguistics.

Here, we will concentrate on the exchange of ideas between Ellenbog and Reuchlin. Two of Ellenbog's letters are included in the contemporary *Letters of Famous Men to Reuchlin* (1514) of 21 January 1510 and of 21 February 1512.[16] The primary aspect of their shared biblical humanism was their interest in polyglotism, that is, their linguistic endeavors in the original languages of the Bible and thus their return to the sources (*ad fontes*), which became the motto of Renaissance humanism. Biblical humanists such as Ellenbog wanted to investigate the original meaning of the Holy Scriptures and what at that time was called the Hebrew truth (*hebraica veritas*) on which Saint Jerome had already written.[17]

Ellenbog was fortunate to have a like-minded abbot as his superior, Abbot Leonhard Widenmann (from 1508 until he died in 1546). He introduced reforms at Ottobeuren according to the Melk Reform of the Benedictine monasteries in the Bavarian-Austrian regions. Ellenbog and Widenmann contributed greatly to the richness of monastic humanism in the southern German-speaking lands. The abbot himself established first contacts with Reuchlin through his letter of 8 October 1508. Further correspondence was carried on mostly by Ellenbog.[18]

---

[13] This biographical sketch largely follows the one provided by Andreas Bigelmair, "Nikolaus Ellenbog (1481–1543)" in Götz Freiherr von Pölnitz, ed., *Lebensbilder aus dem Bayerischen Schwaben* (Munich 1956) 112–139 (with literature up to 1959).

[14] They showed no interest in the study of the sacred languages which Reuchlin promoted; they were more interested in historiography and poetry, according to Paul Richter, "Die Schriftsteller" (1912) 332–333 (see note 49 in Introduction).

[15] Rummel, *The Case*, 16.

[16] In the following excerpts I offer my own translations of this Latin correspondence.

[17] See Sarah Kamin, "The Theological Significance of the *Hebraica Veritas* in Jerome's Thought" in Michael Fishbane and Emanuel Tov, eds., *'Sha'arei Talmon'. Studies in the Bible, Qumran, and the Ancient Near East Presented to Shemaryahu Talom* (Winona Lake, IN 1992) 243–253; Posset, "Polyglot Humanism in Germany Circa 1520 as Luther's Milieu and Matrix", (see note 17 in Introduction).

[18] Incidentally, Jerome Aleander (1480–1542), the later anti-Lutheran papal nuncio, while he was teaching Greek in Paris in 1511, was also supportive of Reuchlin, see Levi, *Renaissance and Reformation*, 217.

In his letter of 8 October 1508, Widenmann praises Reuchlin for his work towards the revival of the liberal arts. He is especially pleased with Reuchlin's books *De verbo mirifico* (The Wonder-Working Word) and *Rudimenta hebraica* (Rudiments of Hebrew). The former is styled as a discussion between three scholars about the significance of Hebrew for the understanding of the Scriptures. The latter is an introduction to the study of Hebrew, but written in Latin, on 621 large-sized pages.[19] The *Rudiments of Hebrew* was appreciated not only by Widenmann, but also by other monks of Ottobeuren, who were eager to learn the 'sacred language' (*s[ancta] lingua*). The monks made plans to hire an instructor of Hebrew for their abbey and asked Reuchlin for his recommendations. Inspired by Saint Jerome who praised the nun Paula of Rome for her studies, the monks of Ottobeuren would be happy if Reuchlin could help them to achieve their desire, to be able at least to read David's Book of the Psalms in Hebrew. If Reuchlin knew of a converted, baptized Jew (*fonte baptismatis renatus*) whom he could recommend, the abbey would be more than happy to hire him as a language instructor.[20]

The abbey of Ottobeuren, with its determination to employ an instructor of Hebrew as early as 1508, appears to have been far ahead of German universities in promoting Hebrew studies. For example, it took ten more years (the summer of 1518) before a professor of Hebrew was hired for the University of Erfurt. He was a baptized Jew by the name of Werner von Bacharach. It appears that the Hebrew professorship there was soon dropped, which may have been why Werner von Bacharach was then recommended for the Hebrew teaching position at Wittenberg. He went to Magdeburg instead, and, in 1523, moved on to Tübingen and then to Ingolstadt.[21] The same shaky position of Hebrew studies can also be observed at the University of Wittenberg. The first instructor who demonstrably taught Hebrew at Wittenberg, in 1513, was a private tutor named Tilman Conradi (or, Thiloninus Philymnus Syasticanus, c. 1485–c. 1522).[22]

---

[19] See Moshe Goshen-Gottstein, "Reuchlin and his Generation", in Arno Herzig and Julius H. Schoeps with Saskia Rohde, eds., *Reuchlin und die Juden* (Sigmaringen 1993) 151–160, here 155.

[20] See RBW 2, 81–82 (no. 147).

[21] See Erich Kleineidam, *Universitas Studii Erffordensis. Überblick über die Geschichte der Universität Erfurt im Mittelalter, 1392–1521* (Leipzig 1969) vol. 2:240–44 (with note 1275 concerning the Hebrew teacher).

[22] On the history of teaching Hebrew at the University of Wittenberg, see Gustav Bauch, "Die Einführung des Hebräischen in Wittenberg: mit Berücksichtigung der

It may be correct to suggest that the University of Wittenberg was blazing the way with regard to humanistic studies when one compares it, say, to the University of Cologne.[23] If we compare Wittenberg to certain monasteries with monastic humanists, the contrast becomes far less striking. In December 1518, the priest-humanist Georg Spalatin at the court of Saxony boasted to Vitus Bild, the humanist at the Benedictine monastery in Augsburg, that at Wittenberg the professor of Hebrew, Johannes Boeschenstein, attracted quite a few hearers (*auditors non pauci*).[24] However, by January 1519 Boeschenstein had left, and Philip Melanchthon substituted until July 1519. Only from June 1521 was there a permanent professorship of Hebrew at Wittenberg, filled by Matthew Aurogallus (Goldhahn, c. 1490–1543), who soon distinguished himself by the publication of a Hebrew grammar (1523) as well as a lexicon on oriental geography.[25] Notably, the abbey of Ottobeuren was, for a short time, the home of an institution of higher learning for their Benedictine members (*Ordenshochschule*), from 1453 to 1544, but it was dissolved during the Schmalkald War in 1546/1547, when the abbey's printing press was also lost.[26]

Returning to the correspondence between Reuchlin and the monks at Ottobeuren, on 11 October 1508, after only three days, Reuchlin responded to Abbot Leonhard's letter of 8 October. He complimented the abbot as a good leader of his monks and lover of the liberal arts. In this, the abbot was a rare bird (*rara avis*) on earth, as he wanted to pursue the "ancient, pure, and original theology of the prophets and visionaries" (*antiquam, puram et originariam theologiam, quae fuit prophetarum atque videntium*). Only the study of Hebrew could lead to the proper understanding (*ad unguem*) of the Scriptures.

Vorgeschichte des Studiums der Sprache in Deutschland", *Monatsschrift für Geschichte und Wissenschaft des Judentums* 48 (1904) 22–32, 77–86; Hans-Jürgen Zobel, "Die Hebraisten an der Universität Wittenberg (1502–1817)" in Julia Männchen and Ernst-Joachim Waschke, eds., *Altes Testament—Literatursammlung und Heilige Schrift* (Berlin 1993) 201–28, here 203 (on Tilmann Conradi).

[23] See Maria Grossmann, *Humanism in Wittenberg, 1485–1517* (Nieuwkoop 1975); Nauert, *op. cit.*; Eckhard Bernstein, "From Outsiders to Insiders. Some Reflections on the Development of a Group Identity of the German Humanists between 1450 and 1530", in Mehl, ed., *In Laudem Caroli for Charles G. Nauert*, 47.

[24] Letter of 10 December 1518 (no. 142), in Schröder, "Der Humanist Veit Bild", 221 (see Chapter on Bild).

[25] See Michael Becht, "Aurogallus", *Lexikon der Reformationszeit*, 50–51.

[26] See Friedrich Zoepfl, "Geschichte der ehemaligen Universität Ottobeuren", *Archiv für die Geschichte des Hochstifts Augsburg* 5 (Dillingen 1916–1919) 517–562; Bigelmair, "Nikolaus Ellenbog (1481–1543)" in *Lebensbilder*, 128–129.

According to Reuchlin, the Hebrew language was the intermediary between God and man (*mediatrix dei et hominum*) through which God chose to make his mysteries (*arcana sua*) known to mortals. He continued that it was hard to believe that scholars dared to interpret the Bible without any knowledge of Hebrew. The abbot would be able to lead his monks away from the muddied, wild rivers back to the purity of the sources (*fontium puritatis*), that is, to the pursuit of Hebrew for the Old Testament and of Greek for the New Testament.[27] The Renaissance humanists who were biblical humanists were convinced that the Hebrews drank from the source, the Greeks from the small creeks, but the Latins from the muddy swamps.[28] In this letter Reuchlin alluded to the metaphors used by contemporaneous humanists for the three ancient languages: Latin is equal to the "stirred up" and muddy rivers, while only the Hebrew and Greek languages are the pure spring waters. As soon as he can find a teacher of Hebrew he will send one to them (which took quite some time, but which finally happened in March 1510). For the time being, the abbot should study Hebrew as much as possible from those Hebrew books he already possesses.[29]

Indeed, over the winter months Ellenbog and the monks studied Hebrew from the books that the abbey owned. On 24 April 1509, he wrote to Reuchlin as the prince of the *literati*, telling him that the *Rudiments of Hebrew* was serving the monks at Ottobeuren well, as they were now sweating over the learning of this language. However, some questions had arisen that he wanted to put to him. First of all, Ellenbog wanted to know the meaning of the expression *Targum*, which Reuchlin mentions so often in his *Rudiments of Hebrew*. Secondly, once Reuchlin's cabalistic studies are concluded, he should send him a copy.

Thirdly, Ellenbog mentions a problem with the spelling of God's name in the form of the tetragram in *De verbo mirifico*, where he finds that the last character in the word 'God' is ה (*h*), while in the Hebrew

---

[27] See RBW 2, 84–85 (no. 148). This letter may make one question the thesis upheld by Goshen-Gottstein, that Reuchlin's "area of interest was not the Bible but knowledge for its own sake", 151.

[28] *Hebrai fontem, Graeci rivulos, Latini paludem bibunt.* This saying is found, for instance, at the Augustinian friary at Lauingen, southern Germany, according to Hedwig Vonschott, *Geistiges Leben im Augustinerorden am Ende des Mittelalters und zu Beginn der Neuzeit* (Berlin 1915; reprint: Vaduz 1965) 103.

[29] See RBW 2, 84–85 (no. 148).

Bible edition that the abbey has borrowed from Conrad Peutinger in Augsburg, the last Hebrew character is ד (*d*). Both Hebrew letters appear somewhat similar to the uninitiated. Ellenbog's letter reveals that by this time he was able to write in both Hebrew and Greek, as he uses Greek letters for 'the word tetragram' (το όνομα τετραγράμματον) and the Hebrew letters for 'Yahweh' with the two differing endings (יהוה, יהוד).[30] His question concerns the four characters of interpunctuation of the Hebrew language that were unknown to Ellenbog. In the conclusion of his letter Ellenbog informs Reuchlin that Abbot Leonhard has ordered Bibles in Hebrew, Aramaic (Chaldaic), and Greek from Venice (without having any success for a Greek Bible). Their abbey wants the Aramaic version, which was translated by the Chaldean Jonathan (ben Usiel, according to the Talmud) whom Reuchlin mentions occasionally in his *Rudiments of Hebrew*. They want Jonathan's version because it is held in such high esteem in the Jewish scholarly world. The monks should no longer be at a disadvantage in this regard because of their lack of knowledge of Aramaic. Therefore, Reuchlin should provide them with a textbook for this language so that they can learn it.

Reuchlin took time to answer Ellenbog's letter, sometime in May 1509. On the concept of *Targum*, Reuchlin explained that it is found in the Talmud and stands for any translation into Aramaic (*interpretationem Chaldaicam*). Concerning his cabalistic studies, he reports that he has nothing published so far. According to Reuchlin, the tetragram is spelled in various versions so that a lessening of its worth (if it were always used in the same way) is prevented; in addition the Jews want to avoid the spelling that was revealed to Moses. As for the characters of interpunctuation, they are a means of accentuation or signs for distinctions similar to the accents in the Greek language. In both Hebrew and Aramaic the same characters are used. Therefore no distinct Aramaic alphabet needs to be learned. Reuchlin informs him further that Aramaic was spoken by the Gallileans, Jesus, and the apostles, and that it is of Syriac origin. The difference between the two languages is comparable to the difference between Low and High German or Dutch and Bohemian.[31]

---

[30] See *Ellenbog Briefwechsel*, vol. 1:47–148 (no. 70); RBW 2, 97 (no. 152), lines 18–21. Hebrew words are read from right to left.

[31] *Quam apud nos Germanos bassae et altae*, *Ellenbog Briefwechsel*, vol. 1:49–50 (no. 71); RBW 2, 101–103 (no. 153).

On 3 June 1509, Ellenbog expressed his gratitude to the *doctissime humanissime* Reuchlin for answering his questions. His abbot would like to invite him to their monastery. In trying to console Reuchlin, who had complained that his books did not sell well, Ellenbog wrote that the esteem of a few scholars was more important than the applause of the masses. Ellenbog asked him for any other books from his pen, as their library so far had only the *Rudiments of Hebrew*.[32]

On 23 July 1509 Ellenbog sent another letter to Reuchlin on a different subject. During his novitiate Ellenbog had collected excerpts from Plato in the Latin translation by Marsilio Ficino[33] which agreed (*adstipulare*) with the Christian faith and were conducive to a moral life. Since his abbey now (1509) possessed its own printing press, he hoped to publish his anthology, *Epitoma Platonicum*.[34] He asked Reuchlin whether he would be so kind as to review his excerpt from *Kratylos* (*ex Cratylo*), check the correctness of words, and emend the text by adding the original Greek characters after the Greek words used. Ellenbog assumed that the reader would draw "greater sweet pleasure" (*maiori suavitate*) from such an edition. Reuchlin should have no problems complying with this request as he was so well versed in Greek and Latin. Ellenbog asked him to be especially careful in handling his manuscript because it was the only copy that existed. He extended greetings from Abbot Leonhard.[35] Ellenbog's project never came to fruition, as only one other of his manuscripts was published, dated 1517, on Saints Felicity, Alexander, and Theodor, whose relics were kept at Ottobeuren.[36]

Ellenbog's knowledge of Greek remained rudimentary, for in 1517 he still needed help with the translation of a Greek prayer to Mary and, in 1525, he was unable to understand a letter from the Benedictine

---

[32] See *Ellenbog Briefwechsel*, vol. 1:50–52 (no. 72); RBW 2, 105–107 (no. 154).

[33] *Opera Latina a Marsilio Ficino* with the addition of his *Theologia Platonica* (Venice 1491); see Lewis W. Spitz, "The *Theologia Platonica* in the Religious Thought of German Humanism", in *Middle Ages—Reformation—Volkskunde. Festschrift für John G. Kunstmann* (Chapel Hill 1959) 118–133, here 119. Spitz mentioned Ellenbog as an example of a "lesser humanist".

[34] See Zoepfl, 245.

[35] See *Ellenbog Briefwechsel*, vol. 1:52 (no. 73); RBW 2, 113–114 (no. 157). On Plato's work, see Timothy M. S. Baxter, *The Cratylus: Plato's Critique of Naming* (Leiden 1992).

[36] *Passio septem fratrum filiorum sanctae Felicitatis. Translatio sancti Alexandri. Passio sancti Theodori martyris*; RBW 1, 150, note 8 and RBW 2, 114, note 4; Bigelmair, "Nikolaus Ellenbog (1481–1543)" in *Lebensbilder*, 121.

Wolfgang Seid[e]l who had written to him in Greek.[37] It was all Greek to him, as he joked that he hardly saluted the Greek language at his doorstep: *Graeca lingua, quam vix a limine salutavi.*[38]

At the end of 1509, Reuchlin responded that due to illness he was unable to comply with the request of emending the excerpts from *Kratylos*; he was returning the manuscript and he hoped that Ellenbog could do the job himself with the help of a Greek dictionary.[39] Ellenbog had acquired such a dictionary from the Augustinian friar Nikolaus Pruckner at Lauingen,[40] which was another south German monastery with humanist members, under the leadership of the learned prior, Caspar Amman.[41]

Ellenbog confirmed in his letter to Reuchlin of 21 January 1510 (one of the letters that made it into the *Letters of Famous Men to Reuchlin*) that his manuscript had been returned to him. He hoped and prayed that Reuchlin would feel better soon so that his expertise might be of benefit to the "whole Catholic Church" (*toti ecclesiae catholicae*); he should put secular work (his job as a lawyer) aside and dedicate himself completely to the study of the divine Scriptures.[42] Ellenbog himself asked his abbot in May 1510 to relieve him from the duties of prior so that he might be able to live the life of a true *monachus* in prayer and studies, including the study of Greek and Hebrew.[43]

In response to a previous request, Reuchlin sent a letter to Ellenbog on 19 March 1510 in which he announced the success of his search for an instructor of Hebrew for the abbey, in the person of a Jewish convert, Johannes (his last name is not known), who was the deliverer of the letter. This may be Johannes Kun, who is listed as 'converted',[44] unless this note refers to a lay brother. Johannes, although not very learned, would nevertheless be able at least to teach the monks the correct Hebrew pronunciation. The new instructor did not expect a

---

[37] See on this RBW 2, 114, note 6.
[38] Bigelmair, "Nikolaus Ellenbog (1481–1543)" in *Lebensbilder*, 125.
[39] See *Ellenbog Briefwechsel*, vol. 1:53 (no. 74); RBW 2, 126 (no. 160).
[40] See *Ellenbog Briefwechsel*, vol. 1:39 (no. 61); RBW 2, 127, note 6.
[41] See Franz Posset, "Amman", BBKL 16 (2000) 49–52.
[42] See *Ellenbog Briefwechsel*, vol. 1:53–154 (no. 75); RBW 2, 128 (no. 161).
[43] See RBW 2, 129, note 7.
[44] RBW 2, 131 (no. 162), n. 7. The family name Kun may be a hint at Jewish origin, like Cohen ('priest' in Hebrew). On other aspects and on the significance of Reuchlin's letter to Ellenbog for a Reuchlin biography, see Augustijn, *Humanismus*, 70–71.

salary, but wished to enlist the support of the abbot and the monks for his ordination to the priesthood (*sacerdotium*). In his letter Reuchlin also wrote of his reverence for the sacred language:

> Thus may God love me since, after I have tried various other studies, nothing from among all other languages connects me more to God than the reading of the Holy Scripture in Hebrew. For, whenever I read Hebrew I feel as if I see God speaking before me—as I consider that this is the language in which God and the angels transmitted their grace to human beings in a supernatural way. When I do that I am shaken by some sort of shudder and by terror, but not without ineffable joy that follows such awe or rather such numbness, a joy which I really would like to call wisdom according to the divine Hebrew verse: "The fear of God is the beginning of wisdom". (Psalm 111:10; see Proverbs 1:7).[45]

To the quotation from Psalm 111:10, given in Hebrew letters, Reuchlin added the Latin translation ("The fear of God is the beginning of wisdom"). Evidently, he was not quite sure whether Ellenbog could handle all the Hebrew words.

The new instructor did not last more than a month at Ottobeuren, as Ellenbog noted in his letter to Reuchlin of 28 April 1510. Yet, they had enough time to learn correct pronunciation.[46] Ellenbog admits in the same letter his difficulties in learning Hebrew by referring to the same problem that Saint Jerome appears to have had in trying to master it. Yet, he would be content with making at least a few small steps in this endeavor.

On 10 April 1511 Reuchlin sent another instructor who was also the letter bearer; a Jew, who had not yet converted. His name is not given. The more friendly (*humanius*) the manner in which this Jew was treated, the better chance there was that he would convert.[47] Their correspondence does not reveal, however, how long this instructor stayed at the abbey.

Reuchlin was summoned to write his expert opinion for the imperial commission under Emperor Maximilian I to investigate a proposal to confiscate the books of the Jews. His opinion was dated 6 October 1510 and addressed to Archbishop Uriel von Gemmingen (1468–1514) of Mainz, chairman of the commission. Reuchlin's cover

---

[45] *Ellenbog Briefwechsel*, vol. 1:54–55 (no. 76); RBW 2, 130 (no. 162).
[46] See *Ellenbog Briefwechsel*, vol. 1:55–65 (no. 77); RBW 2, 137–139 (no. 165).
[47] See *Ellenbog Briefwechsel*, vol. 2:69 (no. 1); RBW 2, 177–178 (no. 175).

letter to the chairman concluded with the statement (in German): "One should not want to take such books away from the Jews, suppress or burn them".[48] In his opinion, the Old Testament could not be interpreted without the commentaries of the Jews, just as one could not do without the Greek language for the New Testament. He added "with due respect" that many teachers in the Church lacked knowledge of the two languages and thus gave a defective interpretation of the Holy Scriptures. From Jewish books flowed the true meaning of the language and understanding of the Bible. It would not be hard to imagine that much evil would arise from burning their books. Reuchlin recommended instead to his Imperial Majesty that for the next ten years the universities in Germany should hire two lecturers each, who would be able to teach Hebrew as the *clementin* had ordered (the wording in Early New High German is: *zwen maister . . . inn hebraeisch sprach . . . wie die clementin anzaigt*).[49] By 'Clementin' he meant a decree of Pope Clement V (1305–1313) that professorships were to be established for the teaching of oriental languages. In this undertaking the Jews should kindly help by lending their books.

When Ellenbog resumed his correspondence with Reuchlin on 30 August 1511 he asked him for an explanation of Jacob's Ladder and the seventy-two angels ascending and descending it, of which Reuchlin had written in the second book of *De verbo mirifico*. More important, though, was his statement to the effect that he would rather trust in Reuchlin's expertise and that he had read the booklet *Hand Mirror* (*Handt Spiegel*, printed in Mainz in 1511)[50] by Johannes Pfefferkorn, a convert from Judaism, with its accusations against Reuchlin. He disagreed with Pfefferkorn and instead sided with Reuchlin, writing to him: "I am eager to proclaim and amplify your praise, your honor".[51] The *Hand Mirror* was written by Pfefferkorn in defense against Reuchlin's opinion and his advocacy of preserving Jewish

---

[48] *. . . man sol nit moegen solliche buecher den iuden abreissen unn die undertrucken oder verbrennen* (cover letter), RBW 2, 158–160, here 160, lines 53–54.

[49] For an English version of the Expert Opinion see Rummel, *The Case against Johann Reuchlin*, Document 3, 86–97.

[50] Full title: *Handt Spiegel Johannis Pfefferkorns wider und gegen die Juden und Judischen Thalmudtschen schrifften*. On Pfefferkorn's writings in German, see Ellen Martin, *Die deutschen Schriften des Johannes Pfefferkorn. Zum Problem des Judenhasses und der Intoleranz in der Zeit der Vorreformation* (Göppingen 1994).

[51] *Ut tuam laudem, tuum honorem praedicare et amplificare studio; Ellenbog Briefwechsel*, vol. 2:74–77 (no. 9); RBW 2, 188–193 (no. 179), here 190, lines 28–29.

books (of 1510). Reuchlin retorted with his *Eye Mirror* (*Augen Spiegel*, printed in Tübingen in 1511),[52] which the theologians of Cologne condemned. Reuchlin was cited before the Inquisition on charges of judaizing. On 7 October 1512 the emperor issued a mandate to confiscate the *Eye Mirror*.[53] The authenticity of the imperial document can no longer be doubted.[54]

Reuchlin defended himself with his *Defense against the Cologne Slanderers*. In 1514, other humanists supported Reuchlin with a letter campaign known as *Letters of Famous Men to Reuchlin*, and, in 1515, further support was published with the *Letters of Obscure Men*, a satire on the scholastic theologians.[55] In 1516, Pfefferkorn defended himself with his *Streitbüchlein* (Little Book of Battle) against Reuchlin, published in Cologne with a nasty title page that shows Pfefferkorn pushing Reuchlin over as he is sitting by his desk. Reuchlin is depicted with a split tongue.[56]

Remarkably, from the beginning of the so-called 'Reuchlin Controversy', the monk from Ottobeuren sided with Reuchlin, as Ellenbog's letter of 30 August 1511 shows. The fact that certain specifically *monastic* humanists sided with Reuchlin is generally overlooked, as happened in a recent publication.[57] In the same letter Ellenbog asked for further information on the tetragram, also known under the Hebrew concept *Semhammaphoras* (*Schem ha-meforasch*, the exact name [of God]), and sent greetings from his abbot,[58] which clearly confirms that the abbot stood by Reuchlin as well.

---

[52] Full title: *Warhafftige entschuldigung gegen und wider ains getaufften iuden genant Pfefferkorn vormals getruckt uβgangen unwarhaftigs schmachbüchlin. Augenspiegel.*
[53] See *Briefwechsel*, vol. 2:625–629. In Early New High German: *nit feyl haben, verkauffen . . ., sonder tzu recht arrestyrt*, RBW 2, 625–627, here 626, lines 24–25; in Latin: *vendere aut emittere nequaquam permittatis, sed . . . per arrestastionem recipiatis* (Appendix IV).
[54] See RBW 2, 628, note 4.
[55] See Rummel's book on Reuchlin. Willibald Pirckheimer came out with his defense of Reuchlin in 1517 (see Rummel, Document 9).
[56] Depiction 3 in Johannes Schwitalla, "The Use of Dialogue in Early German Pamphlets. On the Constitution of Public Involvement in the Reuchlin-Pfefferkorn Controversy", in Andreas H. Jucker, Gerd Fritz, and Franz Lebsanft, eds., *Historical Dialogue Analysis* (Amsterdam and Philadelphia 1999) 111–137, here 129.
[57] Rummel provides as documentation in support of Reuchlin only the *Letters of Obscure Men* (Document 5), the letter of Willibald Pirckheimer of 1517 (Document 8), two letters from Erasmus of 1515 (Document 9), the letters of Hutten of 1520/1521 (Document 12), and Luther's comments (Document 13). Ellenbog's letter (as a document of monastic humanism) would be worthy of being added to this list.
[58] See *Ellenbog Briefwechsel*, vol. 2:74–77 (no. 9); RBW 2, 188–193 (no. 179).

In his response to Ellenbog of 30 September 1511, Reuchlin gave some explanations on the issue of the seventy-two angels. He expressed his joy at being considered worthy of suffering like the prophets who were persecuted (*sic enim persecuti sunt prophetas*, Mt 5:1) and also that Ellenbog and other friends were ready to defend his honor (*propugnator honoris mei*). He sent greetings to the abbot.[59]

Ellenbog indeed used his correspondence with other humanists to defend Reuchlin. We know of his letter to the physician at Memmingen, Jacob Stopel, to whom he sent Reuchlin's *Eye Mirror* on 26 October 1511; Stopel in turn was meant to contact the preacher Jodocus Gay and let him read the *Eye Mirror*.[60] On 12 January 1512, Ellenbog wrote to Reuchlin, thanking him for the copy of his *Eye Mirror*, which would assist him in defending Reuchlin's position. By the fall of that year, however, the *Eye Mirror* had been suppressed throughout the entire empire by the imperial mandate of 7 October 1512.[61] Ellenbog also thanked him for the explanation of the names of the angels, which, however, he still could not figure out. He planned to investigate this further.[62] This he did by contacting other monastic humanists in the Augustinian friary in Lauingen, namely Pruckner and perhaps Prior Amman. Ellenbog also contacted the Hebraist Johannes Boeschenstein in this regard in May 1514. His efforts show no success, however.[63]

Ellenbog took up his correspondence with Reuchlin a few weeks later, on 21 February 1512 (this is the other letter included in the *Letters of Famous Men to Reuchlin*). He expressed joy that Reuchlin was doing well in the circumstances. Might God grant him a long life so that his erudition might benefit the fatherland and he would be a "bright star" (*sydus [sidus] praefulgidum*) to all. His works would live on as *monumenta* after his death. The treasure of his knowledge of languages (*thesaurum cum linguarum interpretatione*) must not stay hidden, as it was God's gift which he must share with others. His abbot (Widenmann) invited Reuchlin to their abbey, and so did Ellenbog. And if Reuchlin happened to learn of a Greek Bible for sale anywhere, he should let him know.[64]

---

[59] See *Ellenbog Briefwechsel*, vol. 2:77–78 (no. 11); RBW 2, 194–197 (no. 181).
[60] See RBW 2, 197, note 17.
[61] RBW 2, 625–627 (Appendix IV).
[62] See *Ellenbog Briefwechsel*, vol. 2:85–86 (no. 23); RBW 2, 229–231 (no. 189).
[63] See RBW 2, 230–231, note 6.
[64] See RBW 2, 260–262 (no. 193).

On 1 August 1513, after a long interval, Abbot Leonhard himself wrote to Reuchlin that Ellenbog was reminding him "day and night" to purchase a Greek Bible for the abbey. Since no such Bible could be bought anywhere, would Reuchlin at least lend to them a Greek version of the Book of the Song of Songs so that the monks at Ottobeuren could make a copy and return it to him immediately afterwards?[65] From 1508 onwards, the monks had wanted to buy a Greek Bible (see letters nos. 147 and 152).

Reuchlin responded right away with a letter to Leonhard on 5 August 1513, letting him know that he did not own a Greek version of the Song of Songs, as he preferred to read texts in their original languages. Translations all too often have many mistakes, he wrote. Therefore, he preferred to read the New Testament in Greek and the Old Testament in Hebrew.[66]

As for Reuchlin's controversy with Pfefferkorn and the theologians at Cologne, Reuchlin informed the monks in the same letter (5 August 1513) that the emperor had ordered all sides (*omnibus partibus*) to be silent, after receiving Reuchlin's *Defensio . . . contra calumniators suos Colognienses* which was actually dedicated to the emperor (March 1513).[67] Reuchlin enclosed in his letter to Abbot Leonhard the text of the imperial mandate of 9 July 1513, which was to be published everywhere and in which the confiscation of Reuchlin's *Defense* was decreed.[68]

On 13 August 1513, Ellenbog sent a brief note to Reuchlin stating that he had had the opportunity to read Reuchlin's letter to his abbot and that he accepted his excuse for not bothering with a Greek version of the Canticle. From now on he, too, would want to read the Old Testament in the native language (*nativa lingua*) of Hebrew alone. Ellenbog also thanked Reuchlin for sending them the text of the imperial mandate against him and, at the same time, repeated the invitation to come and visit them at their abbey.[69] Evidently the monastic humanists at Ottobeuren had no problems with inviting the man whose *Defense* had just been prohibited and confiscated by the emperor. The imperial mandate did not decree

---

[65] See RBW 2, 373–374 (no. 217).
[66] See RBW 2, 375–376 (no. 218).
[67] See RBW 2, 375–376 (no. 218). Such an imperial order (June 1513?) is no longer extant.
[68] The texts in German and Latin are edited in RBW 2, 630–633 (Appendix V).
[69] See *Ellenbog Briefwechsel*, vol. 2:99–100 (no. 47); RBW 2, 396–397 (no. 221).

anything silencing both sides, as Reuchlin had written to the monks. Only Reuchlin's name is mentioned, and the order that his *Defense* is to be suppressed (Early New High German: *untertrucken*; in contemporary High German: *unterdrücken*).[70] As mentioned, on 7 October 1512, the emperor issued his decree for the confiscation of Reuchlin's *Eye Mirror*. In June 1520, the papal court finally condemned and fined Reuchlin.[71]

In March 1516, Ellenbog initiated friendly relations with Erasmus, to whom he wrote: "You [Erasmus] should henceforward add the name of Nikolaus Ellenbog to the list of your friends".[72] Ellenbog was so eager to obtain Erasmus' own Latin translation of the New Testament from Greek that he instructed the carrier of his letter to pay Erasmus in cash for this edition in order to be able to bring the book home right away (letter no. 395). In April, Erasmus accepted the offer of friendship and answered "Nikolaus Ellenbog whom he loves as a brother". In response to Ellenbog's inquiry about Erasmus' new Jerome edition and his Greek/Latin New Testament, Erasmus gave him this information:

> Jerome will be finished next autumn. The New Testament has been rushed into print rather than published, and yet the publication is such that in this class of work I have outstripped all my predecessors... If you judge that the labor which I have spent on the New Testament may do good in the Christian cause, make others study it besides yourself. Farewell, dearest Nikolaus.[73]

It looked as if Ellenbog was set to become not only a supporter of Erasmus and Reuchlin, but also of Luther; but he did not. In later years, he became an explicit opponent of Luther as far as the social implications of Luther's Reformation were concerned. One such concrete implication was the destruction of his abbey's printing press in 1525 during the Peasants' War (it was re-established in 1532).[74] To

---

[70] RBW 2, 631, line 35; in Latin: *supprimere*, 632, line 27 and 633, line 29 (Appendix V).
[71] See the chronology in Rummel, *The Case against Johann Reuchlin*, xvi.
[72] *Nihil inde quaerens nisi vt inter familiares tuos Nicolaum tuum deinceps connumerare velis*, Allen edition, vol. 2:209–210 (no. 395; *The Correspondence of Erasmus*, 252 (letter to Erasmus of 30 March 1516, no. 395).
[73] *The Correspondence of Erasmus*, 273 (letter to Ellenbog of April 1516, no. 402).
[74] See Magnus Bernhard, "Die Buchdruckerei des Klosters Ottobeuren", *Wissenschaftliche Studien und Mitteilungen aus dem Benediktinerorden* 2 (1881) 313–322; C. Viesel, "Die Buchdruckerei des Klosters Ottobeuren", *Memminger Geschichtsblätter* (1952/1953) 1–6. On the popular revolution, see Blickle, *The Revolution of 1525*.

the peasant rebels, the abbey of Ottobeuren became a symbol of exploitation and thus a target. The monastery controlled numerous serfs; some of them lived as far away as the region of Nuremberg and Colmar.[75] In 1540 Ellenbog blamed Luther for the Peasants' War and the attacks on monasteries, as Ellenbog wrote in defense of the servitude of the peasants.[76]

The investigation of the correspondence between the Benedictine monks of Ottobeuren and the lay theologian Johann Reuchlin (up to 1513) indicates that, indeed, at that time monastic humanists thrived in Germany. They were supportive of Reuchlin in his struggle with the theologians of Cologne. It would, therefore, be lop-sided to maintain that only Erasmus of Rotterdam and some anti-monastic humanists such as Ulrich von Hutten, or later Protestant reformers, such as Martin Luther and Philip Melanchthon, supported Reuchlin. The correspondence investigated here demonstrates that, from the beginnings of the 'Reuchlin Controversy', the Benedictine humanists of Ottobeuren sided with this Christian Hebraist. They even hired instructors of Hebrew on his recommendation. In his *Eye Mirror*, Reuchlin suggested that every university in Germany should create positions of Hebrew studies. In this the monastic humanists of Ottobeuren were in the forefront of established institutions of higher learning in the German lands, because they began to hire instructors of Hebrew as early as 1508. Ten years later, the Leipzig humanist Petrus Mosellanus (c. 1493–1524) still had to plead for the study of the biblical languages.[77]

---

[75] See Maps 3 and 4 on the regional distribution of the serfs of Ottobeuren in Peter Blickle, *The Revolution of 1525*, 48 and 54.

[76] Manuscript *De servis et servitude corporali*; see Friedrich Zoepfl, "Der Humanist Nikolaus Ellenbog zur Frage der bäuerlichen Leibeigenschaft", *Historisches Jahrbuch* 58 (1938) 129–135. Ellenbog's anti-Lutheran manuscript is kept at Ottobeuren: *Contra nonulla dogmata Lutheranorum et aliorum nostri temporis haereticorum*.

[77] See his *De variarum linguarum cognitione paranda oratio*; Wim François, "The Plea by the Humanist Petrus Mosellanus for a Knowledge of the Three Biblical Languages. A Louvain Perspective", *Revue d'Histoire Ecclésiastique* 98 (2003) 438–481. Latomus responded with his *De trium linguarum, et studii Theologici ratione dialogus*.

CONCLUSION

By definition, Renaissance monks lived in monasteries with little or no mobility, unlike Renaissance friars who often traveled or were moved, whenever necessary, from friary to friary, always located in major population centers. Monastic humanism comprises monks and friars who normally lived in a community. They were typical Renaissance men, interested in all aspects of letters and sciences, including astronomy (and astrology, which was not yet clearly separated from astronomy). Willibald Pirckheimer's description of humanist theologians as universally educated scholars fits all monastic humanists. According to him, they had to know not only their grammar, dialectic, rhetoric, physics, and metaphysics, but also geometry, arithmetic, music, and astronomy. Furthermore, in his view, a true humanist theologian had studied the three ancient and sacred languages (Latin, Greek, and Hebrew), as well as history and law. Monastic humanists were dedicated to the study of the 'humanities and letters' (*studia humanitatis ac litterarum*). This latter concept appears to have been introduced into the German lands by the middle of the fifteenth century. Universalists, with moral integrity, were the "true theologians" who no longer needed training in scholastic speculations. Instead they should return to the Bible and to the Church Fathers. Thus, Renaissance monks who were humanists are best located in the wider context of late medieval spirituality, theology, and piety (*devotio moderna*) with its 'book culture' (*Buchkultur*) and with its efforts towards reforming the faith and the Church in terms of returning to the original sources (*ad fontes*) of Christianity and to the observance of the original monastic rules.

The concern for spiritual and ecclesiastical reform was shared by both monastic and non-monastic *umanisti* ('humanists'), as they had been called in Italy since 1490. Generally, humanists pursued the ideal of 'learned piety' (*docta pietas*), and as monks (Benedictines and Cistercians) they specifically observed the Rule of Saint Benedict and prayerfully studied the Bible in *lectio divina* (prayerful reading and meditating).

There are certain aspects which to various degrees dominated the lives and works of these monks. Monastic (and, of course, non-monastic) humanists spent much of their time cultivating the art of letter-writing. This included paying attention to Latin grammar and style and to the rules of rhetoric. They collected the letters that they received and that they themselves wrote. In their extensive correspondence, they were also as garrulous as non-monastic humanists. Often they were considered outsiders to the scholastic life of the universities. They 'networked' eagerly in order to support each other and to keep their friendships alive. In addition, they tried to put in print just about anything they thought was noteworthy, or edited famous texts of the past for the first time in the new printing medium (*incunabula*). For this they needed to establish printing presses in their monasteries, and appoint directors for them. Ellenbog, for example, became director of the printing press at his abbey of Ottobeuren.

The general humanist movement back to the sources (*ad fontes*) also brought with it a great interest in historical studies that, for numerous monastic humanists, meant the investigation of the history of their own local monasteries or bishoprics. In the case of Bild at Augsburg this included research on the medieval lives of the local patron saints and the liturgical texts related to their feast days. Others, like Marius at Aldersbach, became significant general historiographers and distinguished verse makers.

Most of the monastic humanists were also biblical humanists. Leontorius excelled as an editor of Latin Bibles and biblical commentaries (and as an editor of the Church Fathers) for publishers at Basel. Ellenbog cherished the magnificent Bible he inherited from his father, still extant at Ottobeuren. Chelidonius composed Latin poems on biblical themes (on the lives of Christ and of Mary) which were printed together with Albrecht Dürer's famous pictures. They clothed biblical and spiritual themes in elegant humanist Latin that made Christian topics attractive, hopefully, even to their less pious humanist colleagues. They were often engaged not only in Latin verse making on biblical and devotional themes, but also on historical subjects and on praise of their friends, or as composers of epitaphs, including some for their own graves. Urbanus at Erfurt, though recognized as a Latinist by his friend Mutianus, is not known as a poet, but instead as a promoter of the Christ-centered poetry of another humanist, the layman Marcus Marulus of Split in Croatia, whose works were sold by Venetian book dealers.

Monastic humanists, as part of the international movement 'back to the sources', wanted not only to return to the origins of their own monastic tradition (observance of the Rule), but also to penetrate the sacred text (*sacra pagina*) on which they meditated and prayed. They wanted to reach the original meaning of the revered Word of God spoken to humankind. However, in order to arrive at the Hebrew Truth of the so-called Old Testament (the Hebrew Scriptures) and at the Greek Truth of the New Testament, they needed to join in the efforts to master these sacred languages, as well as continuing their study of Latin. Their monasteries began to hire teachers of these languages, if they could find them. They spent much of their funds on textbooks and dictionaries of Greek and Hebrew, and much of their time on locating, exchanging, and copying such texts. As for learning Hebrew, they depended on Jewish scholars to teach them, and, as a natural consequence, they became defenders of Johann Reuchlin in his advocacy of preserving Jewish books. The monastic humanists featured here were all more or less explicit supporters of Reuchlin in his defense of Jewish books and in his problems with the authorities.

The biographical sketches presented here demonstrate the broad interest of monastic humanists in the liberal arts and sciences. They made their contributions as Christian poets, music experts, astronomers/astrologers, as historiographers, as biblical humanists, as editors of texts from their Christian heritage—especially the Church Fathers and the Holy Scriptures—and as more or less accomplished Graecians and Hebraists. They were convinced that

> The Hebrews drink from the source, the Greeks from the rivulets, and the Latins from the swamp.
> *Hebräi fontem, Graeci rivulos, Latini paludem bibunt.*

SELECT BIBLIOGRAPHY

Augustijn, Cornelis, *Erasmus der Humanist als Theologe und Kirchenreformer* (Leiden etc.: Brill, 1996).
——, *Humanismus*, trans. into German by Hinrich Stoevesandt (*Die Kirche in ihrer Geschichte. Ein Handbuch*, vol. 2) (Göttingen: Vandenhoeck & Ruprecht, 2003).
Bast, Robert J. and Gow, Andrew C., eds., *Continuity and Change. The Harvest of Late Medieval and Reformation History. Essays Presented to Heiko A. Oberman on his 70th Birthday* (Leiden etc.: Brill, 2000).
Bellot, Josef, "Das Benediktinerstift St. Ulrich und Afra in Augsburg und der Humanismus", StM 84 (1973), 394–406.
Béné, Charles, *Sudbina jedne pjesme. Destin d'un poème. Destiny of a poem: Carmen de Doctrina Domini Nostri Iesu Christi Pendentis in Cruce Marci Maruli* (Zagreb: Nacionalna i sveučilišna biblioteka; Split: Književni krug Split, 1994).
Bernstein, Eckhard, "Der Erfurter Humanistenkreis am Schnittpunkt von Humanismus und Reformation. Das Rektoratsblatt des Crotus Rubianus", *Der polnische Humanismus und die europäischen Sodalitäten. Pirckheimer Jahrbuch für Renaissance- und Humanismusforschung* 12 (Wiesbaden: Harrassowitz, 1997), 137–165.
Bietenholz, Peter G. and Deutscher, Thomas B., eds., *Contemporaries of Erasmus: a biographical register of the Renaissance and Reformation*, 3 vols. (Toronto and Buffalo: University of Toronto Press, 1985–1987).
Bigelmair, Andreas, "Der Briefwechsel von Oekolampadius mit Veit Bild", *Reformationsgeschichtliche Studien und Texte* 40 (1922), 117–135.
——, "Nikolaus Ellenbog (1481–1543)" in *Lebensbilder aus dem Bayerischen Schwaben*, ed. Götz Freiherr von Pölnitz (Munich: Max Hueber, 1956).
Bigelmair, Andreas and Zoepfl, Friedrich, eds., *Nikolaus Ellenbog: Briefwechsel* (Münster: Aschendorff, 1938).
Black, Robert, "Humanism" in *The New Cambridge Medieval History*, ed. Christopher Allmand (Cambridge: University Press, 1997), vol. 7:243–277.
——, *Renaissance Thought* (London and New York: Routledge, 2001).
Blickle, Peter, *The Revolution of 1525: The German Peasants' War from a New Perspective*, translated by Thomas A. Brady, Jr., and H. C. Erik Midelfort from the 2nd edition (Baltimore: The Johns Hopkins University Press, 1981 and 1985).
Buck, August, "Der Rückgriff des Renaissance-Humanismus auf die Patristik", in *Festschrift Walther von Wartburg zum 80. Geburtstag 18. Mai 1968*, ed. Kurt Baldinger (Tübingen: Niemeyer, 1968), vol. 1:153–75.
Cowie, Murray and Marian L., eds., *The Works of Peter Schott (1460–1490)*, 2 vols. (Chapel Hill: University of North Carolina, 1963–1971).
Dall'Asta, Matthias and Dörner, Gerald, eds., *Johannes Reuchlin: Briefwechsel* (Stuttgart-Bad Cannstatt: Frommann-Holzboog, 1999–2003).
D'Amico, John F., *Roman and German Humanism, 1450–1550. Collected Studies edited by Paul F. Grendler* (Aldershot, UK: Ashgate, 1993).
D'Onofrio, Giulio, ed., Matthew J. O'Connell, trans., *History of Theology. III. The Renaissance* (Collegeville, Minn.: The Liturgical Press, 1998).
Ehrenpreis, Stefan and Lotz-Heumann, Ute, *Reformation und konfessionelles Zeitalter* (Darmstadt: Wissenschaftliche Buchgesellschaft, 2002).
Elm, Kaspar, "Monastische Reformen zwischen Humanismus und Reformation", in Lothar Perlitt, ed., *900 Jahre Kloster Bursfelde. Reden und Vorträge zum Jubiläum 1993* (Göttingen: Vandenhoeck & Ruprecht, 1994), 59–111.

Freitäger, Andreas, "Klosterhumanismus. Johannes Cincinnius und die Bildung im Kloster Werden, 1505–1555", in Jan Gerchow, ed., *Das Jahrtausend der Mönche. Klosterwelt Werden 799–1803* (Cologne: Wienand, 1999).
Ganzer, Klaus and Steimer, Bruno, eds., *Lexikon der Reformationszeit* (Freiburg, Basel, Vienna: Herder, 2002). English edition translated by Brian McNeil (New York: Crossroad, 2004).
Gloning, Marian, "Aus der Gedichtesammlung des Abtes Marius von Aldersbach", StM 33 (1912), 76–89.
Gollob, Hedwig, "Der Herkules des Wiener Chelidonius von 1515", *Gutenberg Jahrbuch* (1966), 284–86.
Halporn, Barbara C., *The Correspondence of Johann Amerbach: Early Printing in its Social Context* (Ann Arbor: The University of Michigan Press, 2000).
Hartmann, Alfred, ed. *Die Amerbachkorrespondenz*, 10 vols. (Basel: Verlag der Universitätsbibliothek, 1942–).
Herding, Otto and Mertens, Dieter, eds., *Jakob Wimpfeling: Briefwechsel* (Munich: Wilhelm Fink, 1990).
Hillmann, Thea, "Benedictus Chelidonius von St. Ägidien in Nürnberg", StM 58 (1940), 139–45.
Holzberg, Niklas, *Willibald Pirckheimer: Griechischer Humanismus in Deutschland* (Munich: Wilhelm Fink, 1981).
Höss, Irmgard, *Georg Spalatin 1484–1545. Ein Leben in der Zeit des Humanismus und der Reformation* (Weimar: Hermann Böhlaus Nachfolger, 2nd edition 1989).
Janota, Johannes and Williams-Krapp, Werner, eds., *Literarisches Leben in Augsburg während des 15. Jahrhunderts* (Tübingen: Niemeyer, 1995).
Junghans, Helmar, *Der junge Luther und die Humanisten* (Weimar, 1984; Göttingen, 1985).
Kipf, Klaus, "Bild", *Deutscher Humanismus 1480–1520, Verfasserlexikon*, ed. Franz J. Worstbrock (Berlin and New York: de Gruyter, 2005).
Klugseder, Robert, ed., *850 Jahre Zisterzienserkloster Aldersbach, Festschrift zur Feier der 850. Wiederkehr des Gründungstages* (Vilshofen: Donaudruck, 1996).
Knepper, Joseph, "Jakob Wimpfeling (1450–1528). Sein Leben und seine Werke nach den Quellen dargestellt", *Erläuterungen und Ergänzungen zu Janssens Geschichte des deutschen Volkes* (Freiburg: Herder, 1902; reprint: Nieuwkoop: B. de Graaf, 1965), vol. 3:1–375.
Krause, Carl, ed., *Der Briefwechsel des Mutianus Rufus* (Kassel: A. Freyschmidt, 1885).
Kristeller, Paul Oskar, "The Contribution of Religious Orders to Renaissance Thought and Learning", ABR 21 (1970) 1–155; reprint: *Medieval Aspects of Renaissance Learning. Three Essays* (Durham: Duke University Press, 1974), 95–158.
Le Gall, Jean-Marie, *Les moines au temps des réformes: France (1480–1560)* (Seyssel: Champ Vallon, 2001).
Levi, Anthony, *Renaissance and Reformation. The Intellectual Genesis* (New Haven: Yale University Press, 2002).
Machilek, Franz, "Klosterhumanismus in Nürnberg um 1500", *Mitteilungen des Vereins für Geschichte der Stadt Nürnberg* 64 (1977), 10–45.
Mehl, James V. ed., *In Laudem Caroli for Charles G. Nauert* (Kirksville, Missouri: Thomas Jefferson University Press, 1998).
Moeller, Bernd, "Religious Life in Germany on the Eve of the Reformation", in *Pre-Reformation Germany*, ed. Gerald Strauss (London: Macmillan, 1972), 13–42 (originally published in 1965).
——, "Die frühe Reformation in Deutschland als neues Mönchtum", in *Die frühe Reformation in Deutschland als Umbruch. Wissenschaftliches Symposion des Vereins für Reformationsgeschichte 1996*, eds. Bernd Moeller and Stephen E. Buckwalter (Gütersloh: Gütersloher Verlagshaus Gerd Mohn, 1998).
Müller, Harald and Ziesak, Anne-Katrin, "Der Augsburger Benediktiner Veit Bild

und der Humanismus. Eine Projektskizze", *Zeitschrift des historischen Vereins für Schwaben* 95 (2002), 27–51.
Nagl, J. W. and Zeidler, Jakob, *Deutsch-österreichische Literaturgeschichte. Ein Handbuch zur Geschichte der deutschen Dichtung in Österreich-Ungarn* (Vienna: C. Fromme, 1899).
Newald, Richard, *Probleme und Gestalten des deutschen Humanismus: Studien* (Berlin: Walter de Gruyter and Co., 1963).
Oswald, Josef, "Abt Wolfgang Marius von Aldersbach: Leben und geschichtliche Schriften", in Clemens Bauer, Laetitia Boehm, and Max Müller, eds., *Speculum historiale: Geschichte im Spiegel von Geschichtsschreibung und Geschichtsdeutung* (Freiburg and Munich: Verlag Karl Alber, 1965), 354–74.
——, "Die Gedichte des Abtes Wolfgang Marius von Aldersbach", *Ostbairische Grenzmarken: Passauer Jahrbuch für Geschichte, Kunst und Volkskunde* 7 (Passau: Institut für Ostbairische Heimatforschung Passau, 1964/1965), 310–319.
Overfield, James H., *Humanism and Scholasticism in Late Medieval Germany* (Princeton: Princeton University Press, 1984).
Paulus, Nikolaus, "Wolfgang Mayer, ein baierischer Cisterzienser des 16. Jahrhunderts", *Historisches Jahrbuch* 15 (1894) 575–588 (on Marius).
Porter, Roy and Teich, Mikulás, eds., *The Renaissance in National Context* (New York etc.: Cambridge University Press, 1992).
Posset, Franz, "A Cistercian Monk as Editor of the *Carmen* of the Croatian Humanist Marcus Marulus (died 1524): The German Humanist Henricus Urbanus O.Cist. (died 1538)", CSQ 39 (2004), 399–419.
——, "Benedictus Chelidonius O.S.B. (C. 1460–1521), A Forgotten Monastic Humanist of the Renaissance", ABR 53 (2002), 426–52.
——, "Leontorius", BBKL 19 (2001), 896–900.
——, "Leontorius", *Deutscher Humanismus 1480–1520, Verfasserlexikon*, ed. Franz J. Worstbrock (Berlin and New York: de Gruyter, 2005).
——, "Polyglot Humanism in Germany Circa 1520 as Luther's Milieu and Matrix: The Evidence of the 'Rectorate Page' of Crotus Rubeanus", *Renaissance and Reformation/Renaissance et Réforme* 27 (2003, issued in 2004), 5–33.
——, "'Rock' and 'Recognition': Martin Luther's Catholic Interpretation of 'You are Peter and on this rock I will build my Church' (Matthew 16:18) and the Friendly Criticism from the Point of View of the 'Hebrew Truth' by his Confrère, Caspar Amman, 'Doctor of the Sacred Page'", in Timothy Maschke, Franz Posset, and Joan Skocir, eds., *Ad fontes Lutheri: Toward the Recovery of the Real Luther. Essays in Honor of Kenneth Hagen's Sixty-Fifth Birthday* (Milwaukee: Marquette University Press, 2001), 214–252.
——, "The Benedictine Humanist Vitus Bild (1480–1529): Sundial Producer, Mathematician, Linguist, Poet, Historiographer, Music Expert, Pro-Lutheran, Anti-Zwinglian", ABR 55 (2004), 372–394.
——, *The Front-Runner of the Catholic Reformation: The Life and Works of Johann von Staupitz* (Aldershot, UK: Ashgate, 2003).
——, "Vitus Bild", BBKL 21 (2003), 116–121.
Renaudet, Augustin, *Préréforme et Humanism à Paris 1494–1517* (Paris: Librairie d'Argences, 1916; 2nd, revised edition, 1953).
Reuchlin, Johannes, *De verbo mirifico. 1494. De arte cabalistica. 1517. Faksimile-Neudruck in einem Band* (Stuttgart-Bad Cannstatt: Friedrich Frommann [G. Holzboog], 1964).
Richter, Paul, "Die Schriftsteller der Benediktinerabtei Maria-Laach, mit Textbeilagen. III: Die humanistische Epoche in Maria-Laach mit Rücksicht auf den rheinischen Klosterhumanismus überhaupt", in *Westdeutsche Zeitschrift für Geschichte und Kunst* 17 (1912), 277–340.
Röder, Thomas and Wohnhaas, Theodor, "Die *Stella musicae* des Benediktiners Veit Bild. Eine spätmittelalterliche Musiklehre aus Augsburg", *Jahrbuch des Vereins für Augsburger Bistumsgeschichte e. V.* 32 (1998), 305–325.

Rowland, Ingrid D., "Revenge of the Regensburg Humanists, 1493", *The Sixteenth Century Journal* 25 (1994), 307–22.
Rummel, Erika, *The Case against Johann Reuchlin: Religious and Social Controversy in Sixteenth-Century Germany* (Toronto etc.: University of Toronto Press, 2002).
——, *The confessionalization of humanism in Reformation Germany* (Oxford and New York: Oxford University Press, 2000).
——, *The Humanist-Scholastic Debate in the Renaissance and Reformation* (Cambridge, MA: Harvard University Press, 1995).
Rupprich, Hans, *Der Briefwechsel des Konrad Celtis* (Munich: C. H. Beck, 1934).
Scherbaum, Anna, *Albrecht Dürers* Marienleben. *Form—Gehalt—Funktion und sozialhistorischer Ort.* Mit einem Beitrag von Claudia Wiener (Wiesbaden: Harrassowitz, 2004).
Schneider, Reinhard, "Maulbronns kulturelle Ausstrahlung im Mittelalter", in *Anfänge der Zisterzienser in Südwestdeutschland: Politik, Kunst und Liturgie im Umfeld des Klosters Maulbronn*, eds. Peter Rückert and Dieter Planck (Stuttgart: Thorbecke, 1999).
Schottenloher, Karl, "Der Benediktiner und Humanist Nikolaus Ellenbog in Ottobeuren und sein Briefwechsel (1504–1543)", *Zeitschrift für Bayerische Landesgeschichte* 11 (1938), 468–70.
Schröder, Alfred, "Der Humanist Veit Bild, Mönch bei St. Ulrich: Sein Leben und sein Briefwechsel", *Zeitschrift des Historischen Vereins für Schwaben und Neuburg* 20 (1893), 173–227.
Schwitalla, Johannes, "The Use of Dialogue in Early German Pamphlets. On the Constitution of Public Involvement in the Reuchlin-Pfefferkorn Controversy", in *Historical Dialogue Analysis*, eds. Andreas H. Jucker, Gerd Fritz, and Franz Lebsanft (Amsterdam and Philadelphia: J. Benjamins Publishing Company, 1999), 111–137.
Spitz, Lewis W., *The Religious Renaissance of the German Humanists* (Cambridge: Harvard University Press, 1963).
——, "The *Theologia Platonica* in the Religious Thought of German Humanism", in *Middle Ages—Reformation—Volkskunde. Festschrift für John G. Kunstmann* (Chapel Hill: University of North Carolina Press, 1959), 118–133.
Stupperich, Robert, ed., *Reformatorenlexikon* (Gütersloh: Gütersloher Verlagshaus Gerd Mohn, 1984).
Telesca, William J., "The problem of the commendatory monasteries and the order of Cîteaux during the abbacy of Jean de Cirey, 1475–1501", *Cîteaux* 22 (1971), 154–177.
Verbeke, Gerard and Ijsewijn, Josef, *The Late Middle Ages and the Dawn of Humanism Outside Italy*. Proceedings of the international conference, Louvain, May 11–13, 1970 (Louvain: University Press, 1972; The Hague: Martinus Nijhoff, 1972).
Whitlock, Keith, ed., *The Renaissance in Europe: A Reader* (New Haven: Yale University Press, 2000).
Wiener, Claudia, "Chelidonius", *Deutscher Humanismus 1480–1520, Verfasserlexikon*, ed. Franz J. Worstbrock (Berlin and New York: de Gruyter, 2005).
Wiener, Claudia, Scherbaum, Anna, and Drescher, Georg, eds., *Andachtsliteratur als Künstlerbuch. Dürers* Marienleben. *Eine Ausstellung der Bibliothek Otto Schäfer zu einem Buchprojekt des Nürnberger Humanismus* (Schweinfurt: Weppert Print Media, 2005).
Willibald Pirckheimers Briefwechsel, vols. 1 and 2, ed. Emil Reicke (Munich: C. H. Beck, 1940); vol. 3, ed. Helga Scheible and Dieter Wuttke; vol. 4, ed. Helga Scheible, (Munich: C. H. Beck, 1997).
Wilson, N. G., *From Byzantium to Italy: Greek Studies in the Italian Renaissance* (Baltimore: The Johns Hopkins University Press, 1992).
Wolff, Georg, "Conradus Leontorius. Biobibliographie", *Beiträge zur Geschichte der Renaissance und Reformation: Joseph Schlecht am 16. Januar 1917 als Festgabe zum Sechzigsten Geburtstag*, eds. L. Fischer et al. (Munich and Freising: Dr. F. P. Datterer & Cie [Arthur Sellier], 1917), 363–410.

Worstbrock, Franz Josef, "Aus Gedichtsammlungen des Wolfgang Marius", *Zeitschrift für bayerische Landesgeschichte* 44 (1981), 491–504.
——, *Deutscher Humanismus 1480–1520, Verfasserlexikon* (Berlin and New York: de Gruyter, 2005).
Zoepfl, Friedrich, "Der Humanist Nikolaus Ellenbog zur Frage der bäuerlichen Leibeigenschaft", *Historisches Jahrbuch* 58 (1938), 129–135.

INDEX OF PERSONAL NAMES

Acropolitanus, *see* Bild
Adam and Eve 70, 73
Adelmann, Bernhard (canon) 142, 148, 157
Adrianus Matthaeus (Hebrew instructor) 58
Afra (saint) 141
Agricola, Rudolph (humanist) 6, 24, 95
Aikos (son of Zeus) 61
Alantee (printer) 86
Albrecht von Brandenburg (cardinal) 21
Alcaeus (poet) 74
Alexander (saint) 163
Alkmaion (Alcmeon, Greek legendary maniac) 73
Altdorfer, Albrecht (painter) 86
Ambrose (church father) 53, 55, 152
Amerbach, Boniface 47–49
Amerbach, Bruno 56, 59
Amerbach, Johannes (printer) 36, 38–40, 42–52, 54–60
Amman, Caspar (Augustinian) 145–147, 164, 168
Anna (saint) 76, 92, 97
Annas 74
Anthony (saint) 100
Anubis 78
Aperbachius, *see* Eberbach
Apollo 78, 100, 118
Aristotle 83
Athanasius (saint) 119, 150
Augiensis, *see* Berno von Reichenau
Augustine (church father) 11, 20, 46–47, 53–55, 117, 152
Augustus (emperor) 56
Aurogallus, Matthew (Goldhahn, Hebrew instructor) 160
Aventinus, Johannes (historian) 106

Bacchus (Evius) 35, 122
Bacharach, Werner von (Hebrew instructor) 159
Bandinus (theologian) 87
Barbo, Ludovico (Benedictine) 18
Basilius (saint) 148

Bebel, Heinrich (poet) 40, 135–136
Benedict (saint) 21, 80, 97, 103, 116–117, 135, 173
Benedict XII (pope) 18
Bernard of Clairvaux (Cistercian) 20–21, 45, 70, 102, 112, 115–117, 120, 152–153
Bern[o] von Reichenau (Augiensis, Benedictine) 141
Bessarion (cardinal) 119
Bild, Vitus (Acropolitanus, Benedictine) 23, 28, 133–154, 157, 160, 174
Biondo, Flavio (historian) 46
Blarer, Ambrose (Benedictine) 22
Boeschenstein, Johannes (Hebrew instructor) 143, 145, 160, 168
Bonaventure (saint) 152–153
Brant, Sebastian (lawyer, poet) 37, 39, 43, 52, 61
Breitenladenburg, Kaspar von (Benedictine) 20
Bruschius, Caspar (historian) 96
Bugenhagen, Johannes (Pomeranus, reformer) 150
Burrus, Johannes (Cistercian) 44
Butzbach, Johannes (Benedictine) 97

Caiaphas 72, 74
Cajetan, Thomas (cardinal) 147
Caligula (emperor) 82
Calliope (muse of poetry) 33, 100
Calpinus, Ambrose (Calepin, Augustinian) 55, 145
Camerarius, Joachim (poet, historian) 4
Canappus, Ioannes (Hans Knappe, printer) 127–128
Capnio(n), *see* Reuchlin
Celsus, Cornelius Aulus 56
Celtis, Conradus (poet) 6, 13, 25, 32, 43–44, 65, 81, 136
Chalcondylas, Demetrius (Greek scholar) 35
Charles V (emperor) 84, 86, 104
Charles VIII (king) 34
Chelidonius, Benedictus (Benedictine) 15, 23, 28, 63–93, 120, 174

Ceres (goddess) 118
Christof (Benedictine) 149
Chrysostom, John (theologian) 40, 152–153
Cicero 38, 72, 138
Cimon of Athens 51
Cirey, Jean de (Cistercian) 24, 33–34, 38, 40, 42, 100
Clare (saint) 16, 78–79
Claudius (emperor) 82
Clement V (pope) 166
Clio (muse of history) 100
Cochlaeus, Johannes (priest, humanist) 15, 67, 81–83
Conrad of Halberstadt (de Alemannia, Bible scholar) 51
Conradi, Tilman (Hebrew instructor) 159
Cortese, Gregorio (Benedictine) 18
Corvinus, Antonius (Rabe, Cistercian) 25
Cranach, Lucas (painter) 90–91
Crato, Adam (later, Lutheran preacher) 4
Cressus, *see* Kress
Crotus Rubeanus (Rubianus, humanist) 3–5, 110–113
Cuno, Johannes (Cono, Dominican) 15, 57
Cupid 91
Curvello, Johannes (Benedictine) 97
Cuspidius, *see* Spiess
Cuspinianus, Johannes (poet) 83

Daedalus (craftsman) 75
Dalberg, Johannes von (bishop) 2, 43–44
David (king) 159
Delius 82
Denck, Johannes (later, Anabaptist) 136
Diamond, Jacob (composer) 84
Dionysius (Dionisius, saint) 141, 152–153
Donatus, Aelius 35
Döring, *see* Thöring
Draco, Johannes (Drach, Draconites, canon) 4
Dürer, Albrecht (artist) 21, 66–69, 71, 75, 79–80, 86, 88, 91–92, 129, 174
Duronius, Johannes (Cistercian) 120

Ebendorfer, Thomas (historian, theologian) 104

Eberbach, Peter (Petreius, or Aperbachius, lawyer) 4
Eck, Johannes (theologian, humanist) 15, 87, 89, 147, 157
Ellenbog, Barbara (Cistercian) 157
Ellenbog, Nikolaus (Cubitus, Benedictine) 23, 27–28, 139, 145, 155–171, 174
Ellenbog, Ulrich (physician) 155
Emser, Jerome (theologian, humanist) 15, 40
Epicurus 86
Epitectus [sic], Epitetus 150
Epp, Georg (Dominican) 51
Erasmus of Rotterdam (humanist) 2, 4, 6, 15, 21, 26, 37, 41, 62, 72, 77, 103, 109, 111, 144, 148, 151, 156–157, 170–171
Erinyes (Erinnes) 71
Ernest of Bavaria (duke) 104–105
Eusebius (historiographer) 152–153
Eyb, Albrecht (canon) 46

Faber Stapulensis, Jacobus (Lefèvre d'Étaples, bible scholar) 62, 83
Faustus, Georgius Helmitheus (magician) 124
Felicity (saint) 163
Ficino, Marsilio (philosopher) 123, 163
Foresti, Giacomo Filippo (Augustinian) 19
Francis of Assisi (saint) 117
Frederick III (emperor) 28
Frederick the Wise (elector) 89–90, 105, 124, 139
Froben, Johannes (printer) 46, 50–52, 54–55
Frosch, Johannes (Carmelite) 153
Fug, Johannes (Augustinian) 15
Furter, Michael (printer) 49

Gaguin, Robert (historian) 32
Gay, Jodocus (preacher) 168
Galenus 152
Geiler, Johannes, von Kaisersberg (Kayersberg, preacher, humanist) 15, 39, 120, 129–130
Gemmingen, Uriel von (bishop) 165
George the Rich (duke) 95
Gerson, Jean (theologian) 20, 40, 148
Geryon (monster) 86
Glicon (wrestler) 73
Goldhahn, *see* Aurogallus

INDEX OF PERSONAL NAMES

Graf, Urs (artist) 128–130
Gregory (church father) 80, 152
Gregory of Nazianz (theologian) 150
Gresemund, Dietrich (lawyer) 41
Grimm, Sigmund (printer) 149
Grote, Geert (theologian) 6
Grünewald, Matthias (painter) 99
Grüninger, Johann (printer) 96
Gunther of Pairis (Cistercian) 49

Hadrian VI (pope) 105
Hardenberg, Albert Rizaeus (Cistercian) 25
Haslach, Kaspar (priest) 146
Henry of Rees (Cistercian) 24
Heracles (Hercules) 84, 86
Herbord (Benedictine) 101
Herod (king) 73
Hesiod 112
Hesmann, Johannes (Benedictine) 58
Hessus, Eobanus (poet) 4
Heynlin, Johannes von Stein (de Lapide, Carthusian) 16, 39, 45
Hippocrates 152
Hieronymus Paduanus, *see* Jerome of Padua
Hisolidus, Matthaeus (Hiscold, Hitzschold, Benedictine) 22
Hoeltzel, Hieronymus (printer) 66, 75
Homer 125
Honoratus, *see* Servius
Horace 48, 60, 74, 81, 137
Hugo a Sancto Caro (cardinal) 49–51, 61
Hus, John (priest, reformer) 102
Hutten, Ulrich von (knight, poet) 4, 20, 171

Isis 78

Jacob of Morimond (Cistercian) 38
Jacobus de Bannissis (imperial secretary) 84
Jerome (church father) 41, 56–58, 60, 92, 140, 152, 157–159, 165, 170
Jerome of Padua (Hieronymus Paduanus) 67, 68
Johannes von Gmunden (astronomer) 139
John the Baptist 40, 70, 99
John the Evangelist 40
John of Saxony (duke) 26
Jonas, Justus (canon) 4

Jonathan ben Usiel (Jewish scholar) 162
Joseph (saint) 75
Jouennaux, Guy (Benedictine) 21
Julian (emperor) 150
Jupiter 118

Kaisersberg, *see* Geiler
Kassner, Georg (Cistercian) 25
Kastner, Simon (Cistercian) 95
Kempis, *see* Thomas
Koberger, Anton (printer) 40, 46, 50–51, 54, 118
Knobloch, Johann (printer) 66, 129–130
Kremmbnitzer, Johann (Benedictine) 65
Kress, Anton (Cressus, priest) 83
Kruse, Gottschalk (Benedictine) 22
Kun, Johannes (Hebrew instructor) 164

Lactancius 96, 152, 153
Landinus, Christophorus (commentator on the classics) 35
Lang, Johannes (Augustinian) 4, 15, 124–125, 143
Lang, Matthew (cardinal, of Wellenburg) 84, 105
Lapide, *see* Heynlin
Lascaris, Constantine (Greek scholar) 27
Latomus, Jacobus (theologian) 62
Lefèvre d'Étaples, *see* Faber Stapulensis
Leo X (pope) 4, 90
Leontorius, Conradus (Töritz, Cistercian) 13, 24, 28–62, 100, 174
Leontorius, Henricus (Töritz, Cistercian) 50
Leyb, Kilian (Leib, canon) 15
Linck, Wenceslaus (Augustinian) 15
Linus (musician) 82
Loans, Jehiel (Jewish scholar) 28
Lochau, Martin von (Cistercian) 25
Locher, Jacob (poet) 80, 136–138
Lombard, Peter (theologian) 27, 87
Lucensis, Franciscus (priest) 126
Lucian 143
Luder, Peter (poet) 14
Ludwig of Bavaria (duke) 105
Luna 118
Luscinius, Otmar (Nachtigall, theologian, musician) 143, 145

186 INDEX OF PERSONAL NAMES

Luther, Martin (Augustinian, reformer) 4, 6, 8, 13, 17, 22, 27–28, 46, 62, 65, 72, 79, 87, 89–90, 102–103, 111, 125, 135, 142–144, 146–149, 151–154, 170, 171
Lyra, see Nicholas de Lyra

Mancinus, Dominicus (spiritual author) 67–68
Manetti, Giannozzo (lay theologian) 2
Manlius, Antonius Britonoriensis (Augustinian) 39
Mantuan[us], Baptista (Carmelite) 8, 29, 67, 69, 76, 99, 113, 116, 121, 136, 138
Manutius, Aldus (Aldo Manutio, printer) 5, 27, 96, 119
Marius, Bolfgangus (Lukas Mayer, Cistercian) 25, 28, 32, 66, 93–107, 174
Marschalk, Nikolaus (printer) 27, 115–116
Marulus, Marcus (lay theologian) 2, 86, 97, 111, 126–128, 130–131, 174
Mary
　Annunciation to Mary 74, 76
　immaculate conception 40–41, 92
　Mary Mother of God 77–78
　Mary and John the Baptist (see also deësis) 70
　Mary and Joseph 75
　Mary's assumption 76
　Mary's coronation 76
　virgin 65, 71, 74, 76–77, 80, 91, 97, 99, 118, 163, 174
Mary Magdalene 72, 74
Mary of Hungary (queen) 84
Maximilian I (emperor) 29, 65, 70, 83, 86, 88, 136, 142, 165
Meisterlin, Sigismund (historian) 20, 141
Melanchthon, Philip (lay theologian) 2, 4, 25, 62, 124–125, 143, 160, 171
Menius, Jodocus (Justus Mening, humanist) 4
Metlinger, Peter (printer) 41
Meurer, Michael Haenlein (Michael a Muris Galliculus, Cistercian) 25
Minerva 100
Minos (son of Zeus) 61
Moltzner, Ulrich (Cistercian) 25, 95, 100

Mörlin, Conrad (Benedictine) 140, 142
Mosellanus, Petrus (humanist) 171
Moses 118, 162
Müntzer, Thomas (priest, reformer) 26
Murner, Thomas (Franciscan, poet) 26
Murrho, Sebastian (humanist) 29, 32, 59
Musculus, Wolfgang (Benedictine) 22
Mutianus Rufus, Conradus (canon) 2, 4, 6, 109, 111–113, 115–127, 143, 174

Nachtigall, see Luscinius
Nadler, Jeorius (printer) 140
Nerlius, Bernardinus (printer) 35
Nicholas de Lyra (Francsican) 52, 61
Nider, Johannes (Dominican) 20

Oecolampadius, Johannes (Graecian) 15, 143–144, 147, 149
Öglin, Erhard (printer) 140
Origen[es] 152–153
Orpheus 82, 100
Osiris 78
Otmar, Johann (printer) 138
Otmar, Silvan (printer) 138
Otto of Bamberg (bishop) 101
Otto of Freising (bishop) 83
Ovid 68, 78, 81

Paduanus, see Jerome of Padua
Pandion (king) 68
Pallas Athene (Venus) 86, 91
Paul III (pope) 13
Paul (baptized Jew) 59
Paul of Burgos 52
Paula of Rome 159
Pellican, Conrad (Franciscan) 15, 40, 60, 157
Peter and Paul (apostles) 70
Petrarch, Francis (humanist) 59
Petreius, see Eberbach
Petri, Adam (printer) 54
Petri, Johannes (printer) 46, 50–52, 54
Petz, Georg (Forchemius, humanist) 4
Peutinger, Conrad (humanist) 137, 142, 149, 157, 162
Peutinger, Karl 149

INDEX OF PERSONAL NAMES

Pfefferkorn, Johannes (Jew converted to Christianity) 89, 123, 158, 166–167, 169
Pfeiffer, Heinrich (ex-Cistercian) 26, 125
Philomusus, see Locher
Phoebus (Apollo) 78, 100
Pico della Mirando, Johannes (philosopher) 15
Pindar (poet) 73
Pirckheimer, C[h]aritas (humanist nun) 16, 78–79
Pirckheimer, Georg (Carthusian) 16
Pirckheimer, Willibald (humanist) 14–16, 66–68, 78, 80, 82, 87, 89–90, 144–145, 149–150, 173
Piscator, Hermannus (Benedictine) 20
Plato 163
Plautus 55
Pliny 45, 112
Plutarch 80
Pollux, Iulius 119
Pomponius Mela 82
Procne (wife of Tereus) 68
Proserpina (Persephone) 118
Pruckner, Nikolaus (Augustinian) 164, 168

Quentell, Peter (printer) 67

Rabanus 152, 153
Ragusa, Johannes de (Dubrovnic) 52
Rees, see Henry of Rees
Reginald of Alna (Cistercian) 23
Regiomontanus (astronomer) 139
Reichart, Wolfgang (physician) 153
Reuchlin, Johann (Capnio, lawyer, lay theologian) 2, 4–5, 12, 27–28, 31, 34, 36–38, 43–44, 56–62, 89–90, 95, 111, 119, 123–124, 146, 158–171, 175
Reuter, Conrad (Reitter, Cistercian) 25, 95, 97–98, 100
Rhadamanthys (son of Zeus) 61
Rhegius, Urbanus, see Urbanus
Rosenheim, Peter von (Benedictine) 19–20
Rumpler, Angelus (Benedictine) 23, 97, 100

Sacon, Jacques (printer) 54
Salicetus, Nicolaus (Wydenbosch, Weidenbusch, Cistercian) 24, 96

Sappho (poetess) 74
Sattler, Michael (Benedictine) 22
Schanppecher, Melchior (musician) 140
Schedel, Hartmann (physician) 35, 65, 80–81
Schenck, Wolfgang (printer) 118
Schöffer, Johannes (printer) 21
Scholl, Michael (Cistercian) 58
Schott, Martin (printer) 41
Schott, Peter (humanist) 39–40
Schrott, Johannes (Benedictine) 142, 145
Scotus, Duns (Franciscan) 152–153
Scriptoris, Paul (Francscian) 139
Sedelius, see Seidel
Sedulius, Coelius 68
Segovia, Johannes de 52
Seid[e]l, Wolfgang (Sedelius, Benedictine) 98, 164
Selden, Wernher von (Dominican) 47
Servius, Maurus Honoratus 35
Silberberg, Johannes (physician) 56
Simon, Wolfgang (Cistercian) 100
Simprecht (Simpert, saint) 141
Slatkonia, George (bishop) 65
Sol (god) 118
Solomon (king) 34
Sonfeld, Christophorus (physician) 122
Spalatin, Georg (priest, humanist) 15, 89, 112, 116–117, 119–121, 123–124, 143, 147–148, 154, 160
Spengler, Lazarus (lawyer) 9
Spiess, Heinrich (Cuspidius, humanist) 43
Stabius, Johann (humanist) 86, 137, 139
Staupitz, Johann von (Augustinian, later Benedictine) 8, 15, 17, 65, 90, 104–105, 125
Stopel, Jacob (physician) 168

Tereus 68
Themar, see Werner
Theocritus 91
Theodore (saint) 163
Thiloninus, see Conradi
Thomas (apostle) 73
Thomas Aquinas (Dominican) 23, 152–153
Thomas à Kempis (spiritual author) 20

Thoring, Matthias (Döring, Franciscan) 52
Traversari, Ambrose (Camaldolese monk) 16
Trithemius, Johannes (Benedictine) 14, 29, 36, 40–41, 44, 136
Tritonius, Petrus Athesius (musician) 81

Ulhard, Philipp (printer) 134
Ulrich (saint) 141
Ulrich of Württemberg (duke) 44
Urbanus, Henricus (Cistercian) 4, 6, 26, 28, 97, 109–131, 174
Urbanus Rhegius (humanist, preacher) 4, 112, 151
Uriel, *see* Gemmingen
Utenheim, Christoph von (bishop) 45

Valla, Lorenzo (humanist) 11
Venus 86
Venus and Cupid 90–91
Veronica 70, 73–74
Vestal 78
Virgil (poet) 35, 78, 81, 98–99
Volprecht, Wolfgang (Augustinian) 15

Volz, Paul (Volzius, Benedictine) 21–22

Wagner, Leonhard (Benedictine) 142
Wechtelin, Johannes (artist) 66, 79, 120
Weidenbusch, *see* Salicetus
Werner, Adam, von Themar (poet) 32–33, 100
Werner von Bacharach (Hebrew instructor) 159
Wespechin, Ursula (Cistercian) 157
Wetzhausen, Georg Truchsess von (Benedictine) 81
Weyssenburger, Johannes (printer) 98
Widenmann, Leonhard (Benedictine) 158–160, 162–163, 168–169
William of Bavaria (duke) 105
Wimpfeling, Jacob (priest, humanist) 2, 11, 15, 32, 36–41, 43–47, 59, 61, 95, 115, 136

Zeus 61
Zimmermann, Sigmund (Benedictine) 148
Zwingli, Ulrich (priest, reformer) 104, 144

INDEX OF PLACES

Adelmannsfelden 157
Adwert (Aduard) 24, 25
Aldersbach 32, 66, 93–95, 100–101, 103, 105, 107, 174
Alpirsbach 19, 22
Alsace 19, 21, 49, 59, 157
Altomünster 144
Altzelle 25
Athens 51, 75, 142
Augsburg 20, 23, 81, 104, 133, 137–139, 141–148, 150–151, 153–155, 157, 160–162, 174
Auhausen 81
Aulne 23
Austria 18, 19, 135

Bamberg 101
Basel 17, 36, 38–40, 44–49, 51–52, 54, 56–57, 59, 62, 127, 142, 144, 151, 174
Baumgarten 24
Bavaria 19, 25, 46, 83, 93, 95, 97, 104–105, 133
Bebenhausen 57
Belgium 19
Bergamo 145
Bern 24
Beuditz (near Weissenfels) 26
Biberach 155
Bingen 97
Black Forest 19, 22, 57
Bologna 39, 46, 109
Bosau (Posa) 22
Braunschweig 22
Brixen 81
Burgundy 84
Bursfeld 19–21, 57

Calw 58
Capua 19
Cîteaux 33, 42, 59
Clairvaux 37
Cluny 33
Colmar 29, 42, 59, 171
Cologne 23–24, 67, 89–90, 123–124, 158, 160, 167–168, 171
Constance 22

Constantinople 53
Cracow 155
Crete 122
Croatia 97, 174

Delphi 78
Deventer 6
Dijon 36, 41
Dillingen 146
Donauwörth 142
Dorfbach 93
Dresden 25
Dubrovnic (Ragusa) 52

Ebrach 95
Egypt 75, 78
Eichstätt 46
Engental (Switzerland) 39, 44, 47–48, 52–56, 59–60
England 14, 35
Erfurt 3–5, 26–27, 97, 109, 111, 113, 115, 117–118, 122–125, 127, 130, 142, 159, 174
Ettal 149
Europe 7, 23, 69, 139

Ferrara 109
Florence 16, 35
Forli 46
Formbach, see Vornbach
France 13, 17, 21, 24, 34, 38
Franconia 95, 103
Frankfurt 46, 119, 125
Freiburg 23, 136
Freising 83
Frienisberg 24
Fürstenzell 93

Gelnhausen 113
Georgenthal 26, 113, 115–117, 120–122, 125
Germany 12–14, 19, 21–22, 26, 29–30, 34, 38, 56–57, 63, 78, 80, 82–83, 90, 92, 95, 97, 101–103, 116, 122, 125, 127, 130, 149, 155, 157, 166, 171
Gmunden 139

INDEX OF PLACES

Gotha 2, 5, 26, 109, 113, 115, 117, 120, 122, 125, 142
Greece 13
Güglingen 51

Hannover 25
Heggbach 157
Heidelberg 2, 14, 23, 25, 32, 43–44, 95, 100, 155
Heiligenkreuz 84
Heilsbronn 28, 49
Hirsau 19, 57–58
Höchstädt 133
Holland 19
Hugshofen 21
Hungary 84

Ingolstadt 87, 97, 136–137, 139, 142, 145, 159
Isenheim 99
Italy 12, 20–21, 27, 34, 37, 113, 145, 173

Johannesberg 97

Kaisheim 25, 95, 97–98
Kastl 19
Kößlarn 95

Landshut 95, 98, 100
Lauingen 145–146, 164, 168
Leipzig 22–23, 25–26, 43, 120–122, 171
Lesbos 74
Lizheim 22
Leonberg 29, 58
Loccum 25
Lorch 104
Louvain 77
Low Countries 6
Lower Saxony 25
Luttich 23
Luxembourg 19
Lyon 54

Magdeburg 159
Mainz 20–21, 41, 112, 165–166
Mantua 69, 113
Maria Laach 97, 158
Maulbronn 29–30, 32, 36, 38, 42, 44, 49, 53, 57–60
Melk 19–20, 65, 135, 138, 140, 158
Memmingen 155, 168
Michelsberg 101

Milan 27
Montpellier 155
Morimond 38
Mühldorf 105
Mühlhausen 26, 44

Netherlands 24
Nuremberg 9, 14–16, 23, 35, 38, 46, 50–51, 54, 63, 65–67, 71, 78–79, 81–83, 89, 118, 171

Oppenheim 136
Orb (Urba) 113
Orcus 71
Olympus 71, 77, 82
Orléans 37
Osnabrück 112
Ossa 61
Ottobeuren 23, 27, 145, 155, 157–162, 165, 167–168, 171, 174
Oxford 27

Padua 18–20
Pairis 49–50, 59–60
Paris 16, 23–24, 34, 39–40, 54, 59, 62
Parnassus 78
Passau 93, 95, 102, 104–105
Pavia 46
Pelion 61
Pforzheim 36
Poland 155
Posa, see Bosau
Prague 23

Ragusa, see Dubrovnic
Raitenhaslach 25, 95, 100
Regensburg 106
Reichenau 141
Reifenstein (Eichsfeld) 26
Reutlingen 138
Riddagshausen 25
Rocca di Mondragone 19
Rome 34, 36, 87, 89, 104, 109, 122
Rotthalmünster 95, 97

Salzburg 20, 84, 104–105, 153
Sankt Gallen 20
Sankt Peter 38
Saxony 26, 89, 105, 121, 139, 160
Schlettstatt 39
Schmalkalden 104
Sens 102
Spain 21, 24

INDEX OF PLACES

Speyer 36
Split 174
Sponheim 44
Strasbourg 15, 24, 39–40, 64, 66, 130, 143, 145
Stuttgart 29, 61
Subiaco 19–20
Sussex 35
Swabia 19, 23, 29, 103
Switzerland 19–20, 22, 24, 44, 56, 58, 62, 104

Tartarus (infernal region) 71
Tellus (personified earth) 71, 118
Tegernsee 20, 98
Thebes 73
Thuringia 113
Torgau 121, 122
Trent 104
Tübingen 58, 135, 139, 159, 167

Ulm 157

Vaihingen 58
Valladolid 18
Valley of the Solymi 72
Venice 5, 19, 27, 55, 119, 126–127, 162
Vienna 23, 63, 65, 84–85, 87–89, 96
Vornbach (Formbach) 23, 97

Weissenfels 26
Wiesensteig 137
Wildbad 58
Wimpfen 51
Wittenberg 4–5, 18, 22, 89–90, 124–125, 142, 149–150, 154, 159–160
Worms 2, 43, 44
Württemberg 44

Zeitz 22
Zurich 40

INDEX OF SUBJECTS

ad fontes, *see* back to the sources
Aesopus 148
Alcuinus de Sancta Trinitate (printed by Ellenbog) 155
Amplexus Bernardi 21, 70–71
Annales sive Chronicon (by Marius) 94, 101–102, 105
Antidotarius animae (by Salicetus) 24, 96
anti-scholastic 116
Aramaic 162
astrologer, astrology 139, 155, 157, 173
astronomer, astronomy, astronomical 139–140, 148, 155, 157, 173
Athanasius 119
Augenspiegel/Eye Mirror (by Reuchlin) 90, 124, 167–168, 170–171
Augsburg Confession 154

back to the sources (*ad fontes*) 21, 26–27, 77, 158, 161, 173–174
Bernard Renaissance 118
Bible, *Biblia* 50–52, 61, 169, 173
Bible concordance 51, 52
biblical humanism/humanist(s) 1, 12, 44, 61, 145, 161, 175
book culture (*Buchkultur*) 6, 173
Brethren of the Common Life 6
Brevis Germaniae Descriptio (by Cochlaeus) 82
Brigittine monastery 227

Cabala, cabalistic 38, 161–162
[Carmen] contra poetas impudice loquentes (by Mantuan) 136
Carmen Dactylicum Alcmanium (by Chelidonius) 73
Carmen de bello Norico/Song about the Bavarian War (by Marius) 95, 101
Carmen de doctrina domini nostri (by Marulus) 97, 126–128, 130
Carmen de laudibus sacre scripture (by Butzbach) 97
Carmen de passione (by Mancinus) 68
Carmen de passione Christi (by Marius) 97

Carmen paschale (by Sedulius) 68
Carmen rithmicum (by Leontorius) 42
Carmina in Vitam Sancti Benedicti (by Locher) 80
Cathalogus (by Marius) 105
century of reform 6
Cerberus 71
Chaldaic 162
Christ's suffering, Passion 65, 67, 81, 100
Christ-centered poetry 28, 174
Christ as trophy of God 81
Christi Fasciculus (by Marius) 66, 97–98, 106
Chronicon urbis et ecclesiae Maguntinensis (by Piscator) 20
Chronographia Augustana/Ein schöne Cronick (by Meisterlin) 141–142
Church Father(s) 7, 14, 17, 53, 173–175
civic humanism, humanists 1, 9–10
classical (Latin, antiquity) 2, 8, 11, 74–75, 78, 81, 91, 98
Collecta quorundam priuilegiorum ordinis Cisterciensis 41–42
College of Saint Bernard
  in Leipzig 121
  in Paris 23, 34
College of Saint Jacob in Heidelberg 32, 95
Colloquia (by Erasmus) 151
Commentaria bibliorum (by Pellican) 40
commentary on Romans (by Erasmus) 233
Compendium musicae (by Meurer) 25
confessionalization of humanism 12, 14, 89, 133, 154
Contra turpem libellum Philomusi defensio (by Wimpfeling) 136, 138
Council of Basel 102
Council of Constance 18–19, 102
Council of Trent 79, 104
courtly humanism 1
Creed
  Apostles' Creed 70, 150–151
  Nicene Creed 150

cross-centered piety 67
culture of reform 6
curial humanism 1

Decastychon—ad ymaginem crucifixi
  (by Curvello) 97
De arte cabalistica (by Reuchlin) 54
De civitate Dei (by Augustine) 54
De conceptu et triplici candore Mariae virginis (by Wimpfeling) 40
De consolatione theologiae (by Gerson) 148
De illustribus viris ac sanctimonialibus (by Epp) 51
De integritate (by Wimpfeling) 11, 46, 115
De patientia (by Mantuan) 121
De professione religiosum (by Valla) 11
De rerum inventoribus (by Virgil) 98
De Roma triumphans (by Biondo) 46
De rudimentis Hebraicis (by Reuchlin) 28, 57, 59–60, 119, 159, 161–163
De scriptoribus ecclesiasticis (by Trithemius) 36, 60, 65
De sacrosancta trinitate (by Bandinus) 87
De statu animae (by Meurer) 25
De suorum temporum calamitatibus (by Mantuan) 138
De verbo mirifico (by Reuchlin) 36–37, 159, 161, 166
deësis 70, 100
Defensio/Defense against the Cologne Slanderers (by Reuchlin) 123, 167, 169–170
deformation/reformation 8, 12–13
descent into hell 70, 150
devotio moderna 6, 173
Dialogus de Hercule/Dialogue about Hercules (by Marulus) 86
Dialogues of Gregory the Great 80
Dictionarium [graecum] Ambrosii (by Calpinus) 54–55, 145
diet
  of Augsburg (1518) 139, 147
  of Augsburg (1530) 104, 154
  of Constance (1507) 81

Eckius dedolatus/Eck planed down (by Pirckheimer) 87
Ehrenbuch (memorial book, Honors Book) 141
Elegia F. Benedicti Chelidonii Norici 65
Elementale Lipsiensium 146

Enchiridion (by Erasmus) 37
episcopal humanism, humanists 2, 43
Epistolae Merulae 119
Epistle 42 (by Bernard) 45, 102
Epitoma Platonicum (by Ellenbog) 163
Erasmianism 9
Erotemata (by Lascaris) 27
Eucharist (Olympic bread) 72, 74, 144, 149
evangelical truth, see *veritas*
eve of the Reformation 6, 16, 28, 67, 75, 91
Epitome in divae parthenices Mariae/ Excerpts from the Story of the Holy Virgin (by Chelidonius) 75
Eye Mirror, see *Augenspiegel*

Facetarium (by Bebel) 135

Gesta Friderici (by Otto of Freising) 83
Glycon/glicon 73
grammar 10, 14, 27
Graecian, Greek study 16, 27, 40, 43, 57, 59, 62, 113, 115, 122, 124–125, 136, 142, 144–145, 150, 163–164, 166, 169–170, 175
Greek concepts 61, 67, 71–72, 76, 116, 118, 143–144, 149, 162–163
Grund vnnd Schriftliche anzaygungen (attributed to Bild) 134

Hand[t] Spiegel/Hand Mirror 166
Hebraist(s), study of Hebrew 12, 36, 58–60, 62, 83, 119, 145–146, 157, 159–162, 164–165, 167, 169, 171, 175
Historia horarum canonicarum de S. Hieronymo vario carminum genere contexta (by Bild) 140
historiography, historiographer, historiographical 2, 13, 20, 23, 49, 83, 93, 101, 174
humanist Latin 60, 72, 77–78, 80, 91, 96, 118

Idyll (by Theocritus) 91
Iesuida seu De passione Domini (by Jerome of Padua) 69
image and word, see *pictura et eloquentia*
In aliquot Lutherana paradoxa Dialogus (by Marius) 103
In sacram synodi (by Leontorius) 45

Institutio bene vivendi/Instruction on How to Lead a Virtuous Life (by Marulus) 126, 127
Institutiones musicae (by Luscinius) 143
Interpretatio in librum Psalmorum (by Bugenhagen) 151

Jewish books 12, 27, 89, 123, 165–166, 175

Klosterhumanismus, see monastic humanism
Kratylos 164

Landshut War 100
Large Passion 67–69
Last Supper, *see* Eucharist
Latin poets, poetry 10, 25, 29, 32–33, 36, 39–41, 46, 65–87, 93, 96–101, 126–131, 135–138, 174
law(yer) (jurist, canon law[yer]) 2, 9, 14, 19, 37, 39–41, 56, 95, 109, 123, 145, 158, 164, 173
layman, laymen 2–4, 171
Leipzig Disputation 22
Letters of Famous Men to Reuchlin 5, 57, 89, 158, 164, 167–168
Letters of Obscure Men 4–5, 89, 109, 167
liberal arts 109, 140, 175
Life of the Holy Bishop Otto of Bamberg (by Herbord) 101
Little Passion 66–69, 72, 78–79
Lord's Supper, *see* Eucharist
Lucubrationes (by Oecolampadius) 144
Lucubratiunculae (by Gresemund) 41
Lucubratiunculae (by Schott) 39–40

Magnum Etymologicum Graecae linguae 119
Margarita poetica (by Eyb) 46
Marienleben/Life of Mary 78–79, 129
Mass explanation (commentary, by Heynlin) 17, 45
Melopoiae 81
Meteorologia (by Aristotle) 83
modern devotion, *see devotio moderna*
monastic humanism 1, 5–6, 8–14, 16–18, 26–28, 44, 91, 113, 133, 160, 167, 171, 173–175
multi-lingual, *see* polyglotism
music, musician 14, 25, 81–82, 84, 140, 143, 145, 173, 175
Musica figurata (by Schanppecher) 140

Name of God (tetragram) 37, 161–162, 167
name of Jesus 37–38
national humanism 13

Olympic bread, *see* Eucharist
On Consideration (by Bernard) 102
Opera of Ambrose 55
Opera of Augustine 54
Opera of Virgil 35
Operationes in Psalmos (by Luther) 150
Oratio rhythmica (by Pseudo-Bernard) 96
Ordo et numerus summorum pontificum (by Marius) 105
Orthographia (by Marschalk) 115

Parish ministry, *see* pastoral care
Parthenice prima, sive Mariana (by Mantuan) 138
Parthenice secunda, sive Catharinaria (by Mantuan) 138
Passio Christi (by Geiler) 120, 129–130
Passio domini (by Jerome of Padua) 67, 69
Passio Iesu Christi (by Chelidonius) 66, 68, 120
Passio Jesu Christi aus den vier Evangelien (by Seidel) 98
pastoral care 34, 91, 95
Peasants' War 21–22, 26, 103, 125, 149, 170–171
pictura et eloquentia 72
pietas/piety 8, 67, 75, 100, 112–113, 121, 173
Poetae Christiani veteres 96
polyglotism, polyglot (multi-lingual) 2, 5, 38
Praise of Folly (by Erasmus) 37
Pro Archia poëta oratio. Pro M. Marcello oratio (by Cicero) 138
Proba centum scripturarum (by Wagner) 142
Pyrgopolinices (by Plautus) 55

Quadrivium Grammatices (by Cochlaeus) 82

Rectorate Page (by Crotus) 3, 110–112
Reformatio Prediger Ordens (Dominican) 18
Reformationis monasticae vindiciae seu defensio (Benedictine) 17

Resolution[e]s (by Luther)   144, 147
rhetor(ic,) rhetorical   10, 14, 45, 173
Roman humanists   1
Rosetum memoriale (by Peter von Rosenheim)   20
Rudiments of Hebrew, see *De rudimentis Hebraicis*
Rule
  of Saint Augustine   11, 117
  of Saint Benedict   21, 34, 103, 116, 135, 173, 175
  of Saint Francis   117

sacred philology, see three sacred languages
Saint Lorenz Church   82, 83
Saint Mary Church   109
Schmalkald War   160
Scholasticism (schools), scholastic(s)   3, 8, 14, 173–174
Scripture(s), see Bible
sect (*secta*)   11, 104, 116
Semhammaphoras, see Name of God
Sentences (by Lombard)   87
Sergius (by Reuchlin)   43
sodalitas, sodality, sodalities   5, 44, 137
Stations of the Cross (Way of the Cross)   70, 73
Statuta synodalia Basiliensia (by Christoph von Utenheim)   45
Stella musicae (by Bild)   140
Streitbüchlein / Little Book of Battle (by Pfefferkorn)   167
'Struggle between lust and virtue' (by Chelidonius)   84, 85

studia humanitatis   14, 173
sundials   139, 157
Supplementorum chronicorum (by Foresti)   19
Syriac   162

technology of printing, printing press   9, 16, 36, 118, 127, 155, 160
Tetrachordum Musices (by Cochlaeus)   82
tetragrammaton/tetragram, see Name of God
The Twelve Articles (by Rhegius)   151
Theologia Germanica (edited by Luther)   148
three sacred languages, ancient, biblical languages (Hebrew, Greek, and Latin), trilingual ideal   5, 13–14, 27, 29, 37, 56, 62, 119, 138, 145, 153, 159, 161, 168, 171, 173, 175
Triumphal Arch   86–88
Triumphal Procession   87

Veritas
  archetypa   27
  evangelica, evangelical Truth   27, 142, 147
  graeca, Greek Truth   143, 175
  hebraica, Hebrew Truth   27, 158, 175
Vocabularium Iulii Pollucis   119
Votorum monasticorum tutor (by Marius)   103
Vulgate   62, 72, 76

Afterword

DR. POSSET'S METICULOUSLY RESEARCHED presentation of the world of late-fifteenth- and early-sixteenth-century humanist monks through the lens of bio-bibliographies introduces us to a handful of its lesser-known denizens—for many students of the period, only the name of Chelidonius may be familiar, especially to art historians, or the name of Henricus Urbanus. And yet Posset's biographies insist that they were hardly an isolated phenomenon: the world of monastic humanism was broad, perforce international, and relatively well-populated even if our knowledge of its range and depth is limited. Needless to say, Posset's brief survey touches only those humanists who, strictly speaking, can be called monks, which leaves out regulars like Erasmus, and laymen like More, both of whom disputed with monks (e.g., John Batmanson, a Carthusian) over humanistic topics like Greek philology. Posset has sketched out the parameters of a vibrant if cloistered world.

Students of the period see in the accounts of these men—citizens of the church, their particular orders, and the empire in the early decades of the sixteenth century—a society that will be utterly changed within a generation. The Reformation will sweep away much of the monastic world, and forever alter those institutions it did not erase. It is as if we are reading an account of Edwardian Britain on the eve of the First World War: we see a world that is precious, confident, and doomed. Posset does not dwell on the elegiac, nor does he need to. When we read the biography of Leontorius, a monk of Maulbronn, who was employed to produce "spontaneous verse" for his bishop's drinking parties in 1496 or that in a direct inversion of the impulse that drove Saint Benedict from the decadence of Rome to Subiaco, the Benedictine monk Chelidonius moved to Vienna to be closer to the imperial court of Maxmilian I, we sense the storm brewing that eliminated, almost overnight, half the 1,500 Benedictine monasteries in Europe, and every single house of regulars in England.

Posset's sketches make it clear that the scholarship generated by these monks is far from trivial, despite the occasional verse for drinking parties. Humanists in the Renaissance, and regulars among them, long labored under the stigma of being mere ornaments while the real heavy lifting was done by scholastic theologians. But that stigma itself quickly evaporated as the century's interest in biblical criticism and patristic scholarship deepened. And it was this vigor—centered around a clash in epistemologies—that fueled much of the scholarship that has come down to us from men whose public career was made possible by their ability to work outside the cloister. The philological interests of men such as Reuchlin and Erasmus, whose names frequent these accounts, were taken up by other authors, and despite the lamentable overenthusiasm for classical terminology, such as describing the eucharist as "panis olympicus," the monks described here made significant contributions to the Christian humanist corpus which was even then redefining ecclesiastical scholarship. Posset's encapsulated studies go a long way towards modernizing the image of early modern monks by showing them as the forerunners of modern academic authors—they network incessantly, they are impressively mobile in an age not known for easy relocation, and they are passionate about their books. Reading is a sacred activity.

Posset obviously kept an eye out for the telling details he mined the letters of these obscure men. We are treated to many details that in themselves speak volumes: Leontorius asking Amerbach for a hair shirt—not for himself, he protests, despite Amerbach's heady religious influence—but for a nun of his acquaintance, to be sent in plain wrapping so as to prevent gossip or writing to Froben about needing new glasses: "When I put two pairs of these spectacles together on my nose, I see much further and more clearly; if I add a third, they are almost equal to a thicker and more curved lens." The image of this scholar laboring under three sets of spectacles as he helps to edit the complete works of Augustine in eleven volumes gives us pause.

But clearly the main contribution of this volume lies in an area none of its subjects anticipated: these men, and indeed the philological and theological interests that inform their writing, were poised on the edge of a rapidly growing abyss the dimensions of which they were only dimly aware. This is best seen in the case of Vitus Bild, a monk of Augsburg, whose blend of Biblicism and monasticism was at the time unremarkable. He lived a monk in the heartland of the reform, and died eight years after Luther's formal rejection of religious vows in 1521. Posset identifies him as "an evangelical Catholic monk", something of a contradiction to the popular conception of the

Reformation although common enough to scholars of this protean era. Naturally, Bild wore various hats—secretary, Latin teacher, poet, priest, polymath (he studied astronomy, music, philology, theology), cartographer, historian, and procurer of sundials for Frederick the Wise. In none save perhaps the last was he especially distinguished, and perhaps therein lies his interest to us although to his peers he may have been quite ordinary. With dozens of his co-religious, he certainly moved along the bright periphery of Augsburg, corresponding with those in the center like Oecolampadius, Spalatin, and even Luther himself while remaining decidedly in the background. Perhaps one of the most useful aspects of Posset's sketch is to demonstrate how deep that background must have been. With an outsized figure like Luther on center stage in Augsburg, dozens if not hundreds of fascinating characters were relegated to the shadows. After the Peasant's War Bild lost contact with the chief reformers but his interest in the kernel of their message endured. In his own words, taken from a letter to Spalatin, he embraced Luther's new Biblicism yet retained his monastic vocation: "The Gospel in which God instructed me through Martin [Luther], the most faithful servant of his vineyard, is so deeply rooted in my heart that I despise everything else." Whether Bild would have remained a monk had he lived longer is hardly the point and is in any case unanswerable. Yet his accommodation should warn those who would engineer a conflict between the Reformers and humanists where men such as he saw none.

Posset's short concluding chapter highlights the salient features of these monastic *umanisti* and draws out common features with their non-monastic peers, chief among which were love of language and a reinvigorated Biblicism. Indeed, the humanistic enterprise itself—far from being simply an interest in Hebrew, Greek, and Latin and a leaning toward rhetoric over logic and metaphysic, was profoundly oriented toward a reinvigorated apprehension of the fruits of Christian faith. And in that, certain monks had long held sway even if they could not be considered *umanisti* because they decisively predate the Renaissance, or lacked an interest in trilingual scholarship; the Carthusians are prominent among this group. They lie at the center of the changes even then unfolding in the scholarly world and the wider context of Western Christendom. And while only a few of their members—John Batmanson in England, Gregor Reisch in Germany—would qualify as humanists strictly speaking, the order sponsored the translation and dissemination of works centered on the vita Christi for diverse populaces: readers and non-readers, lay and ordained, regular and secular. Forbidden by their constitution to preach or hold parishes, they long adapted their monastic charism to adapting and transmitting the wisdom of the cloister.

From the early twelfth century with the dissemination of the Carthusian *Scala Claustralium* of Guigo II (appearing in England as the *Ladder of Monks*), texts streamed out of Carthusian monasteries on the Continent and permeated the devotional lives of religious and lay alike. The thirteenth century *Somme le Roi* (printed later by Caxton as the *Royal Book*) spawned many vernacular catechetical texts, and later in the century an anonymous compilation of *The Chastising of God's Children* popularized the Dutch mystic Jan van Ruusbroec. But it was left to the fourteenth and fifteenth centuries to fully capture the outpouring of teachings from religious life, and the Carthusians were foremost in translating and disseminating them not only in England but throughout Europe. In the mid-fourteenth century appeared the anonymous The *Abbey of the Holy Ghost* (printed by de Worde in 1496) for "all those that ne may not be bodily in religious, that they may be ghostly." Later in the century Walter Hilton, a canon not a Carthusian, wrote his *Epistle on the Mixed Life* which quickly joined his *Scale of Perfection* as a standard for lay devotion. The *Meditationes Vitae Christi* (by de Caulibus, earlier ascribed to Bonaventure) was translated by Nicholas Love (Carthusian prior of Mount Grace) as *Myrrour of the Blessed Lyf of Jesu Christ* and contains adapted paraphrases of Scripture despite Archbishop Arundel's 1411 restrictions on translating Scripture, and another Carthusian of Sheen translated the *Speculum Devotorum* (*Mirrour for Devout*) also based on the *Meditationes*. At the close of the fifteenth century, de Worde printed Adam the Carthusian's *The xii Profits of Tribulation*.

The Carthusians weren't alone in writing, translating, and disseminating monastic erudition. Since its foundation in 1415, the Bridgettine house at Syon (across the Thames from the Carthusian house of Sheen) was a fountain of devotional texts. Many of its monks had been fellows at Cambridge (e.g., William Bonde, author of *A Consolation of Timorous Consciences*, and John Fewterer), or chaplains to archbishops and noblemen (e.g., Richard Whitford, author of *A Werke of Preparacion to Communion or Howselyng* and *A Werke for Householders* addressed to "them that have the guiding or governaunce of any company") and its library contained thousands of texts.

Since the publication of volume 9 of the Corpus of British Medieval Libraries: Syon with the Libraries of the Carthusians (2001: eds. Vincent Gillespie and A .I. Doyle) we now have an inventory of late medieval and early modern monastic reading, and it is exceptionally rich. As expected, there are many texts on contemplation, but so too we find much Augustine; Aquinas, including the *Epistola de modo studendi*; Petrarch's *De remediis utriusque fortunae*, Plutarch's *De liberis educandis*; Pico's *Opera*; English translations of Paul's letters; and Langton's *Interpretationes nominum hebraicorum*. Equally interesting is the history of lending books to other houses less well-endowed, suggesting a lively circulation of texts among religious houses throughout England. As with the monastic humanists Posset sketches, these monks and nuns demand a reinterpretation for their roles in spreading authentic monastic theology. The devotional life of the vast majority of medieval and early modern Christians would be virtually empty of non-imagistic texts were it not for the activities of the Carthusians and members of other religious orders.

To take but one example of how deep this tradition ran, we need only look at England's most exemplary humanist, Sir Thomas More. Living among the London Carthusians while training for a legal career, More translated the *Life of Pico* (the London Charterhouse had just received perhaps the first copy in England). Two and a half decades later, while awaiting execution in the Tower for his refusal to sanction Henry VIII's schism, he penned his last works—the witty *Dialogue of Comfort against Tribulation* and the profound meditation on Christ's agony in Gethsemane: *De Tristitia Christi*. For these he used, among other texts, Love's *Meditations on the Life of Christ*, the anonymous *Chastysing of God's Children*, William Flete's *Remedies against Temptation*, Walter Hilton's meditations on Psalms 90 and 91, the anonymous *Six Masters on Tribulation* and the *Tretyse of Love* (based on the thirteenth-century monastic *Ancrene Riwle*). Each of these is found in the Carthusian and Syon catalogues, from where it is likely More borrowed them.

In his compelling account, Dr. Posset invites us to re re-envision the Reformation and see the depth and richness of its monastic theology by holding up to us a few of its lesser-known practitioners. They are proxies for thousands of other monks whose names do not come down to us, and whose activities remain invisible: "et sunt quorum non est memoria, perierunt quasi non fuerint, et nati sunt quasi non nati."—But of others, there is no memory, for when they ceased, they ceased, and they are as though they had not lived (Sir 44.9).

Seymour Baker House
Erstwhile Dwyer Chair of Humanities
Professor of Church History
Mount Angel Seminary

List of International Book Reviews

of the First Edition of Renaissance Monks (2005)
in chronologischer order

1. Seymour Baker House, in *Renaissance and Reformation* 28 (2004 [issued in 2005]) 131-133.
2. Erika Rummel, in *Renaissance Quarterly* 59 (2006) 573-575.
3. Barry Collett in *Ecclesiastical History* 57 (2006) 594-595.
4. Kathleen O'Neill, OSCO, in *Cistercian Studies Quarterly* 41 (2006) 387-389.
5. Harald Müller, in *H-Soz-u-Kult (Humanities – Sozial und Kulturgeschichte)* 11 October, 2006 [in German].
6. Michael Basse, in *Zeitschrift für Kirchengeschichte* 117 (2006) 362-363 [in German].
7. Stephen Parkinson, ed., in *The Year's Work in Modern Language Studies* 67 (2007) 592.
8. Thomas Sullivan, OSB, *in The American Benedictine Review* 58 (2007) 105-107.
9. Dennis D. Martin, in *The Catholic Historical Review* 93 (2007) 164-166.
10. William Hyland, in *Sixteenth Century Journal* 38 (2007) 784-785.
11. Asaph Ben-Tov, in *H-German, H-Net Reviews*, March, 2007.
12. Anders Jarlert in *Church History and Religious Culture* 87 (2007) 96-97.
13. François Wim, in *Revue d'histoire ecclésiastique* 102 (2007) 600-602.
14. R. N. Swanson in *The Heythrop Journal* 49 (2008) 343-344.
15. Duane A. Rudolph, in *Biography* 31 (2008) 303-305.

Collected Works

1. *The Two-Fold Knowledge: Readings on the Knowledge of God Selected and Translated from the Works of Saint Bernard of Clairvaux*
2. *Pater Bernhardus: Martin Luther and Bernard of Clairvaux*
3. *Luther's Catholic. Christology: According to His Johannine Lectures of 1527*
4. *Respect for the Jews*
5. *Catholic Advocate of the Evangelical Truth: Marcus Marulus (Marko Marulić) of Split (1450–1524)*
6. *Renaissance Monks: A Group Portrait of Monastic Humanism*

www.ingramcontent.com/pod-product-compliance
Lightning Source LLC
Chambersburg PA
CBHW062022220426
43662CB00010B/1441